# SOCIOLOGICAL THEORY AND CRIMINOLOGICAL RESEARCH: VIEWS FROM EUROPE AND THE UNITED STATES

# SOCIOLOGY OF CRIME, LAW AND DEVIANCE

Series Editor: Mathieu Deflem
(Volumes 1–5: Jeffrey T. Ulmer)

Recent Volumes:

SOCIOLOGY OF CRIME, LAW AND DEVIANCE
VOLUME 7

# SOCIOLOGICAL THEORY AND CRIMINOLOGICAL RESEARCH: VIEWS FROM EUROPE AND THE UNITED STATES

EDITED BY

## MATHIEU DEFLEM

*University of South Carolina, Columbia, SC, USA*

**ELSEVIER**
JAI

Amsterdam – Boston – Heidelberg – London – New York – Oxford
Paris – San Diego – San Francisco – Singapore – Sydney – Tokyo

JAI Press is an imprint of Elsevier

JAI Press is an imprint of Elsevier
The Boulevard, Langford Lane, Kidlington, Oxford OX5 1GB, UK
Radarweg 29, PO Box 211, 1000 AE Amsterdam, The Netherlands
525 B Street, Suite 1900, San Diego, CA 92101-4495, USA

First edition 2006

**British Library Cataloguing in Publication Data**
A catalogue record for this book is available from the British Library

ISBN-13:   978-0-7623-1322-8
ISBN-10:   0-7623-1322-6
ISSN:      1521-6136 (Series)

For information on all JAI Press publications
visit our website at books.elsevier.com

Printed and bound in The Netherlands

06 07 08 09 10 10 9 8 7 6 5 4 3 2 1

Working together to grow
libraries in developing countries

www.elsevier.com | www.bookaid.org | www.sabre.org

ELSEVIER    BOOK AID
            International    Sabre Foundation

# CONTENTS

# LIST OF CONTRIBUTORS

| | |
|---|---|
| *Ronald L. Akers* | Department of Criminology, Law and Society, University of Florida, FL, USA |
| *Robert D. Crutchfield* | Department of Sociology, University of Washington, WA, USA |
| *Stacy De Coster* | Department of Sociology, North Carolina State University, NC, USA |
| *Mathieu Deflem* | Department of Sociology, University of South Carolina, Sloan College, SC, USA |
| *Imke Dunkake* | Forschungsinstitut für Soziologie, Universität zu Köln, Köln, Germany |
| *Nigel G. Fielding* | Department of Sociology, University of Surrey, Guildford, UK |
| *Karen Heimer* | Department of Sociology, University of Iowa, Iowa City, IA, USA |
| *Susanne Karstedt* | School of Criminology, Education, Sociology and Social Work, Keele University, Keele Staffordshire, UK |
| *Sanjay Marwah* | Sociology and Anthropology Department, Guilford College, Greensboro, NC, USA |
| *Ross L. Matsueda* | Department of Sociology, University of Washington, WA, USA |
| *Fritz Sack* | Institut für Kriminologische Sozialforschung, Universität Hamburg, Hamburg, Germany |
| *Joachim J. Savelsberg* | Department of Sociology, University of Minnesota, Minneapolis, MN, USA |

*Karl F. Schumann*          Universität Bremen, Bremen, Germany

*René van Swaaningen*       Department of Criminology, Erasmus
                            University Rotterdam, Rotterdam,
                            The Netherlands

*Halime Ünal*              Department of Sociology, Mugla University,
                            Sosyoloji Bolumu, Mugla, Turkey

# INTRODUCTION: THE BEARING OF SOCIOLOGICAL THEORY ON CRIMINOLOGICAL RESEARCH

## Mathieu Deflem

### ABSTRACT

*Modern criminology is unthinkable without the contributions of sociology and sociological theory. Yet, not all criminology is sociological in orientation and, far more troublesome, not all sociologically minded criminological work is resolutely and thoroughly grounded in theory. The chapters in this book address various ways in which insights from sociological theory have been helpful in the contributing authors' criminological research. Revealing the global reach and nationally distinct variations in the practice of sociological theory and criminology, this volume is explicitly trans-atlantic in terms of its contributors and the topics and theories they discuss.*

No discipline has made a greater theoretical contribution to the research domain of criminological research than has sociology. Of course, the birth and development of criminology are historically rooted in systems of knowledge that were intimately connected to the practical and administrative demands of criminal justice policy (Pasquino, 1991; Foucault, 1978).

Sociological Theory and Criminological Research: Views from Europe and the United States
Sociology of Crime, Law and Deviance, Volume 7, 1–6
Copyright © 2006 by Elsevier Ltd.
ISSN: 1521-6136/doi:10.1016/S1521-6136(06)07001-1

But, it is likewise the case that modern criminology as it has matured toward an independent scholarly activity is firmly grounded in sociology and other social-science disciplines (Garland, 1992). The triple alliance of criminology, criminal statistics, and police that existed during the early days of the criminal sciences has thus been replaced in serious social-science scholarship on crime and its control by an alliance of theory, methods, and research. It is the role of theory in this nexus in the area of criminological sociology that this volume is devoted to.

The authors in this book present chapters that highlight the value of sociological theorizing in their respective efforts in criminological research. The chapters do not merely involve discussions about the ideal value of sociological theory for research nor about the relation between the field of criminological sociology and the discipline of sociology at large. Instead, they present concrete analyses and discussions of how sociological theory has actually been useful to the author's own criminological research. Presenting this volume, we collectively aim to show that some of the very best criminological work is distinctly informed in useful and varied ways by sociological theory.

## SOCIOLOGICAL THEORY AND CRIMINOLOGY

Not only was criminological thinking until the late-19th century not distinctly sociological, even when the earliest generation of criminologists focused on the social (rather than the biological or mental) correlates of crime, their analyses were not particularly informed by the theoretical insights from the burgeoning discipline of sociology. Most famously, the work of the Belgian astronomer Adolphe Quetelet rested on a simplistic inductivism to construe the perspective of the 'average man' (Quetelet, 1835). Because it lacked any serious theoretical inspiration, Auguste Comte thought very little of Quetelet's work and particularly despised his perversion of the term of 'social physics,' for which reason Comte had to cook up the neologism 'sociologie' (Comte, 1839).

While the sociological classics did not discuss crime and criminal justice as central elements in their analyses of the transformations of modern society, the research domain of criminology was not entirely neglected by the founders of the discipline. Probably best known today is Emile Durkheim's (1895) discussion on the normality of crime. Yet, unlike his penetrating analysis of suicide in the modern era, Durkheim did not conduct a systematic empirical research of crime, instead merely relying on the category of crime to develop his theoretical argument that normal and pathological social facts can be distinguished on the basis of their average existence in a particular stage of development in a society. While a control theory of criminal or deviant behavior might be developed out of Durkheim's twin notions of regulation and anomie, and while the notion of the normality of crime anticipates the constructionist perspective of crime and deviance, neither theoretical tradition as it exists in criminology today has emanated directly from Durkheim, instead having taken on other theoretical avenues to develop.

Probably most thorough of all criminological interests among the sociological classics was the work of Ferdinand Tönnies (Deflem, 1999). Although generally known only for his theory of *Gemeinschaft* and *Gesellschaft*, Tönnies wrote 3 books, 22 papers, and 9 review articles on various topics of crime, in addition to 17 methodological papers on criminal statistics. However, Tönnies' contributions to the sociology of crime have been almost entirely neglected.

It would be foolish now, a hundred years later, to try and reconstruct any part of the sociological classics to fit the model of contemporary sociological theorizing in the criminological domain beyond the actual historical lineages that exist in theory development. Yet, what can be observed is that whatever the place was that the likes of Durkheim and Tönnies attributed to crime within the totality of their oeuvre, the theoretical and/or empirical attention they paid to crime was always part and parcel of a comprehensive vision of sociology and an integrated perspective of the relation between theory and research.

There is no doubt that the heydays of modern American sociology that came in the footsteps of the European classics have brought about the major stimulus for the development of sociological theorizing in criminological research until today. I hope there is no bias on my part involved in stating as a matter of fact that the most important initial impetus for the development of a theoretically sound criminological sociology came from Robert Merton's (1938) seminal article on anomie and opportunity structures. Whatever its merits and limitations, it was Merton's typology of types of deviant behavior and his theories of anomie and strain that produced a wealth of empirical and theoretical discussions like no other contribution at the time (and arguably since).

A close second in degree of influence, although developed already from the early 1930s onwards, were the penetrating works of the early Chicago School of sociology that were focused on the social ills of crime in the urban settings of industrial society. Anticipating the emerging theoretical insights that would later crystallize around symbolic interactionism, the contributions of Clifford Shaw and Henry McKay (Shaw & McKay, 1942) stand out as another important point of departure for research and theorizing in criminological sociology. Emanating from within the Chicago tradition, also, we have a third important building block in the work of Edwin Sutherland and his development of differential association theory (Sutherland, 1939).

In the period after World War II, criminological sociology underwent a proliferation of theorizing and research that, in its scope and richness, has not been witnessed since and may well never be experienced again. New lines of research were explored and novel insights in theory tested and applied in a pace so fast that even an entire book devoted to sociological theory and criminological research, such as ours, can only unravel a fragment of the relevant issues. Importantly, the endeavors in criminological sociology in the immediate post-war era not only took up a central place within the discipline as a whole, but many theoretical ideas in our subfield were also central to sociological theorizing as such. And it is in this precise sense that our present era is different. Whether or not we agree that the development of sociological research domains into new separate disciplinary areas involves an intellectual Balkanization (Horowitz, 1993), it is clear that criminological sociologists today cannot lay claim to the same centrality in the discipline of sociology – and most definitely not with respect to theoretical developments. What is, in my mind, most tragic about this development is not that some work in criminological sociology today is not well grounded in sociological theory, but that the insights of criminological sociology are also not sufficiently recognized in the discipline at large even on the occasions when remarkable theoretical advances are made in our specialty area. This situation is undeserved and unjust. Serious criminological sociology, as this book shows, relies on and develops sound theoretical ideas and models. And serious criminological sociologists, like the representatives of any another disciplinary subfield, realize that core epistemological and theoretical issues are at stake in how their specialty enterprise and sociology as a whole are constituted. It is in this precise sense that the present volume hopes to contribute to bring theory back into criminological sociology.

## AN OVERVIEW OF THE CHAPTERS

This book offers no less than 10 informative chapters and 2 commentaries. Written by some of the leading practitioners of criminological theory and research today, the chapters reveal some of the strengths of criminological sociology in its reliance on insights from sociological theory. Because we are fortunate to have two expert commentators for each part of this volume, a brief overview of the contents may suffice.

The chapters in Part I deal with various empirical and theoretical issues in criminological sociology revolving around the twin models of macro- and micro-analyses. Karl Schumann opens the discussions by offering an empirical analysis of the relation between work and crime in the German context from the viewpoint of life-course perspectives and insights from Max Weber's work on the Protestant ethic. Also on the basis of an empirical study, Imke Dunkake investigates school truancy as a form of deviant behavior on the basis of ideas derived from expectancy value theory, Pierre Bourdieu's capital perspective, and Robert Merton's anomie and strain theories. Moving to a more distinctly theoretical discussion, Sanjay Marwah and Mathieu Deflem investigate Merton's anomie-and-opportunity-structures theory from the viewpoint of some of the criticisms that have been raised against this perspective and in the light of one of Merton's final essays in this intellectual tradition. Ross Matsueda continues the theoretical discussion by investigating the value of certain important ideas in the work of George Herbert Mead for criminological research surrounding the notion of self and the concept of human agency. Karen Heimer, Stacy De Coster, and Halime Ünal move on in a social–psychological direction by contemplating on some of the critical consequences of the socialization into hegemonic gender definitions for juvenile delinquency. Ronald Akers, a leading theorist of criminological thought whose work needs no introduction, concludes Part I by offering a very thoughtful and astute commentary on the preceding chapters.

Part II of our volume addresses issues that pose questions of crime in intimate connection with pressing matters of dimensions of criminal justice. As such, our criminological attention is broadened. Nigel Fielding and Joachim Savelsberg both tackle social control issues very distinctly in their respective chapters. Fielding discusses dynamics of law enforcement, especially police training and police culture, from the viewpoint of the formative role of biography, while Savelsberg, in a likewise autobiographically contextualized manner, argues for the value of Weberian analysis on the basis of ideal types in the case of empirical research on sentencing and sentencing guidelines. Next, Robert Crutchfield returns to crime issues in an intellectually informed manner by relating crime problems to the structures of social inequality and social stratification. Susanne Karstedt takes a different route in bringing in emotions in the study of crime and criminal justice. In the best European tradition, René Van Swaaningen again leads us to a broad and high view by tackling important epistemological concerns in criminological thought and practice. Finally, we are fortunate to have Fritz Sack, one of the central players in the institutionalization of German (and European) criminological sociology, conclude our volume by commenting on the chapters in Part II. With Fritz, I hope that readers will have reason to conclude that this volume shows that the works of sociological scholars of crime and social control can be and will be perceived to be sociological in the very best tradition of our discipline.

# REFERENCES

Comte, A. (1839). *Cours de philosophie positive (Tome quatrième)*. Paris: Bachelier.

Deflem, M. (1999). Ferdinand Tönnies on crime and society: An unexplored contribution to criminological sociology. *History of the Human Sciences, 12*(3), 87–116.

Durkheim, E. ([1895] 1982). *The rules of sociological method*. New York: Free Press.

Foucault, M. ([1978] 1991). Governmentality. In: G. Burchell, C. Gordon & P. Miller (Eds), *The Foucault effect* (pp. 87–104). Chicago: University of Chicago Press.

Garland, D. (1992). Criminological knowledge and its relation to power: Foucault's genealogy and criminology today. *British Journal of Criminology, 32*, 403–422.

Horowitz, I. L. (1993). *The decomposition of sociology*. New York: Oxford University Press.

Merton, R. K. (1938). Social structure and anomie. *American Sociological Review, 3*, 672–682.

Pasquino, P. (1991). Criminology: The birth of a special knowledge. In: G. Burchell, C. Gordon & P. Miller (Eds), *The Foucault effect* (pp. 235–250). Chicago: University of Chicago Press.

Quetelet, A. (1835). *Sur l'homme et sur le dévelopment de ses facultés, ou Essay de physique sociale*. Paris: Bachelier.

Shaw, C. R., & McKay, H. D. (1942). *Juvenile delinquency in urban areas*. Chicago: University of Chicago Press.

Sutherland, E. H. (1939). *Principles of criminology* (3rd ed.). Philadelphia: J.B. Lippincott.

# PART I:
# FROM MACRO TO MICRO MODELS
# IN CRIME AND DELINQUENCY
# ANALYSIS

# WORK AND CRIME: CAN THE MISSING LINK BE UNDERSTOOD THROUGH MAX WEBER'S PROTESTANT ETHIC ☆

Karl F. Schumann

## ABSTRACT

*The relationship between work and crime has been neither empirically nor theoretically settled. Equivocal results do not correspond well with most of the theories employed. This paper suggests a new understanding. Based on the data of the Bremen school-to-work-cohort-study, it looks at the work–crime issue from a life-course perspective. On the one hand, variables measuring aspects of work or unemployment did not show in multivariate analyses significant effects on delinquency. On the other hand, there are interventions by the juvenile or criminal justice system that have an effect on work biography. Selectivity patterns of the criminal justice*

☆ This paper condenses results of the Bremen school-to-work-study, which lasted 13 years. That longitudinal study was funded by Deutsche Forschungsgemeinschaft and the University of Bremen as part of the Special Research Unit 186 "Status Passages and Risks in the Life Course." In the preparation of this article, I started from a paper, Beate Ehret and myself presented at the ASC annual meeting in Denver in 2003, but revised substantially its theoretical and empirical content.

**Sociological Theory and Criminological Research: Views from Europe and the United States**
**Sociology of Crime, Law and Deviance, Volume 7, 9–28**
Copyright © 2006 by Elsevier Ltd.
**All rights of reproduction in any form reserved**
**ISSN: 1521-6136/doi:10.1016/S1521-6136(06)07002-3**

*system seem to honor puritan notions like 'idleness leads to crime.' Insofar that attitude shapes formal social control and – as can be shown – reduces subsequently the options available for delinquent persons in their work biography, Max Weber's "The Protestant Ethic and the Spirit of Capitalism" offers the best theoretical framework to understand the specific relationship between work biography and crime.*

## WORK AND CRIME: THEORETICAL AND EMPIRICAL PROBLEMS

The relationship between crime and work has been a topic of theoretical and empirical efforts in criminology since decades. One of the major questions to be answered is whether unemployment leads to crime. Research has been conducted at the macro level using aggregate data as well as at the micro level using individual data with equivocal results (Schumann, 2003a, Chapter 1). The following short overview is by no means meant as being comprehensive, rather it shall provide a first idea of the variety of theoretical starting points.

At the macro level, the theoretical framework mostly referred to is Merton's (1957) *anomie theory*. However, empirical support has been very limited. Theodore G. Chiricos, who has published various articles on the relationship between unemployment and crime, summed up the evidence (Chiricos, 1987) and found only few studies which did not support the well-known "consensus of doubt" (Cantor & Land, 1985). However, Chiricos pointed out that even if generally the findings were equivocal, some studies which were based on smaller aggregates (e.g. cities) and looked at property offenses tended to show positive correlation between unemployment and crime (Chiricos, 1987, p. 199). A convenient theoretical explanation was deduced from anomie theory: shrinking labor markets especially in inner cities help to legitimize illegal ways to obtain funds for living. Certainly, Robert K. Merton's (1957) anomie theory can offer some theoretical understanding for those findings on the aggregate level, while the linking of unemployment and crime on the macro level is neither empirically nor theoretically very compelling.

Researchers who used individual data also referred occasionally to anomie theory, especially for studies on the effects of unemployment on crime. For studies at the individual level, Merton's approach was reconstructed as *strain theory* which perceives crime as one of the possible responses of a given person to the discrepancy between universally held goals or aspirations, when legitimate means to achieve these goals are not available. Also regarding the impact of other aspects of working, for example the quality of work (e.g. skilled or unskilled work), the lengths jobs are held during life and the levels of earnings, anomie theory seemed to have something to offer. Agnew (1992) noted that frustration caused by income inequality (presumably caused in part by lack of access to satisfactory jobs) could erode occupational goals and values and encourage criminal behavior. Or, in the words of Uggen (1994):

> To the extent that one's job is economically rewarding and personally satisfying, one discerns progress toward success goals and is unlikely to adopt a deviant role adaptation (p. 4).

Even with explications like that it becomes unclear what particular aspects of work may have a protective effect against crime. Just earning sufficient money? Do something you like to do? The term 'success goals' seems to correspond with Merton's culturally acclaimed goals but can in fact be understood also more generally. This indicates the general problem with the application of criminological theories on the work–crime issue: the theories are so general that they grasp only very formal aspects of work (to have work or not, to earn legitimate money, to have a job to his liking), but miss any specific mechanism which might link work to conformity.

The other theoretical options, which have been employed to interpret individual data, especially control theory and rational choice theory, do hardly better. According to *control theory*, bonding follows from the commitment to the current job and to the achieved occupational career. By working one builds a stake in conformity that is unlikely to be jeopardized by committing criminal acts. A second bonding effect comes from involvement. Since working eats up so much of the daily time, there is little left for idleness (cf. Hirschi, 1969). This view is actually shared with economic theories of crime, which assume a zero-sum-situation between time spent with legal and illegal work. Again, this framework is very general (working consumes the time necessary to commit crimes) or tautological (working as a conform activity stabilizes conformity). Whether or not bonding through work emerges might depend on the type and quality of work. It is difficult to believe that any kind of work, e.g. a badly paid or exploitative one, contributes to bonding to the existing social order. Empirically it is difficult to study the relationship; bonding by involvement for example, that is, the blockage of committing crimes by the actual lack of time available for it, would demand the use of cross-sectional data. But cross-sectional analysis does not allow to conclusively settle the causal order. For that lagged data would be necessary. But if a lagged data set is used, the researcher constructs essentially an implausible relationship: e.g. after having spent a year with a time-consuming job, why should one be expected to commit no crimes in the following year? Or, after being unemployed in year 1, why should one be expected to commit crimes during the next year (especially if the unemployment has been terminated eventually)? The assumption of stability of the work situation over time is not always granted.

Moreover, we know from longitudinal studies that reciprocal effects exist. In studying the relationship between unemployment and crime, Thornberry and Christenson (1984) demonstrated by using longitudinal data that there are effects in both directions, which has encouraged Thornberry (1987) to develop the *interactional theory*. Such reciprocity however indicates that one has to include more aspects in the analysis to understand what is going on than what control theory usually refers to.

The *rational choice theory* or economic theory weights the payoffs of crime against the losses in normal life. Under the assumption that an individual makes choices between legal and illegal work, the individual will prefer illegal work if that becomes more rewarding. Low educational attainment, putting adolescents and young adults at risk of unemployment or achieving only low paying jobs may lead to participation in income-generating criminal activities.

> If the legal labor market opportunities appear weak, a youth is less likely to make adequate investment in acquiring the human capital necessary for success in the legal labor market (Bushway & Reuter, 1997).[1]

Looking at the work–crime relationship, rational choice theory would suggest that obtaining training for skilled jobs should increase the perceived payoffs and rewards of legal work, thus diminishing the chance of criminal involvement, if the legal labor market is strong and can provide jobs to those adequately trained. In contrast, if returns coming from illegal work exceed those stemming from legal work, a person may well prefer to commit illegal acts.

The question is, how appropriate that theoretical framework is to grasp the connection between work and crime, if there is any. In fact empirical results quite often do not back that assumption very well. In a comprehensive overview on research, Fagan and Freeman (1999) have convincingly argued that legal and illegal work are not exclusive like a zero-sum-game, but can very well accompany each other. They summarize various shortcomings of the research on work and crime, which may be of general importance. Firstly, they criticize the conceptualization of the relationship of crime, perceived as illegal work, and legal work as mutually exclusive. Rather, they contend that the relationship should be perceived as potentially additive. Various types of combinations, ranging from employee theft over tax evasion to drug dealing using a legal occupation as cover indicate the possibility that legal and illegal work can be combined in attempts to doubling up the returns. Secondly, they take from ethnographic as well as longitudinal research the insight that individuals move in and out of legal and illegal activities, that they may enter illegal work while still in school and create a mortgage thereby for difficulties throughout their adult working life. Having been incarcerated in adolescence may reduce the earnings by later legal work as well as the stability of work contracts.

The arguments of Fagan and Freeman raise doubts on the soundness of theoretical frameworks used to study the association between unemployment and crime. It appears that the above-sketched theories are too general to help understand the work–crime relationship as it emerges and changes throughout one's lifetime. Hardly one of those theories has gained substantial empirical support or has even been developed any further by research in this field. This raises the question whether we should not look for a new theoretical framework, which could explain effects visible in longitudinal data better. So far most of the theories mentioned have been confronted with aggregate or individual data, using cross-sectional or lagged time-order designs using data from two points in time to study causal relationships. The insights of the life-course approach, which is not a theory but rather a way to study issues by using longitudinal data of a wider timespan and looking at reciprocal and accumulative effects, suggest more complex designs. It may be necessary to focus more on the impact societal institutions, like agents of social control and gate-keepers on the labor market, have on the life-course and how those are intertwined with the behavior of actors (see Leisering & Schumann, 2003). By looking at institutions which affect the life course, that is by studying the work–crime relationship with regard to the meso-level, one actually starts to look for an ideological link, which explains the relationship between work and crime.

## METHODS

This paper is based on the results of the Bremen school-to-work-study, which is a prospective cohort study of the life course of juveniles starting at the beginning of their school-to-work transition. The data set covers the 10 years following their exit from school through the enrollment in apprenticeships of the majority of the cohort and the early years of their working life. The research looks at their crime patterns based on self-reports as well as official data. Thereby, it is possible to study the relationship between work life and offending during the adolescent and young adult years. The cohort is constituted by students who left schools of the city of Bremen after completion of the compulsory number of 9 years of schooling in 1989. The cohort was selected at the *Hauptschule* or *Sonderschule*, which essentially provides basic education. In this article only a selection of the many results is presented,[2] observed by using various types of statistical analyses like event history analysis, logistic regressions with the dependent variable being measured with nominal, ordinal and interval scaling. However, the results are robust and rather independent from the type of statistical analysis.

The cohort of early school-leavers was selected to allow for the study of the impact of the German system of apprenticeships on the school-to-work transition. In contrast, high school graduates would for the most part not enter apprenticeships but rather continue with higher education at colleges or universities.

The interview data have been collected at five panel waves (Fig. 1). At the first wave in May/June 1989, the mean age of the cohort members, who at that time still went to school, was 16.6 years. 45% of the cohort were female, 55% male. The proportion of minority youth in the cohort was 17%.

After the youths had exited school in July 1989, they have been re-interviewed four times thereafter in intervals of 2–3 years, namely in 1993, 1995, 1997 and 2000. The attrition was reasonably over time, reducing the cohort from 424 to 376 in 1997, the number dropped however in 2000, 11 years after the first interviews, to only 333 persons.[3]

In addition to this standardized data collection with the so-called 'macro panel,' a qualitative five-wave-panel study was conducted. In 1989, 60 members of the cohort were selected and thereafter contacted five times during the years 1989 and 1997 for explorative open interviews. The interviews took place in 1989, 1990, 1992, 1994 and 1997. To take care for attrition in the so-called 'micro panel,' losses were filled up in 1992 and 1997 so that altogether 79 persons of the macro panel also became members of the micro panel over the years. From those qualitative data the individual assessments of the progress of the occupational development was gained as well as accounts the youth gave on their deviancy including their interpretation of the relationship between work and crime.

The dependent variable delinquency has been measured by self-reports, providing for the years 1989 through 1999 annual data on some 34 types of

| | Standardized Interviews MACRO-PANEL | Qualitative Interviews MICRO-PANEL | Official records | Selfreported Delinquency (code for years) |
|---|---|---|---|---|
| Before July 1989 | May/June (N=732) 1st wave | | | A (Starting at age 14) |
| After July 1989 | | December N=60 1st wave | | B |
| 1990 | | September N=60 2nd wave | | |
| 1991 | | Interviews by phone June | | |
| 1992 | December N=426 2nd wave | April N=48 3rd wave | | C |
| 1993 | | | | D |
| 1994 | | April N=57 4th wave | *BZR*-record Research N=1221 | E |
| 1995 | June N=376 3rd wave | | *Court records Study* N=86 | F |
| 1996 | | | | G |
| 1997 | April N=370 4th wave | September N=52 5th wave | BZR-records update N=415 | H |
| 1998 | | | | I |
| 1999 | | | | J |
| 2000 | April N=333 5th wave | | | K |

*Fig. 1.*  Research Design.

offenses; most of them were aggregated to indices on property, violence and drug-related crimes. While the majority of the analyses were completed for those three different indices, they were also added including various other crimes to a total index of delinquency for some analyses. In addition we collected official data for the macro panel cohort members at the German central registry (BZR), where all decisions by prosecution and court are registered, measuring the criminal activities of all cohort members from the age of 14 years up to the year 1999. In the questionnaires delinquency has been measured using a bi-annual retrospective, which may have caused some underreporting for the more remote years (1990/1991, 1993, 1995). Of course, a variety of variables used in criminological research have been covered in the questionnaires. In addition, between July 1989 and December 1999, the vocational training or substitutes for it and the enrollment into the labor force were measured month-by-month in a calendar, so that every change could be accounted for and any phase of unemployment could be measured in its duration.

Additionally, a study of the court records of cohort members was conducted to find out whether or not progress in their vocational careers affected the court decisions. For those cohort members who gave their agreement, the files of cases against them handled by the prosecution and court offices in Bremen were qualitatively analyzed and coded to find out if background information on success or failure during apprenticeships and the subsequent work life were considered in the decision making about dismissals or conviction.

## OBTAINING VOCATIONAL SKILLS AND DEVIANCE

The Bremen school-to-work-study was designed to find out whether or not success in obtaining a vocational training by graduating from an apprenticeship would contribute to the termination of juvenile delinquency. Most German criminologists are convinced that the successful completion of apprenticeships is a valid predictor for conformity in later life.[4] Considering that the age-curve of delinquency peaks around the age of 18, the subsequent decline is expected to be more visible, if a vocational training after leaving school has been completed. Accordingly, the main hypothesis of this research was *the more successful a juvenile is in accomplishing the apprenticeship (that is, graduating from it), the less delinquency he or she will commit.*

A brief explanation of the apprenticeship system in Germany seems necessary.[5] This system, jointly organized by state schools and private industries, provides vocational training for some 360 occupations (handicrafts, technicians, services, work in administration and health sector, etc.). An apprenticeship lasts for between 2 and 3 years and consists of attending state-run vocational schools for one or two days per week and of specific job-training, provided by industry or shop owners. Apprentices are being paid about one-fourth of the regular salaries in the particular trade, which makes them convenient workers for many employers. The majority of Germany's youth either enters an apprenticeship after leaving school or continues to higher education. In fact almost 90% of our sample has entered an apprenticeship at some point in time in their adolescence, and two-third have eventually graduated from it.

Using the data of the second wave, which were collected roughly 3 years after most of the cohort members had begun their apprenticeships, it was possible to have a first test of the hypothesis: it was falsified. A final judgment was however postponed until the data of the third wave, collected in 1995, were in, after most of the cohort had finished their apprenticeship. In that multivariate analysis (the data were collected $5\frac{1}{2}$ years after the youths left school) the hypothesis was falsified again. Thus, it became definite that the supposed protective effect of vocational qualifications was not supported by the data. Some of the results were: after leaving school, all male members increased the frequency of their delinquency, but the apprentices were among those who increased the *most*. The qualitative data, collected for the smaller 'micro panel,' allowed to explain that surprising fact: among the successful apprentices were some who led a *"double life"* (see Dietz, Matt, Schumann, & Seus, 1997, pp. 247–250, for details; Böttger, 2003, pp. 105–107). They did an excellent job at work but enjoyed to commit offenses during weekends.

Moreover, the prevalence of delinquency of those obtaining successfully their occupational qualification and those failing to complete or to enter an apprenticeship at all was almost *equal*. This was true also for the mean frequency of offending. Property offenses were even more frequently committed by *apprentices* compared to unskilled workers. Drug taking was *as frequent* among apprentices as among unskilled or unemployed.

In a regression analysis of the frequency of delinquency during 1993 (Table 1), none of the variables measuring success of qualification (as listed in the variable groups *occupational typology* and *subjective dimension*) contributed to the explanation. The model showed significant negative effects for the variables age, female sex, minority status and positive attitude toward vocational school, and – expectable – positive effects for the frequency of delinquency in the preceding year, but also – by controlling for prior delinquency – for being sanctioned by the Juvenile Justice System in the preceding year and for substitution of apprenticeship contracts with subsequent start of a new contract. The conclusions regarding those results are: labeling effects seem to effect an increase of delinquency, as do problems during an apprenticeship which cause a substitution of the contract. In contrast, neither successful graduation from the apprenticeship system nor

***Table 1.***  Multiple Regression: Delinquency (Frequency) in 1993.

| Independent Variables | Total | Property | Drug Use/ Sales | Assault |
|---|---|---|---|---|
| Intercept | — | — | — | — |
| Age | −0.003 | −0.067 | −0.071 | 0.039 |
| Male | +0.271** | 0.235** | 0.215** | 0.130** |
| Minority | −0.121** | −0.002 | −0.109* | −0.137** |
| **Informal social control** | | | | |
| Living with parents | −0.067 | −0.062 | −0.156** | −0.050 |
| Parents know | 0.021 | 0.071 | 0.062 | −0.025 |
| Partner know | −0.003 | 0.065 | −0.013 | −0.012 |
| Have difficulties with demands at work | 0.064 | 0.155** | 0.107* | 0.066* |
| Clique | 0.019 | 0.089† | 0.073 | 0.031 |
| **Graduation** | | | | |
| No graduation/school for children with special needs | −0.032 | −0.053 | −0.058 | 0.000 |
| Graduated with honor | 0.048 | −0.043 | 0.025 | 0.012 |
| Equivalent to German realschule | 0.044 | 0.039 | 0.079 | −0.009 |
| **Occupational Typology** | | | | |
| Continues apprentice | 0.065 | 0.015 | 0.077 | −0.019 |
| Interrupted apprentice | −0.004 | −0.018 | −0.009 | −0.010 |
| Apprentice after training scheme | 0.013 | 0.075 | −0.033 | −0.013 |
| Failed/drop out | −0.030 | 0.067 | 0.029 | −0.055 |
| Never apprenticeship | 0.040 | 0.041 | 0.085 | 0.012 |
| Change of job | 0.104* | −0.018 | 0.041 | 0.098* |
| Unemployment (cum) | 0.041 | −0.002 | 0.009 | 0.042 |
| **Occupational school** | | | | |
| I liked it | −0.100* | 0.058 | −0.034 | −0.035 |
| I didn't like | −0.049 | −0.013 | −0.046 | −0.019 |
| I did well | 0.016 | −0.045 | −0.051 | 0.062 |
| I did poorly | 0.037 | 0.047 | 0.092† | 0.042 |
| I was truant | 0.044 | 0.110† | −0.013 | 0.074 |
| **Subjective dimension** | | | | |
| Satisfied with apprenticeship | −0.002 | −0.019 | −0.016 | −0.020 |
| Assessment of own finances | 0.069 | 0.059 | 0.046 | −0.019 |
| Job of your liking | 0.031 | −0.001 | 0.007 | 0.059 |
| **Court contact** | | | | |
| History | 0.020 | −0.015 | 0.023 | 0.118* |
| In year 1992 | 0.104* | 0.012 | 0.147** | 0.075 |
| **Delinquency prior year** | | | | |
| Total-C | 0.374** | — | — | — |
| Assault-C | — | 0.084 | — | — |
| Property-C | — | — | 0.217** | — |
| Drugs-C | — | — | — | 0.475** |
| $R^2$ | 0.39 | 0.18 | 0.25 | 0.40 |

†$p < 0.1$;
*$p < 0.05$;
**$p < 0.01$.

failing to obtain that degree of qualification seems to be relevant for the development of delinquency.

Some additional findings were: being unable to obtain an apprenticeship-contract or being kicked out of an apprenticeship might be considered as failure; however, neither of those developments seems to increase the crime risk among youths, who experienced that bad luck. To the contrary, their prevalence of property crimes was *lower* than the mean prevalence of the remaining cohort. Moreover, there was no statistical difference between the frequency of this group and the most successful group of graduates from apprenticeships. It is to be expected that unemployment may hit unskilled workers more often than the remaining cohort; however, we did not find significant higher delinquency for the year they became unemployed. This was true also if we looked at delinquency in the subsequent year following the one of being unemployed.

One result, however, was surprising: while the group of unskilled workers had lower self-reported delinquency, their official crime rate was actually *higher*. Apparently, they were more often caught by police and prosecuted for their offenses. This gap between self-reports and registered offenses seems to indicate selection effects of the formal control agencies.

## GETTING ESTABLISHED IN THE LABOR MARKET

For those who graduated from apprenticeships, the transition into the labor market can be considered successful if they manage to find jobs fitting the level of their skills. If they work in unskilled jobs thereafter, the vocational training did not pay, the human capital did not produce the expected returns. We might formulate as a hypothesis, *that those graduates who have to face such poorer working conditions might be more delinquent than those who got skilled jobs.* This turned out to be not the case. The successful group persisted at their delinquency level for some time, as did the unsuccessful group, which did *not increase* their delinquency. Neither increase nor decrease of delinquent activities of persons who graduated from apprenticeships (or from equivalent forms of training to obtain skills) was affected by variables related to the quality of work, at least not immediately. The following models explain increase and decrease of delinquency for the whole period following the graduation from apprenticeships (Tables 2 and 3).

Increase is significantly larger for those who had obtained a skilled job after graduation from apprenticeship and for those who had been convicted; increase is reduced by getting established in stable work as well as by getting

***Table 2.*** Transition Rate Model: Delinquency Increase after Graduation from Apprenticeship (Odds and Odds-Ratios).

| Delinquency Increase | Total | Property | Drug Use/Sales | Assault |
|---|---|---|---|---|
| Intercept | 0.838 | 0.486* | 0.240*** | 0.143*** |
| Female | 0.440 *** | 0.415*** | 0.396*** | 0.117*** |
| Parenthood | 0.591 | 0.493 | 0.561 | 0.991 |
| Current occupational status | | | | |
|   Housework | 1.487 | 1.355 | 0.000 | 3.970 |
|   Unemployed | 0.952 | 0.962 | 1.031 | 1.248 |
|   Unskilled | 1.223 | 1.354 | 0.526 | 1.369 |
|   Other | 0.576 | 0.753 | 0.523 | 1.171 |
|   Skilled work after apprenticeship | 1.648* | 2.006** | 1.457 | 1.325 |
|   Skilled work – stability | 0.623* | 0.623$^\dagger$ | 0.465* | 0.484$^\dagger$ |
| Court contact | | | | |
|   Prosecution dismissal §45 | 0.791 | 0.905 | 0.293* | 0.425 |
|   Court dismissal §47 | 1.440 | 1.320 | 1.112 | 2.311$^\dagger$ |
|   Convicted | 1.432 | 1.078 | 1.992* | 4.758*** |
|   Clique | 1.317 | 1.152 | 1.137 | 1.986* |
|   Not living with parents/partner | 1.218 | 1.476$^\dagger$ | 0.860 | 0.755 |
| Level of delinquency | | | | |
|   1–5 offenses | 0.589** | 0.555* | 1.317 | 0.082*** |
|   6–10 offenses | 0.751 | 0.892 | 7.035*** | 1.179 |
|   Time | 0.799*** | 0.776*** | 0.861* | 0.796* |
| Delinquency (prior year) | | | | |
|   Assault | 0.998 | 1.004 | 0.989 | 1.013 |
|   Property | 1.002 | 1.003* | 1.001 | 1.001 |
|   Drug use/sales | 0.998 | 0.992 | 1.004 | 0.995 |
|   Traffic and other offenses | 1.003 | 1.001 | 1.004* | 1.007*** |

$^\dagger p < 0.1$;
$^* p < 0.05$;
$^{**} p < 0.01$;
$^{***} p < 0.001$.

older. We may neglect the foreseeable effects of former levels of delinquency on an increase or decrease model.

The decrease model shows smaller effects. Decrease is hindered by convictions and by peer groups. For violence we find an effect toward decrease if diversion has been practiced by judges. Again, variables relating to work status are irrelevant. And – not surprisingly – decrease is more often the case among females.

***Table 3.*** Transition Rate Model: Delinquency Decrease after Graduation from Apprenticeship (Odds and Odds-Ratios).

| Delinquency Decrease | Total | Property | Drug Use/Sales | Assault |
|---|---|---|---|---|
| Intercept | 0.897 | 2.504* | 0.585 | 3.999 |
| Female | 1.717* | 1.272 | 0.837 | 6.490 |
| Parenthood | 1.125 | 1.415 | 1.564 | 0.726 |
| Current occupational status | | | | |
| Housework | 4.172 | 3.724 | 0.962 | ∞ |
| Unemployed | 0.893 | 1.330 | 0.810 | 1.034 |
| Unskilled | 0.846 | 1.134 | 0.975 | 0.888 |
| Other | 1.024 | 0.502$^\dagger$ | 2.017 | 1.841 |
| Skilled work after apprenticeship | 1.189 | 0.780 | 1.324 | 0.659 |
| Skilled work – stability | 0.788 | 1.543 | 0.970 | 0.879 |
| Court contacts | | | | |
| Prosecution dismissal §45 | 1.268 | 1.031 | 0.640 | 1.429 |
| Court dismissal §47 | 0.434* | 0.718 | 0.855 | 4.559* |
| Convicted | 0.570* | 1.137 | 0.274** | 0.630 |
| Clique | 0.597* | 0.555* | 0.564$^\dagger$ | 0.545 |
| Not living with parents/partner | 0.846 | 0.830 | 0.591 | 0.702 |
| Level of delinquency (prior year) | | | | |
| 1–5 offenses | 0.665$^\dagger$ | 0.599$^\dagger$ | 1.900$^\dagger$ | 0.242 |
| 6–10 offenses | 1.631$^\dagger$ | 1.214 | 0.834 | 0.461 |
| Time | 1.003 | 0.901 | 1.058 | 1.130 |
| Delinquency (prior year) | | | | |
| Assault | 1.014 | 1.018 | 0.993 | 0.992 |
| Property | 0.990* | 0.991* | 1.001 | 1.002 |
| Drug use/sales | 0.992$^\dagger$ | 1.002 | 0.996 | 1.008 |
| Traffic offenses and other | 0.999 | 1.000 | 0.999 | 1.002 |

∞ = An exact value is not calculable because the denominator equals zero.
$^\dagger p < 0.1$;
$^* p < 0.05$;
$^{**} p < 0.01$.

Altogether it seems that the trajectory of vocational training and work seems to be quite unrelated to the frequency and prevalence of offending. The quantitative analyses, the qualitative findings and a comparative data analysis, based on the Bremen data set as well as the Denver Youth Survey data set (Huizinga, Schumann, Ehret, & Elliott, 2000), point consistently into that direction. If this is true, it would be misleading, for example, to use knowledge about performance in vocational training and work or unemployment as predictors for later delinquency. This conclusion, however, needs to be qualified.

## EFFECTS OF CRIMINAL SANCTIONING ON THE WORK LIFE

It was already pointed out that unskilled workers have been more often registered while they had reported delinquency at a *lower* level than the rest of the cohort. This indicates selectivity by the law enforcement agencies in their patterns of persecution. Additional selectivity was found in sentencing decisions which were also related to the work life. If delinquent youths were sanctioned by the justice system, their occupational skills seemed to influence the level of sanctioning; unskilled workers were facing harsher reactions. In a specific analysis Panter, Prein, and Seus (2001) looked at the effects of unemployment and lacking skills on sanctioning by judges in property offense cases. They found significant effects (Table 4).

The sanctioning level increases with regard to age (18 or older), severity of the offense, but also if the offender was unskilled or unemployed. From the qualitative analysis of court records, various cases were found in which good progress in the work career led to leniency, while in the case of unemployment, imprisonment appeared legitimate (see Panter et al., 2001, pp. 170–181). Actually, similar results have been reported for the United States by Chiricos and Bales (1991) and Nobiling, Spohn, and DeLone (1998) as well as for the

***Table 4.*** Ordinal Logitmodel: Sanctioning in the Juvenile Justice System for Property Offenses.

| Parameter | $\beta$ |
|---|---|
| $\alpha 1$ (Juvenile court dismissal) | $-2.19^{**}$ |
| $\alpha 2$ (Conviction) | $-4.98^{***}$ |
| Female | $-0.77$ |
| 18 years or older | $2.06^{**}$ |
| Second offense | $-1.30$ |
| Severe offense | $2.14^{**}$ |
| Unskilled | $1.74^{*}$ |
| Unemployed | $1.87^{*}$ |

*Source:* Panter et al. (2001, p. 168); translated by the author.
$^{*}p<0.05$;
$^{**}p<0.01$;
$^{***}p<0.001$.

UK by Crow, Richardson, Riddington, and Simon (1989), to mention just a few studies which demonstrated that unemployment increases the risk of being incarcerated.

In addition, we found: those who became subject of criminal persecution tended to experience in the subsequent time negative developments in their working trajectory; they dropped out of the apprenticeships more often or they were more often downward mobile in regard to the quality of their jobs (Table 5).

These findings correspond actually with the results of life-course-research in the US. Bushway (1996) found that arrests reduced the earnings in later work life, the same finding was reported by Grogger (1995). Fagan and Freeman (1999) concluded therefore that negative effects of being incarcerated on the subsequent work life are definite (p. 142).

The conclusion based on those research results would be: while, in general, there seems not to be much of a link between the trajectory of vocational education and work on the one hand and the persistence of offending on the other, at least not until early adulthood (that is until the age of about 25), the decision-making processes of criminal justice system

***Table 5.*** Transition Rate Model: Risk of Negative Occupational Events.

| Variable | Dropout from Apprenticeship | | | Downward Occupational Mobility | | |
|---|---|---|---|---|---|---|
| | $\beta$ | Significance | $\alpha$ | $\beta$ | Significance | $\alpha$ |
| Intercept | −4.0641 | *** | 0.0172 | −3.8287 | *** | 0.0217 |
| Male | −0.6979 | *** | 0.4976 | −0.3304 | ** | 0.7187 |
| Child | 0.4380 | | 1.5497 | 0.6758 | *** | 1.9657 |
| High school graduation | −0.7101 | ** | 0.4916 | −0.5002 | *** | 0.6064 |
| Delinquency | | | | | | |
| Drug use | 0.5214 | ** | 1.6844 | 0.1826 | | 1.2003 |
| Property | 0.0986 | | 1.1036 | 0.1299 | | 1.1387 |
| Traffic and other offenses | −0.2815 | | 0.7547 | 0.0115 | | 1.0116 |
| Assault | 0.7574 | *** | 2.1327 | 0.5837 | *** | 1.7926 |
| Court contact | | | | | | |
| Convicted | 0.4191 | | 1.5207 | 0.8235 | ** | 2.2785 |
| Dismissal §47 | 1.0470 | *** | 2.8492 | 0.7335 | | 2.0823 |
| Dismissal §45 | 0.6616 | * | 1.9379 | −7.1659 | | 0.0008 |
| Traffic offense | −0.5331 | | 0.5868 | 0.6570 | | 1.9290 |

*$p<0.05$;
**$p<0.01$;
***$p<0.001$.

may produce such a link during the later adult life, either by furthering unemployment as a consequence of sanctioning or by selecting harsher sanctions for those with lesser skills. Thus, as also Sampson and Laub (1997) have observed, in the later phases of the life course there may be an accumulation of disadvantages, which – at least for some members of the society – can in fact imply or constitute a relationship between work and crime. For the majority of delinquent persons, insofar they managed to avoid law enforcement, such relationship does not seem to exist.

## LEARNING FROM MAX WEBER

How can these findings be explained? It seems not very fruitful to seek theoretical approaches based on unemployment or the work life of the offender, which might explain criminal behavior, at least not during adolescence and the early adulthood; empirically, there seems to be little relationship to be explained. Rather it looks promising to look for a theoretical framework to understand why law enforcement agencies have everyday routines which discriminate against persons who lack working skills or a higher educational level, who have unstable work life or who experience unemployment. I believe that Max Weber's "The Protestant Ethics and the Spirit of Capitalism" offers the appropriate answer (Weber, 1906/1965).

In his seminal study Weber raised the question, if and how far religious influences helped to specify and expand the spirit of capitalism throughout the world. The term 'spirit of capitalism' was explicated by referring to Benjamin Franklin's "Advice to a young tradesman" (Franklin, 1748/1840); Weber (1965) mentioned the principles 'time is money', 'credit is money', 'money can make money' and others (p. 41). In his view the capitalist ethos implies a rationality, which includes calculation of returns, a systematic style of working by performing it as a 'calling' and a specific conduct of life (Lebensführung), which focuses on the augmentation of money. Weber (1965) sees especially middle class entrepreneurs as supporters of that spirit (p. 55); the big businessman supports it only insofar as he does not spend his money but reinvests it. The worker, however, has to learn that spirit, so that he can overcome the traditionalist orientation: that one needs only so much money as is necessary to survive. Under the traditionalist orientation a worker will, if the piece-work wage increases, produce less, not more (1965, p. 49).

Weber analyzed the religions of the world by looking for correspondences with this spirit and found especially in Calvinism and in Baptism, but also in the Methodist church and in Pietism such links ("Wahlverwandschaften")

(Weber, 1965, p. 115). Especially, Calvinism teaches that success in the working life indicates predestination for the eternal life. Self-control and ascetic lifestyle are important. Pleasure and idleness are considered as being thoroughly bad (1965, p. 167). Waste of time is extremely objectionable. Weber (1965) summarizes: "Work is the most ascetic way and the specific prevention against all temptations of 'unclean life'" (p. 168).[6] However, not any type of work, only skilled work is what God demands. The skilled worker spends his time methodically, in contrast to the casual laborer (1965, p. 171). Thus, in the protestant ethic, notwithstanding differences between Calvinism, Puritanism and Methodism, it is definite that work is the primary means to make sure to be among the chosen few. Unequal distribution of goods indicates Gods providence (1965, p. 185).

Those religious movements became economically effective through their educational efforts. Weber elaborated on this, especially after his visit to the USA in 1907, where he studied the religious orientations of Baptist sects, of Mennonites and Quakers. He pointed at the practices within those – how he calls them – sects to audit, control and punish the way of life of their members (1965, p. 296).[7] Church members have permanently to live up to those ethical expectations.

The sociological importance of that ethos lies in Weber's view less in the message itself but rather in the positive and negative sanctioning of the respective lifestyles. While Weber mentioned only the religious educational efforts (e.g. by Sunday schools and social control in the parish) as mechanisms to permeate this spirit into the minds of the people, one can think of many social institutions which share this effort: the school system teaching middle-class values, the apprenticeship system training skills as well as virtues related to work and life conduct, and also the juvenile and adult courts. The spirit of capitalism based on the protestant ethic seems to have hegemonic quality, which grants a consistent orientation in institutions of socialization and social control. This has been overlooked so far because it is so obvious. One might even say: there seems to exist a "prison for thoughts" (Quensel),[8] created by the common shared values of the protestant ethic in the industrial societies, which makes everybody believe that there must be a connection between not working and crime. Of course criminologists also, searching for empirical evidence for this connection, are inmates of that prison as well.

Further research, using longitudinal data to study in depth the interrelations between deviance, sanctioning and success and failure in the work life in a more comprehensive way than has been possible in this research (e.g. using a longer timespan with a cohort of a larger size) may provide a clearer understanding of the work–crime (non)-relationship by controlling for influences of institutional interventions. For the time being it seems important to bring to the attention of the law enforcement agencies the empirical finding that their everyday routines, insofar they are built on an ideologically legitimized selectivity, produce eventually the link between work life and crime, which the ideology assumes as granted: a typical case of self-fulfilling prophecy.

## NOTES

1. Quoted from the internet publication www.ncjrs.org/works/chapter6, p. 2.
2. See Schumann (2003a, b) for a more comprehensive report of results.
3. Since for the whole cohort of school-leavers (in 1989, $n = 732$) data on their registered crimes could be collected, the structure of attrition could be controlled beyond the use of statistical data collected in the first wave. Using both sources it turned out that only between the third and fourth waves a significant loss of registered persons took place. Besides that only the loss of females was significant, if one compares wave 1 with wave 5; changing their names after getting married caused apparently problems in tracking them over 10 years.
4. For an overview, see Schumann (2003a, pp. 28–33).
5. More information can be obtained from Hamilton (1990) and Schumann (1995).
6. Translated by the author.
7. The topic has been elaborated in Weber's article "Die protestantischen Sekten und der Geist des Kapitalismus" (The protestant sects and the spirit of capitalism), written in 1920, which the German edition of the 'Protestant Ethic' of 1965 also contains.
8. Quensel (1982) characterized with this term the usual reasoning to defend the prohibitive drug policy.

## REFERENCES

Agnew, R. (1992). Foundations for a General Strain Theory of crime and delinquency. *Criminology, 30*, 7–88.
Böttger, A. (2003). Berufsausbildung und Delinquenz – eine qualitative Analyse. In: K. F. Schumann (Ed.), *Berufsbildung, Arbeit und Delinquenz* (pp. 89–114). Weinheim and München: Juventa.
Bushway, S. D. (1996). *The impact of a criminal history record on access to legitimate employment*. Unpublished doctoral dissertation. Carnegie Mellon University.
Bushway, S. D., & Reuter, P. (1997). Labor markets and crime risk factors. In: L. Sherman, D. Gottfredson, D. MacKenzie, J. Eck, P. Reuter & S. Bushway (Eds), *Preventing crime: What works, what doesn't, what's promising* (Chapter 6). Washington: NCJRS.

Cantor, D., & Land, K. (1985). Unemployment and crime rates in Post World War II United States. *American Sociological Review, 50*, 317–332.

Chiricos, T. G. (1987). Rates of crime and unemployment: An analysis of aggregate research evidence. *Social Problems, 34*, 187–212.

Chiricos, T. G., & Bales, W. D. (1991). Unemployment and punishment: An empirical assessment. *Criminology, 29*, 701–724.

Crow, I., Richardson, P., Riddington, C., & Simon, F. (1989). *Unemployment, crime and offenders*. London: NACRO.

Dietz, G.-U., Matt, E., Schumann, K. F., & Seus, L. (1997). *"Lehre tut viel ...".* *Berufsbildung, Lebensplanung und Delinquenz bei Arbeiterjugendlichen*. Münster: Votum.

Fagan, J., & Freeman, R. B. (1999). Crime and work. In: M. Tonry (Ed.), *Crime and Justice*, (Vol. 29, pp. 225–390). Chicago: University of Chicago Press.

Franklin, B. (1748/1840). *Advice to a young tradesman. Works* (Vol. II) Boston: Tappan, Wittemore and Mason.

Grogger, J. (1995). The effects of arrests on the employment and earnings of young men. *The Quarterly Journal of Economics, 110*, 51–71.

Hamilton, S. F. (1990). *Apprenticeship for adulthood: Preparing youth for the future*. New York: Free Press.

Hirschi, T. (1969). *Causes of delinquency*. Berkeley: University of California Press.

Huizinga, D., Schumann, K. F., Ehret, B., & Elliott, A. (2000). *Training for the labor market and juvenile delinquency. A comparative study of the impact of different systems of school-to-work-transition in the USA and Germany*. Unpublished final report to the German-American Academic Council, Boulder and Bremen.

Leisering, L., & Schumann, K. F. (2003). How institutions shape the German life course. In: W. R. Heinz & V. W. Marshall (Eds), *Social dynamics of the life course* (pp. 193–209). New York: Aldine de Gruyter.

Merton, R. K. (1957). Social structure and anomie. In: *Social theory and social structure* (pp. 131–160). Glencoe: Free Press.

Nobiling, T., Spohn, C., & DeLone, M. (1998). A tale of two counties: Unemployment and sentence severity. *Justice Quarterly, 15*, 459–485.

Panter, R., Prein, G., & Seus, L. (2001). Per Doppelpass ins Abseits! Zur Kontinuität von Interpretations- und Handlungsmustern in Arbeitsmarkt und Strafjustiz und deren Konsequenzen. In: L. Leisering, R. Müller & K. F. Schumann (Eds), *Institutionen und Lebensläufe im Wandel* (pp. 157–189). Weinheim and München: Juventa.

Quensel, S. (1982). *Drogenelend*. Frankfurt: Campus.

Sampson, R. J., & Laub, J. H. (1997). A life-course theory of cumulative disadvantage and the stability of delinquency. In: T. P. Thornberry (Ed.), *Developmental theories of crime and delinquency* (pp. 133–161). New Brunswick: Transaction Publishers.

Schumann, K. F. (1995). The deviant apprentice. The impact of the German dual system of vocational training on juvenile delinquency. In: J. Hagan (Ed.), *Delinquency and disrepute in the life course* (pp. 91–103). Greenwich, CT: JAI.

Schumann, K. F. (Ed.) (2003a). *Berufsbildung, Arbeit und Delinquenz*. Weinheim and München: Juventa.

Schumann, K. F. (Ed.) (2003b). *Delinquenz im Lebensverlauf*. Weinheim and München: Juventa.

Thornberry, T. P., & Christenson, R. L. (1984). Unemployment and criminal involvement. *American Sociological Review, 49*, 398–411.

Thornberry, T. P. (1987). Toward an interactional theory of delinquency. *Criminology, 25*, 863–891.
Uggen, C. (1994). Innovators, retreatists and the conformist alternative: A job quality model of work and crime. Paper presented to the ASA meetings in Pittsburgh 1992, Revised, unpublished.
Weber, M. (1906, reprint/1965). *Die protestantische Ethik und der Geist des Kapitalismus.* München und Hamburg: Siebenstern.

# TRUANTS AND THE FAMILY: AN EMPIRICAL STUDY OF DEVIANT BEHAVIOR IN EARLY ADOLESCENCE

Imke Dunkake

## ABSTRACT

*The central aim of this article is to analyze family factors influencing truancy. To examine these family factors, a theoretical framework is proposed on the basis of Anomie Theory. It is extended by the Expectation Value Theory and the concepts of social and cultural capital. Using data from the German PISA Study 2000, we estimate indirect as well as direct effects on truancy. The results show that terms of social and cultural capital, poor school achievement and the attachment to deviant peers are important predictors. Controlling for school achievement results even suggest a weak positive relation between socioeconomic status and truancy.*

## INTRODUCTION

In Europe, the discussion on truancy is primarily influenced by pedagogical and medical scientists who define this term quite often as a symptom of an

Sociological Theory and Criminological Research: Views from Europe and the United States
Sociology of Crime, Law and Deviance, Volume 7, 29–56
Copyright © 2006 by Elsevier Ltd.
All rights of reproduction in any form reserved
ISSN: 1521-6136/doi:10.1016/S1521-6136(06)07003-5

abnormal, neurotic or phobic personality. The dominance of medical science in the research field of truancy is partly due to its historical roots in psychiatry research (Healy, 1915; Broadwin, 1932). Currently, there is still no agreement on a clear definition. Skipping school, truancy, absenteeism, school refusal, school tiredness or school phobia are concepts quite often used synonymously for a similar phenomenon: the unexcused absence from school. Even though there is no agreement on the definition, it is possible to state that "school phobia" and "school refusal" are terms describing the unexcused absence caused by psychological dispositions (e.g. Tyerman, 1968; Corville-Smith, Ryan, Adams, & Dalicandro, 1998).

From a sociological point of view, truancy can be defined as deviant behavior since it is, in most societies, a violation of the legal norms of the social system requiring regular school attendance (e.g. van Petegem, 1994). Moreover, in the majority of Western countries, frequent absenteeism is classified as an administrative offense, which can cause fines or even imprisonment for the legal guardians. Already one hundred years ago, scientists characterized truancy as an indicator of neglect and dissocial behavior (Kline, 1898; Healy, 1915). Healy and Bronner (1926, p. 171) titled truancy as the "kindergarten of crime", and a number of publications, starting in the 1940s with Shaw and McKay (1942), identified truancy as an important predictor for further delinquency (Glueck & Gleuck, 1950; Farrington, 1980; Loeber & Farrington, 1998). Recent studies mainly focus on the influence of different agents of socialization, especially the impact of the family. For instance, May (1975) and Tibbenham (1977) found truants to be members more often of large families than non-truants. Also, the negative influence of a broken home (Elliott, 1975) and an inconsistent style of parenting were significantly related to truancy (Sommer, 1985; Fergusson, Lynskey, & Horwood, 1995). Without question, the majority of these studies could contribute a lot to the understanding of truancy and pave the way for prevention strategies, but most of them are not theoretically guided. Therefore, the purpose of this paper is to develop a theory explaining the influence of the family on truancy. We will apply the Anomie Theory and extend it with the concepts of social and cultural capital. Secondly, we empirically test the theoretical model using the national German PISA Study 2000.

## ANOMIE THEORY

One of the oldest and the most influential theories explaining deviant behavior is the Theory of Anomie (Strain Theory), originally developed by

Durkheim (1983 [1897]). In 1938, Merton adopted essential assumptions of Durkheim's Theory and expanded it in "Social Structure and Social Theory", published in 1957. Merton distinguishes between a cultural and a social structure of society. 'Social structure' is a pattern of social relationships. 'Cultural structure' defines both, the goals of action (e.g. prosperity, social recognition) – which are primarily influenced by the middle class – and the institutionalized legitimate means, such as norms, rules and values necessary to achieve the cultural goals. Merton generally hypothesizes the level of anomie within a society to result from a discrepancy between cultural and social structure (Merton, 1968, p. 216). The position of individuals within the social structure particularly influences their possibilities to access the institutionalized means. In contrast to the members of the middle and the upper classes, members of the lower classes possess fewer resources to achieve culturally defined goals. Therefore, they experience a stronger social pressure to find non-established and, possibly deviant ways to achieve those goals.

According to Merton, there are five possible individual modes of adaptation to compensate for the strain between cultural goals and institutionalized means: conformity, innovation, ritualism, retreatism and rebellion. *Conformity* occurs when individuals accept the culturally defined goals and the related socially legitimate means of achieving them. Merton suggests that within a stable society, most individuals remain conformists. However, Merton is primarily interested in the question of how the restricted access to socially approved goals and/or means leads to deviant behavior. The second type of adaptation is named *innovation*. This type occurs if cultural goals are aspired, although the access to legitimate means is limited. Members of lower social classes are disadvantaged, notably concerning the goal 'prosperity'. Often, they do not have legitimate means to achieve prosperity, which in turn makes it more likely for them to apply illegitimate means (p. 198). *Ritualism* can be defined as deviant behavior only in a restricted sense, since the individual adapts the goals to the means. Individuals abandon the goals they once believed to be within their reach and dedicate themselves to their current means (p. 203). *Retreatism* involves rejecting the cultural goals of prosperity and social recognition as well as the socially legitimate means of achieving it. The retreatist withdraws from society. In this context, Merton especially refers to social outsiders (p. 207). *Rebellion* marks an exceptional case, as this type does not adapt to the given goals and means, but actively tries to challenge them.

Anomie Theory has been criticized for different reasons (e.g. Lemert, 1964). In the following, we will discuss two of the most important criticisms mentioned in the literature. First, Merton does not explain the transfer from the macro- (social structure) to the micro-level (modes of adaptation). He posits a gap in the social structure between institutionalized means and goals, which results in individual types of adaptation, but he does not offer an explanation about the function of agents of socialization, for example, the family, which mediates between the macro and micro level. Second, the Anomie Theory does not specify under which conditions the different types of adaptation occur. Therefore, we need a Theory of Action explaining the formation of the four different types of adaptation. Before supplementing the Anomie Theory by a Theory of Action and integrating the family as a mediator between the social structure and individual modes of adaptation, we first will describe how truancy can be explained within the Anomie Theory.

To do so, it is necessary to make assumptions about the general goals of students. Because it is not always possible to theoretically deduce all relevant goals, we will concentrate on two types of individual goals: educational success and social recognition as well as prosperity. Educational success is subordinated to social recognition and prosperity as cultural goals, and it functions as a means to these goals. Legitimate means to achieve educational success might be measured by different indicators of school achievement, e.g. reading literacy or repeating a class. Summarizing the paragraph, the following hierarchy of goals and means emerges obvious: school achievement – educational success – prosperity/social recognition.

Anomie Theory does not claim a connection between factors of social structure and legitimate means for achieving educational success. Still, there are various research findings in the field of class-specific socialization, which prove a positive relation between a low socioeconomic status (SES) of the family of origin and a failure in meeting the requirements asked by the educational system (Rossides, 1990; Ornstein & Levine, 1985). Anglo-American studies could even show a direct negative connection between the social status of the family of origin and illegitimate absence from school (Tyerman, 1968; Farrington, 1980). Based on these results, we can assume that juveniles with a poor socioeconomic background often fail to accomplish the expectations of the educational system, and therefore are in higher risk for truancy.

Concerning truancy, the individual types of adaptation might be interpreted as follows (Table 1):

*Conformity* (*the "proper" student*): The student has internalized the cultural goal "educational success", and in addition, possesses the legitimate means necessary to achieve this goal. Truancy does not take place in this case.

**Table 1.**  Modes of Adaptation and Types of Truancy.

| Modes of Adaptation | Types of Truancy | Culturally Approved Goals (Educational Success, Prosperity) | Institutionalized Means (School Achievement) |
|---|---|---|---|
| Conformity | The "proper" student | + | + |
| Innovation | Active truancy | + | – |
| Ritualism | Passive truancy | – | + |
| Retreatism | Complete truancy | – | – |
| Rebellion | Truancy as protest | +/– | +/– |

*Note:* (+), Acceptance; (–), rejection; (+/–), rejection of existing goals and means and substitution of new goals and means by the individual.

*Innovation ("active truancy")*: The student accepts "educational success" as an immediate goal in order to attain a professional position that offers financial security, social recognition and prosperity, but he does not have the legitimate means to reach the accepted goal. According to Merton (1968), the lack of legitimate means results from a socioeconomic disadvantage of the family of origin. The innovator tries to find ways other than regular school attendance (e.g. part-time work, acceptance by deviant peers) in order to achieve the goals established by the society.

*Ritualism ("passive truancy")*: The student does not accept the purpose of going to school. A regular school attendance takes place just because it is a matter of routine: students attend school because everybody attends school. That is why, in most of the cases, school efforts only meet minimal demands. The characteristics of passive truancy (physically present, but not showing any interest) are compatible to Merton's type of ritualism and often function as a precursor of active truancy (Schreiber-Kittl & Schröpfer, 2002).

*Social retreatism ("complete truancy")*: Social retreatism can be characterized by lethargic behavior. Neither the cultural goals nor the institutionalized means are accepted. In contrast to the rebel, this type does not strive to find alternatives to the missing goals and means. Following Merton (1968), social retreatism often results from frustrating experiences, that is, if both goals and means had been accepted, but did not turn out to be effective. Because of bad experiences, students refuse to go to school as it no longer makes sense to them.

*Rebellion ("truancy as protest")*: Students refuse to go to school because they want to protest against the goals and means of the school as an institution. In contrast to the type of social retreatism or the ritualist, the rebel tries to find alternative goals and means. Intense absence from school is no passive truancy, but rather expresses dissatisfaction about the existing conditions. Truancy that is approved by the parents can be interpreted as a type of rebellious adaptation which is passed on from one generation to another. This is the case if parents believe school attendance to be wrong for educational, religious or ideological reasons, and make their children stay at home or be taught in educational institutions other than public schools.

Defining school achievements as the means and educational success as the goal, the following hypotheses can be stated about students of the innovator type:

**H1.** The lower the SES of the family of origin is, the worse the school achievement will be.

**H1a.** The worse the school achievement is, the more likely students will try to achieve goals like social recognition or economical prosperity aside from school.

**H1b.** The more the students follow up their goals aside from school, the more frequent truancy will occur.

Merton's (1968) ritualist type of adaptation characterizes students whose academic achievement is satisfactory, but who do not strive for educational goals and who internally isolate themselves from being taught in school. Since these students are physically present during the lessons, they cannot be defined as active truants. Rebellion will not be taken into consideration here, as those students barely have the means to develop alternatives to the legally stipulated school attendance.

*Expansion of the Anomie Theory by Expectancy Value Theory*

Anomie Theory is focused on the social, not on the individual conditions of deviant behavior. In order to make precise assumptions about individual decisions, we will combine the Anomie Theory with the Expectancy Value Theory, focusing on the innovative type of adaptation. In this context, truancy can be understood as a result of cost–benefit analysis (Burgess, Gardiner, & Propper, 2002). If regular school attendance does not ensure the student the opportunity for prosperity and social recognition, the innovator is behaving rational if he aims for alternative activities. One alternative to reach prosperity would be a side job. Of course "prosperity" is a relative term in this instance, since a student's income is not comparable to the income of a person with a vocational education. Still, if a student has the choice between a side job, which offers some income and a school career, which is perceived as an offer without any perspective, it seems rational to decide for the former. The acceptance by peers might compensate the lack of social recognition by the educational system. In schools, students with poor achievement are confronted with their failure everyday – especially stressed through comments by teachers or classmates – therefore, it is more likely that they adapt a negative self-perception. To compensate this negative feedback, it is, from a student's point of view, reasonable to attach himself to peers who share values and norms aside the values represented by the school system. According to the Subculture Theory (Cohen, 1955), it is likely that these alternative patterns of values, norms and beliefs imply, in the sense of a counterculture, deviant values, and consequently cause deviant behavior. If students find alternatives to school attendance that are of high gain and if truancy does not involve too many costs, the student is more likely to refuse school. Students with a poor school performance prefer those alternatives because their future prospects of a secure and financially lucrative employment are negative. Thus, the benefits from a regular school attendance will be rated as very low. As a specification of Hypothesis 1 we assume:

**H2.** The lower the perceived benefit of school attendance is, the more likely the student is to do a side job or to aim for acceptance through deviant peers.

In summary, we can illustrate the hypotheses in the following graph (Fig. 1). The initial point is the SES of the family: the lower the SES of the family, the worse the school performance of the student. If the means are restricted (poor school achievement), it is rational from the student's point of view to use other means to reach the goals of prosperity and social recognition. In our example, such alternatives are a side job and the contact with deviant peers. Adolescents who value these alternatives more than regular school attendance are more likely to play truant. To identify whether the predictors effect truancy in the theoretically deduced or other direct ways, we will empirically test different possible relations. The theoretically deduced relations (indirect) are marked by continuous lines; other direct relations are pictured by dashed lines.

### Integration of Family Factors

In the first section, we specified the assumption of the Anomie Theory by supplementing the Expectation Value Theory to the phenomenon of

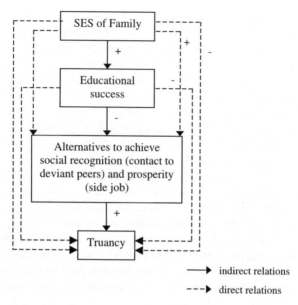

*Fig. 1.* Merton's Anomie Theory Extended by the Value-Expectation Theory
(Innovator).

truancy. In the following section, we will integrate assumptions on the
family into our model. Even if Merton recognized the importance of the
family and underlined the function of the family as a status setter (Merton,
1968, p. 212), he did not elaborate on the connection between social status,
family and the individual types of adaptation. Class-specific resources like
economical, cultural or social capital are transmitted via the family to the
offspring. Thus, the social status of the family determinates to which extent
parents are able to transfer the means to reach the societal goals of prosperity and social recognition to their child in the process of socialization. To
specify the Anomie Theory on the meso-level, it is necessary to find concepts
that meet two criteria: first, it should be the intention of this concept to
explain differences in the school achievement, and second – in dependence
on Mertons means-goal discrepancy – the socioeconomic deprivation of the
family should be seen as a causal factor to explain the distinction in school
achievement. One possibility to fill the gap of the Anomie Theory regarding
the meso-level is the integration of different forms of capital. In the sociology of education, two concepts are discussed in particular, which are
appropriate to these criteria: the cultural and the social capital.

### *Poor School Achievement as the Result of Low Cultural Capital*

For a long time, the sociology of education focused on the relation between the economical capital of the family and the success in schooling. Additionally, to the traditional understanding of capital as economical capital, Bourdieu (1983) extended the concept of capital by cultural and social capital. Cultural capital describes educational resources, and social capital is defined as "the aggregate of the actual or potential resources which are linked to the possession of a durable network of more or less institutionalized relationships of mutual acquaintance and recognition" (Bourdieu, 1983, p. 190). These three forms of capital are not self-sufficient units, but they are rather transformable into each other. For example, educational resources (cultural capital) can be transformed into economic capital, as a high level of education enables an individual to gain an occupational position with a substantial income. Another characteristic of the relation between economic, social and cultural capital is the dominance of the economic one (Bourdieu, 1985, p. 11). Especially, in societies characterized by a differentiated self-regulated market, the economic capital dominates the cultural and the social capital. Consequently, families who possess a high economic capital also have considerable opportunities to gain social and cultural capital. To explain the discrepancy in school achievement of students with different social backgrounds, Bourdieu (1983) focuses on the cultural capital. Analogous to Merton (1968), his theory is based on the assumption that society is primarily influenced by the norms and values of the middle class. This dominance of middle class values is also reflected in the school system, since it is one of the most influential institutions to establish basic norms and values of the society. Students whose families of origin have a low social status and therefore have limited access to cultural capital are disadvantaged to reach a high level of education in comparison to their counterparts of the middle and upper classes. This disadvantage might be expressed in less-internalized achievement motivation, reading skills or restricted access to cultural assets. Following Bourdieu (1983), cultural capital can exist in three variants:

1. In the *embodied state*, describing patterns of thought and action, values and cognitive skills, which the individual inheres in the process of socialization. All these dimensions of the embodied state of cultural capital are primarily affected by the intellectual capacity of the family.
2. In the *objectified state*, taking the form of cultural goods like pictures, books, dictionaries, musical instruments, etc. On the one hand, objectified

cultural capital can be seen as a transmutation of the economic capital into the form of the right of property (e.g. acquisition of a precious painting). On the other, it gains a high symbolic value solely based on the embodied cultural capital. The possession of objectified cultural capital alone does not automatically lead to the pleasure of, or the intellectual preoccupation with the object. In order to enjoy these, the owner needs a certain amount of embodied cultural capital, internalized in the process of socialization.

3. In the *institutionalized state*, it exists in the form of academic credentials, diplomas and honors, creating a certificate of cultural competence which confers on its holder a conventional, constant, legally guaranteed value with respect to power (Bourdieu, 1983, p. 190).

### *Poor School Achievement as the Result of Low Social Capital*

The concept of social capital is an elusive one and has been defined in various ways. Especially, since Coleman's (1988) work many studies have approved the efficacy of some dimensions of social capital as influencing school achievement (e.g. Isreael, Beaulieu, & Hartless, 2001). Next to the relation between social capital and school achievement, numerous studies also verified social class differences on parent's participation in school education (e.g. Lareau, 1996; Epstein, 1987). For the further implementation, we will adapt the concept of social capital described by McNeal (1999). In his study "Parental Involvement as Social Capital: Differential Effectiveness on Science Achievement, Truancy and Dropping Out", McNeal (1999) constitutes a direct relation between a low social capital of the family and the dependent variables of poor school achievement, truancy and dropping out. Complementary to McNeal (1999), we also hypothesize an indirect effect of social capital on truancy, mediated by a poor school achievement.

Avoiding a specific definition of social capital, McNeal points at three elements, which are characteristic for this capital: (1) form of social capital, (2) norms of obligation and reciprocity and (3) resources. The term '*form*' refers to the structural aspects of the social relations, like span of the network, intensity of the relationships or structural holes. *Norms* of obligation and reciprocity are characteristic for the relationship within a social network. Social capital is the result of investments in a social relationship, based on the expectation of a return on this investment or based on the philosophy "quid pro quo". A fundamental element of this relation is a sense of trust, obligation or norm of reciprocity. The third element is the availability of resources. Parents are endowed with various levels of physical, human and cultural capital.

McNeal identifies four dimensions of the social capital which have a strong impact on poor school achievement and truancy: (1) parent–child discussion, (2) PTO network (parent–teacher organization), (3) monitoring and (4) educational support strategies. Underlying the assumption that all these dimensions are indicators of the parental interest in the child's school performance, it can be stated: the stronger the interest of the parents, the more effort the child may invest in its school career to accomplish the expectations. And, the more effort the child invests in the school career, the less likely he/she will disengage from schooling. Furthermore, the parental involvement is an instrument of social control. The more information parents accumulate on the school career of their child – through conversation with the child on school issues or with teachers about the development of their child – the faster they are informed about difficulties and the faster they can intervene. The effectiveness of the function of social control is especially relevant in terms of parent–child discussion and PTO networks.

1. *Parent–child discussion*: This dimension measures the degree to which parents and children actively engage in conversations pertaining to education. Discussion topics involve school-related activities, planning the school program or problems in the school. Beyond the definition of McNeal's parent–child discussion, we also define communication on general literacy issues as a relevant element of this dimension.
2. *PTO network*: The second element of parental involvement is the PTO, intensively analyzed by Coleman and Hoffer (1987) in their study of private and public high schools. If parents participate in school activities – by volunteering, for example – and if they keep regular contact with teachers and other parents, they will be more likely informed if their child is failing in school.
3. *Parental monitoring*: A third aspect of parental involvement is parental monitoring. It is assumed that a strong monitoring by the parents evokes greater investments by the child to improve the educational performance (McNeal, 1999, p. 125). In the tradition of the Control Theories (Toby, 1957; Hirschi, 1969; Sampson & Laub, 1993), we can distinguish between direct (e.g. supervision) and indirect (e.g. attachment) forms of control. McNeal refers to direct forms of control like limiting time for watching TV, checking homework or requiring chores (McNeal, 1999, p. 125).

4. *Educational support strategies*: The last element is direct parental involvement in the educational process, especially through educational
   support strategies (helping with homework or preparation for tests).
5. *Home affective environment*: Beside the dimensions discussed by McNeal,
   we will supplement the theoretical model by another predictor, giving
   information on the quality of parent–child relation: the home affective
   environment. Since social capital is defined by the "structure of relation
   between actors and among actors" (Coleman, 1988, p. 98), and trust-
   worthiness of the social environment is a central aspect of this relation, it
   is reasonable to assume that the quality of a home affective environment
   is an important predictor for the development of intellectual tasks and
   social competence (e.g. Estrada, Arsenio, Hess, & Holloway, 1987). This
   results in a positive impact on school achievement.

Considering the hypotheses formulated previously, we can expand the assumptions on the relation between SES, cultural and social capital, school
achievement and alternatives to reach prosperity as well as social recognition as follows:

**H1.** The lower the SES of the family of origin is, the less access the
student has to social and cultural capital.

**H2.** The less access to cultural and social capital, the worse the school
achievement of the student.

**H3.** The worse the school achievement, the more likely students try to
achieve goals like social recognition or economical prosperity aside from
school.

**H4.** The more students follow up their goals aside from school, the more
frequent the truancy.

Analogous to Fig. 1, continuous lines display the theoretically deduced
relations (indirect), and dashed lines represent the other possible direct relations in Fig. 2.

## DATA AND METHODS

The Programme for International Student Assessment (PISA) is an international large-scale assessment study. It was initiated by the Organization
for Economic Cooperation and Development (OECD) and provides the
OECD member countries with internationally comparable data about their
educational systems. PISA is a long-term project, planned to span three

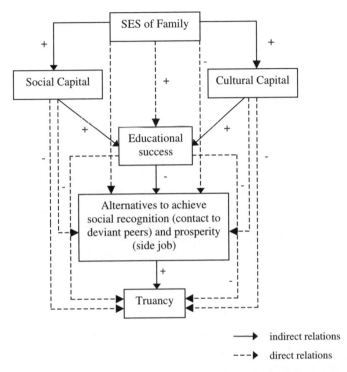

*Fig. 2.* Merton's Anomie Theory Extended by Social and Cultural Capital (Innovator).

assessment cycles. Each cycle covers the three domains of reading literacy, mathematical literacy and scientific literacy. For the first cycle, the assessment took place in the year 2000, with a primary focus on reading literacy. A total of 180,000 students from 28 OECD member countries and four non-OECD countries participated in this assessment. This empirical analysis is undertaken using the national German PISA Study 2000, which is an extension of the international sample, making it possible to address questions that are of particular relevance to the German education system. In a first step, the subsample of German students in the international sample ($N = 5,073$, 219 schools) was enlarged to 33,809 (1,460 schools) cases. A representative sample was selected of the total population of the 15-year-olds enrolled in educational institutions: first, the educational systems of the participating countries were broken down by key characteristics such as regions and school types. Within these subdivisions (school type within the federal state), schools were sampled randomly. Second, 15-year-old students were selected within the sampled schools, again at random. In the second step, the consortium added a series of supplementary national options to the international survey. These supplementary surveys took place on a second testing day and contained information on topics like family, peers, relation to teachers and leisure time. Besides the students, parents were also asked to fill in a questionnaire on the second testing day, which was aimed at collecting information on the SES and on the school career of the child.

To reproduce the proportions in the population, and not the ones in the disproportional multistage PISA sample, it is necessary to weight the sample according to the proportion of students in the population. For the present analysis, we use a sample weight developed by the PISA consortium (Baumert et al., 2002). Analogue to the analysis of Baumert et al. (2002), students attending special schools ($N = 752$) and vocational schools ($N = 211$) are excluded, because in terms of achievement, they are not comparable to students attending public schools.

A major problem of analyzing the national PISA sample is the large number of missing data. Besides the efficiency loss due to missing data, nonresponse can cause serious identification problems of the population parameters. Next to variables measuring the SES, also indicators assessing characteristics of peers, information on school achievement and parental involvement partly exhibit missing values up to 25 percent. To minimize the loss of cases that answered all the other items relevant to this analysis, interval- and categorical-scaled variables with at least five items and normal distribution were substituted using the expectation maximization (EM) algorithm.[1] By means of this imputation, we are able to use almost 88 percent ($N = 29563$) of the sample in comparison to only 49 percent ($N = 16112$), not utilizing imputation.

## Measurement of the Dependent Variable

The information on the dependent variable truancy is based on the student's self-reported statements. Even if one assumes truancy to be underestimated within the sample because frequently truant adolescents could not be met at school even after a number of attempts, there are hardly any alternative methods. Truancy was measured by asking students how often they skipped school lessons in the last two weeks. The response categories ranged from never (1), 1–2 lessons (2), 3–4 lessons (3), to five or more lessons (5).

Using the imputated and weighted dataset, 29,563 students responded to the question of truancy. Responses to this item were predictably skewed (M = 1.16, SD = 0.51), with 88.0 percent ($N = 26,013$) stating that they never skipped school, 9.1 percent ($N = 2,684$) were truanting 1–2 lessons, 1.4 percent ($N = 412$) 3–4 lessons and 1.5 percent ($N = 454$) missed 5 school lessons or more. To distinguish truancy in a "harmless range" and truancy as an indicator for an endangered school career, the categorical variable was dichotomized: students truanting 5 lessons or more (1) and those not skipping school at all or skipping lessons less than 5 times (0).

## Measurement of the Independent Variables

### Indicators of SocioEconomic Status

To assess the SES of the family, we used the International Socioeconomic Index of Occupational Status (ISEI), which was derived from student responses on parental occupation. ISEI captures the attributes of occupations that convert parent's education into income (Ganzeboom, De Graaf, & Treiman, 1992). The values of the index ranged from 16 (low) to 90 (high) with a mean of 48.84 and a standard deviation of 15.47.

### Social Capital

With the expectation of the PTO network, all dimensions of the social capital mentioned by McNeal (1999) could be measured by at least two indicators. Three five-item scales were used to assess intensity of *parent–child discussion* on educational issues. Students were asked: (1) How often their parents talk to them about political and social topics ($M = 2.51$, $SD = 1.27$), (2) How often they talk about school-related issues ($M = 4.06$, $SD = 1.01$) and (3) How often they take meals in common ($M = 4.66$, $SD = 0.87$). The last variable is included, because sharing a family meal often implies communication among the members. In this context, Hess and Handel (1959) referred to the importance of "table talks", in which family members have discussions, talk about experiences in job or school life or about problems. Response options ranged from never (1) to few times a week (5).

To measure *educational support strategies*, two variables were assessed: first, two five-point rating scales, indicating how often mother and father support the child in doing homework (1 = never to 5 = several times a week). Because the correlation between these two variables is highly significant (Spearman's $\rho = 0.60$), the mean of both variables was used for multivariate regression analysis. By doing so, the problem of multicollinearity was avoided ($M = 2.42$, $SD = 1.22$). Second, we used information on how often students have private lessons outside the school to operationalize direct parental involvement. "Private lessons" was measured by a scale of six items, each ranking from 1 to 3 (1 = never, 2 = sometimes, 3 = regular). Students were asked if they have had in the last three years: (1) additional tuition, (2) extra German lessons in a private school, (3) other extra lessons in a private school, (4) extra classes to learn working techniques, (5) private lessons in German and (6) private lessons in other subjects. The internal consistency was sufficient, with Cronbachs $\alpha$ of 0.60 (M = 1.16, SD = 0.31). Even if the parents are not directly involved in this process, it is likely that they are the ones financing the private lessons and therefore supporting the academic achievement of the child.

*Parental monitoring* was assessed by two variables ("movies" and "homework"). First, the frequency of watching violent, horror or porno movies (1 = never to 5 = 6 times or more; M = 2.11, SD = 0.99) in the last two weeks; and second, the frequency of being behind schedule finishing homework (1 = never to 4 = always; M = 2.82, SD = 0.80). *Home affective environment* ("home environment") was a composite constructed by utilizing three five-point item scales, implying the following questions and statements: (1) Are you able to talk to your parents about problems? (2) Would you raise your own children, as your parents raised you? and (3) I feel comfortable at home. Cronbachs $\alpha$ for this scale was 0.72. Scores on the composite variable for all respondents ranged from 1 to 5 (M = 3.77, SD = 0.88).

## Cultural Capital

Of all three forms of cultural capital, we are only able to measure two dimensions: the objectified and embodied state. Objective cultural capital was operationalized using an additive index based on four dichotomous variables. Students were asked if the following cultural assets are available at home: classical literature, poetry, art works and a piano. These items are reliable with $\alpha = 0.62$ (M = 2.45, SD = 1.30). The second item was established by asking the parents how often they read books to their child in early childhood (1 = never to 5 = almost daily). On average, the parents read once or few times a week to their offspring (M = 4.21, SD = 0.97).

## School Achievement

School achievement[2] was assessed by two variables: first, the subjective evaluation of skills in German; and second, information if the student skipped or repeated grades. The first indicator was a four-point-scale item (1 = disagree to 4 = agree), where students rated the statement "I am a hopeless case in German" (M = 1.90, SD = 0.89). The frequency of skipping or repeating grades ("school development") was measured by a five-point-scale item (M = 2.33, SD = 0.59), indicating if the student was in comparison to peers, one year ahead in school (1), equal (2), one year behind (3), two years behind (4) or more than three years behind (5).

### *Alternatives to Gain Prosperity and Social Recognition*

To measure the extent of a side job, respondents were asked "How many hours a week do you spend on a side job" (1 = never to 7 = 11 hours or more). On average, students are working 2–3 hours a week (M = 1.81, SD = 1.45). Attachment to deviant peers was assessed by a composite scale of three five-point items (1 = do not agree at all to 5 = agree completely). The scale consists of the following variables: (1) whether the peers solve problems without discussion, (2) whether the peers ignore the law to reach interests of the group and (3) how often in the last year peers were involved in fights with other groups. The scale was moderately reliable with Cronbachs $\alpha = 0.67$ (M = 2.30, SD = 0.93).

### *Control Variables*

Control variables are migration status of the parents, family status and gender (1 = male, 2 = female) of the respondents. Migration status was assessed by a dichotomized variable that indicates whether both parents were born in Germany (0) or if at least one parent was born in a foreign country (1). Family status was coded by a trichotomized variable (1 = living with both parents, 2 = living with one parent, 3 = living with no parent).

## RESULTS

To test the relations of dependent variables on social and cultural capital, school achievement, alternatives to gain prosperity, social recognition and truancy, we conducted three types of analyses. First, ordinary least squares (OLS) regression is performed to compute the effect of SES and control variables on social and cultural capital. Second, to determine the relative contribution of each predictor and to examine the difference in the predictive value of the independent variables, we ran stepwise OLS regression equations for the following dependent variables: "school development", which measures school achievement and "deviance of peers", which models the alternative to reach prosperity. Regression estimates on the second indicator assessing school achievement (subjective appraisal in German) will not be presented. This is because the proportion of explained variance is very low

($R^2 = 0.06$) and there are no substantial differences of the important predictors in comparison to the dependent variable "school development". OLS results on the second alternative (side job) are only shortly discussed, also because of a very small proportion of explained variance ($R^2 = 0.03$). Collinearity and autocorrelation (Durbin Watson Test) were not found. Coefficients of OLS analysis are presented in form of standardized estimates ($\beta$). Finally, to determine the predictors of respondent's truancy, stepwise binary logistic regression was computed to test all theoretical relevant variables of the model (Table 5). The relative explained variance of each model in comparison to Model 1 is displayed in the last lines of Tables 3, 4 and 5.

The OLS estimates of SES and control variables on the indicators measuring social and cultural capital are presented in Table 2. Apart from the dependent variable "homework not in time", the SES displays significant positive effects ($p = 0.001$) on all items. Therefore, we can preliminarily support Hypothesis 1. Even though significant effects can be identified for most of the items measuring social and cultural capital, it is obvious that the SES has the strongest influence on three dependent variables: "cultural assets" ($\beta = 0.35$), "read to child" ($\beta = 0.22$) and "talk about politics" ($\beta = 0.23$). Relatively high proportions of variances are found for the variables "watching violent or x-rated movies" ($R^2 = 0.25$), with the strongest effect by gender ($\beta = -0.46$), "cultural assets" ($R^2 = 0.13$) and "read to child" ($R^2 = 0.09$). In all other cases, the proportion of explained variance has to be valued rather low with $R^2$ varying between 0.01 and 0.06.

Table 3 displays the results of stepwise multivariate OLS analysis on the dependent variable "school development". The inclusion of control variables and SES (Model 1) leads to an $R^2$ of 0.08, with the strongest explanatory power by the migration background and the SES of the parents. Girls perform better than boys, children living with a single or no parent are repeating more grades compared to children living with both parents and juveniles whose parents have a migration background repeat more grades than children whose parents are both German.

Entering indicators assessing social capital slightly increases the proportion of explained variance about 3 percentage points to an $R^2 = 0.11$. With the exception of the frequency on talks about school issues and of the indicators measuring parental educational support strategies, the bias of all estimates coincides with the hypotheses formulated in Chapter 2. Contrary to the assumptions, we find a positive impact of parental support (private lessons and parental help) on a poor school achievement. Consequently, we can deduce that the indicators of parental support are primarily modelling the *need* for support, because of poor school achievements. A similar conclusion can be

**Table 2.** OLS Regression Estimates for Social and Cultural Capital on Control Variables and SES (Standardized Regression Coefficients).

| | Talk About Politics | Talk About School | Share Meals | Parent Help | Priv. Less. | Movies | Home-Work | Cultural Assets | Read to Child | Home Environment |
|---|---|---|---|---|---|---|---|---|---|---|
| | β | β | β | β | β | β | β | β | β | β |
| Gender | −0.05 | 0.00 (ns) | −0.01 (ns) | 0.05 | 0.02 | −0.46 | 0.09 | 0.10 | 0.05 | −0.01 (ns) |
| Ref. Single parent | — | — | — | — | — | — | — | — | — | — |
| | −0.02 | −0.00 (ns) | −0.12 | −0.10 | 0.01 (ns) | 0.04 | −0.09 | −0.05 | −0.03 | −0.06 |
| No parent | −0.02 | −0.03 | −0.10 | −0.04 | 0.03 | 0.02 | −0.03 | −0.03 | −0.04 | −0.06 |
| Migration | 0.01 (0.05) | 0.06 | −0.03 | −0.06 | 0.03 | 0.07 | 0.02 | −0.01 (ns) | −0.16 | −0.02 |
| SES | 0.23 | 0.03 | 0.05 | 0.02 | 0.05 | −0.15 | 0.00 (ns) | 0.35 | 0.22 | 0.06 |
| $R^2$ | 0.06 | 0.01 | 0.03 | 0.02 | 0.01 | 0.25 | 0.02 | 0.13 | 0.09 | 0.01 |

*Notes:* $N = 29563$, all predictors are highly significant ($p = 0.001$), predictors not being significant (ns) or significant on a 0.01 or 0.05 level are listed in parentheses; reference category is "living with both parents".

***Table 3.*** OLS Regression Estimates for School Development on Control Variables, SES, Social- and Cultural Capital (Standardized Regression Coefficients).

|                              | Model 1 | Model 2   | Model 3   |
| ---------------------------- | ------- | --------- | --------- |
|                              | $\beta$ | $\beta$   | $\beta$   |
| *SES/control variables*      |         |           |           |
| Gender                       | −0.11   | −0.06     | −0.06     |
| Ref.                         | —       | —         | —         |
| Single parent                | 0.04    | 0.04      | 0.04      |
| No parent                    | 0.05    | 0.04      | 0.04      |
| Migration                    | 0.19    | 0.18      | 0.17      |
| SES                          | −0.15   | −0.12     | −0.10     |
| *Social capital*             |         |           |           |
| Talk about politics          |         | −0.08     | −0.07     |
| Talk about school            |         | 0.02      | 0.02      |
| Shared meals                 |         | −0.04     | −0.03     |
| Parental help                |         | 0.06      | 0.07      |
| Private lessons              |         | 0.09      | 0.09      |
| Homework                     |         | 0.01 (ns) | 0.01(ns)  |
| Movies                       |         | 0.12      | 0.11      |
| Home environment             |         | −0.03     | −0.03     |
| *Cultural capital*           |         |           |           |
| Cultural assets              |         |           | −0.02     |
| Read to child                |         |           | −0.04     |
| DF                           | 5       | 13        | 15        |
| $R^2$                        | 0.08    | 0.11      | 0.11      |
| $R^2$ in comparison to Model 1 | —     | 0.06      | 0.03      |

*Notes:* $N = 29563$, all predictors are highly significant ($p = 0.001$), predictors not being significant (ns) or significant on a 0.01 or 0.05 level are listed in parentheses; reference category is "living with both parents".

drawn for the positive effect of "talk about school" ($\beta = 0.02$). It seems the more students talk about school issues, the more problems they might have, in part due to poor school performance. Another strong predictor, next to migration background and SES in Model 2, is the frequency of watching violent or x-rated movies ($\beta = 0.12$). Completing homework in time has no significant effect. The inclusion of items measuring cultural capital (Model 3) does not increase the level of explained variance. Still, both indicators have a highly significant negative influence on the school development.

**Table 4.** OLS Regression Estimates for Deviant Peers on Control Variables, SES, Social and Cultural Capital, and School Achievement (Standardized Regression Coefficients).

| | Model 1 | Model 2 | Model 3 | Model 4 |
|---|---|---|---|---|
| | $\beta$ | $\beta$ | $\beta$ | $\beta$ |
| *SES/control variables* | | | | |
| Gender | −0.25 | 0.06 | −0.06 | −0.05 |
| Ref. | — | — | — | |
| Single parent | 0.07 | 0.03 | 0.03 | 0.02 |
| No parent | 0.04 | 0.02 | 0.02 | 0.02 |
| Migration | 0.07 | 0.04 | 0.03 | 0.02 |
| SES | −0.12 | −0.05 | −0.03 | −0.02 |
| *Social capital* | | | | |
| Talk about politics | | −0.05 | −0.04 | −0.03 |
| Talk about school | | 0.07 | 0.07 | 0.07 |
| Shared meals | | −0.05 | −0.05 | −0.05 |
| Parental help | | 0.03 | 0.03 | 0.03 |
| Private lessons | | 0.06 | 0.06 | 0.05 |
| Homework | | −0.16 | −0.16 | −0.16 |
| Movies | | 0.37 | 0.37 | 0.36 |
| Home environment | | −0.08 | −0.08 | −0.07 |
| *Cultural capital* | | | | |
| Cultural assets | | | −0.05 | −0.04 |
| Read to child | | | −0.02 | −0.02 |
| *School achievement* | | | | |
| School development | | | | 0.06 |
| German skills | | | | 0.02 |
| DF | 5 | 13 | 15 | 17 |
| $R^2$ | 0.09 | 0.27 | 0.28 | 0.28 |
| $R^2$ in comparison to Model 1 | — | 0.27 | 0.04 | 0.05 |

*Notes:* $N = 29563$, all predictors are highly significant ($p = 0.001$), predictors not being significant (ns) or significant on a 0.01 or 0.05 level are listed in parentheses; reference category is "living with both parents".

The regression estimates of all theoretically relevant variables on the extent of peer delinquency are presented in Table 4. A low SES of parents affects the probability of contact to deviant peers in a positive way ($\beta = -0.12$). Even if the $\beta$ coefficient is losing effect, its influence is highly significant in all the following models.

In accordance to many sociological and criminological studies, we also find peers of males to be more deviant in comparison to females. To live with a single parent or no parents as well as a migration background of parents is significantly related to get in contact with deviant peers. The second model, with the different social capital dimensions introduced, increases the overall explanatory power by another 18 percentage points to an $R^2$ of 0.27. The most influential estimates found in Model 2 are "homework not completed in time" ($\beta = -0.16$) and "home affective environment" ($\beta = 0.37$). Parallel to the results of regression analyses on school development, the variables "talks about school", "parental support" and "private lessons" have a positive impact on peer delinquency. All other terms are corresponding with the hypotheses pictured in Fig. 2. In the third model, we find no significant changes in comparison to Model 2. Although the two terms of cultural capital are highly significant negative, in the sense of the lower the cultural capital, the more deviant the peers, the $R^2$ of 0.27 only increases by 1 percentage point. Also in Model 4, in which the indicators of school achievement are added, no relevant changes are identifiable. As hypothesized, both variables assessing school achievement show a highly significant positive coefficient. Restrictively, we have to point out that the explained variance of these two indicators in comparison to Model 1 is very low ($\beta = 0.03$).

Results on stepwise OLS regression analysis on the second alternative of practising a side job are not presented, since the explained variance is very low with $R^2 = 0.03$. Nevertheless, summarizing the most important results, we will just mention predictors being significant on the 0.001 level and the effect of the SES. The analyses showed that talking about political issues, rarely sharing a family meal, attending private lessons, watching violent or x-rated movies, an inadequate family environment, restricted access to cultural assets and grade repeating have a positive impact on the frequency of a side job. A low SES of the parents is associated with an intensive pursuit of a side job, although the coefficient is only significant on a 0.05 level.

Table 5 presents estimates of the effects of all theoretically relevant variables on truancy. For our analysis, we chose a stepwise binary regression model that includes groups of variables linked to the theoretical assumptions. The standardized $\beta$ coefficients (odds ratio) are quoted. Percentage effects are calculated with the following transformation: $(\exp(\beta)-1)100$.

Model 1 comprises the control variables: gender, family status, parent's migration status and SES of the parents. Girls skip classes less than boys. Students living with no parent are truanting more in comparison to students living with both parents. To live with a single parent has only a significant

***Table 5.*** Stepwise Binary Logistic Regression for Truancy on Control Variables, SES, Social and Cultural Capital, and School Achievement (Odds Ratio).

| | Model 1 | Model 2 | Model 3 | Model 4 | Model 5 |
|---|---|---|---|---|---|
| | Exp($\beta$) | Exp($\beta$) | Exp($\beta$) | Exp($\beta$) | Exp($\beta$) |
| *SES/control variables* | | | | | |
| Gender | 0.24*** | 0.51*** | 0.52*** | 0.56*** | 0.58*** |
| Ref. | — | — | — | — | — |
| Single parent | 1.34** | 1.00 | 0.98 | 0.95 | 0.91 |
| No parent | 5.25*** | 2.75*** | 2.63** | 2.46** | 2.53** |
| Migration | 1.44*** | 1.34** | 1.27* | 1.16 | 1.13 |
| SES | 0.99 | 1.00 | 1.00 | 1.01* | 1.01* |
| *Social capital* | | | | | |
| Talk about politics | | 1.06 | 1.09* | 1.11* | 1.10* |
| Talk about school | | 0.94 | 0.94 | 0.93 | 0.92 |
| Shared meals | | 0.86*** | 0.86*** | 0.86*** | 0.88*** |
| Parental help | | 1.08 | 1.09 | 1.08 | 1.08 |
| Private lessons | | 1.17 | 1.20 | 1.11 | 1.03 |
| Homework | | 0.42*** | 0.42*** | 0.43*** | 0.47*** |
| Movies | | 1.73*** | 1.70*** | 1.64*** | 1.40*** |
| Home environment | | 0.81*** | 0.82*** | 0.83*** | 0.86*** |
| *Cultural capital* | | | | | |
| Cultural assets | | | 0.91* | 0.92* | 0.93* |
| Read to child | | | 0.86*** | 0.86*** | 0.86*** |
| *School achievement* | | | | | |
| School development | | | | 1.38*** | 1.33*** |
| German skills | | | | 1.31*** | 1.31*** |
| *Alternatives* | | | | | |
| Deviant peers | | | | | 1.52*** |
| Side job | | | | | 1.10*** |
| DF | 5 | 13 | 15 | 17 | 19 |
| Nagelkerke $R^2$ | 0.06 | 0.18 | 0.18 | 0.19 | 0.21 |
| $R^2$ in comparison to Model 1 | — | 0.17 | 0.02 | 0.04 | 0.10 |

*Notes:* $N = 29563$, reference category is "living with both parents".
*$p < = 0.05$;
**$p < = 0.01$;
***$p < = 0.001$.

negative effect in Model 1, but turns out to be insignificant in the following steps. Noticeably, the strongest predictor is the variable "living with no parent". It raises the risk of truancy in comparison to students living with both parents about 421 percent. This means that especially students living in a children's home and therefore students, who have quite often less intensive relations to attachment figures, are truanting from school. In contrast to the assumption of the unmodified Anomie Theory, suggesting a low SES of the family raises the probability to become a truant, we find no significant SES effect in Model 1. All in all, the proportion of explained variance has to be rated rather low with $R^2 = 0.06$.

The inclusion of indicators of social capital (Model 2) leads to a loss of explanatory power of the variable "living with a single parent". Of the variables modelling the dimension "parent–child discussion", rarely or not sharing a collective family meal shows a significant negative ($p = 0.001$) effect on the risk of truancy ($-14$ percent). Both variables measuring parental monitoring – "time spent watching x-rated movies" ($+73$ percent) and "homework not completed in time" ($-58$ percent) – are highly significant. Living in a family with a negative home environment increases the risk of truanting by about 20 percent ($\exp(\beta) = 0.81$, $p = 0.001$). These explanatory terms also keep their highly significant and considerable $\beta$ coefficients in the following models. In contrast, both variables measuring parental support strategies show – consistently – no significant effect on the outcome of truancy. The cumulative explained variance in this model has increased about 12 percentage points. Model 3 displays no relevant changes within the indicators previously mentioned. From the two predictors measuring cultural capital, absence of cultural assets increases the probability of truancy only about 9 percentage points ($\exp(\beta) = 0.91$, $p = 0.05$). A stronger negative effect is identifiable for the item "reading to child" ($-14$ percent).

The entering of indicators of school achievement (Model 4) leads to interesting changes. Both items have a highly significant negative effect on truancy. A low self-assessment of achievement in German raises the risk of truancy by about 31 percent and a school career, characterized by repeating grades, heightens the risk of truancy by about 38 percent. It is worth mentioning that in comparison to Model 1, these two terms explain only 4 percent of variance. Controlling for school achievement, the previous negative effect of migration status is losing explanatory power. The SES finally shows not a strong, but positive influence on truancy ($\exp(\beta) = 1.01$, $p = 0.05$). This result leads to the opposite hypothesis on the relation between SES and truancy as assumed by the unmodified Anomie Theory. We will describe this result in greater detail below. The final model additionally includes the alternatives to a regular school attendance: "side job" and "deviant peers". In dependence on Hypothesis 4, both items have a strong positive effect on truancy, which is also reflected in the high proportion of explained variance in comparison to Model 1 ($R^2 = 0.10$). The broader the attitude of deviance within the peer group ( + 52 percent) and the more time the student spends on a side job ( + 10 percent), the higher the probability of truancy. The total explained variance is $R^2 = 0.21$.

Summarizing the results of binary regression analysis on truancy, we find the gender of the respondent and living with no parent to be the most important predictors of the control variables. Of the dimensions which are modelling social capital, all indicators assessing parental monitoring, a negative home environment and rare sharing of a family meal have a strong effect on the risk to skip classes. In comparison to Model 1, the power of explanation entering indicators of social capital rises strongly ($R^2 = 0.17$). Also, a lack of cultural capital in the family household increases the probability to play truant, although the power of explanation is by far not as strong as for the indicators measuring poor school achievement and the contact to deviant peers as well as the practice of a side job. Of the latter ones, especially belonging to a deviant peer group has a strong impact on truancy. More interesting, controlling for school achievement, it is shown, that students whose family of origin occupy a high SES are at last in risk of becoming truants. As a result, students with status inconsistency are the ones skipping school. Considering the strong positive relation between the SES of the parents and school performance in the German educational system, as frequently verified (e.g. Baumert et al., 2002), we find students not sharing the same socioeconomic background – and therefore, also not sharing the same lived-in world as their classmates – to be in risk to become truants. In this context, the status of an "outsider" could be an important cause. Certainly, this result needs more detailed research.

## DISCUSSION

The SES of the parents shows highly significant effects on almost all indictors assessing social and cultural capital, apart from "finishing homework in time". Therefore, we can confirm Hypothesis 1. We also find a negative impact of the SES on the school career, even though the effect slightly loses power of explanation controlling for social and cultural capital. This implies that both forms of capital are interceding between social status and school achievement (Hypothesis 2). Similarly, we can identify a strong direct effect of SES on peer delinquency; yet, this effect loses most power of explanation entering variables of social capital, which on their part influence peer delinquency. Again, a mediating effect is announced. This result verifies Hypothesis 3. Although we find a significant negative effect of school achievement on the probability to get in contact with deviant peers, we have to state that the additional contribution of these variables to the explanation of deviance of peers is restricted. Focusing on the results of stepwise binary regression analysis on truancy, we find only weak effects of the SES on truancy when controlling for school achievement. Moreover, the effect turns out to be the opposite as assumed in the hypothesis. Students whose parents have a high SES and who perform poorly in school are the ones playing truant. Especially, variables assessing the social capital and deviance of peers were significantly related to student's truancy. The latter relation supports Hypothesis 4. All in all, we can state that the integration of social and cultural capital contributes positively to the understanding of the family effects on truancy, and allows a more detailed analysis of family factors, than the original Anomie Theory does.

Unfortunately, there were some limitations to this research. First of all, it is very reasonable to assume that social and cultural capitals have a stronger impact in childhood than in early adolescence, when peers increasingly take over the functions of the family. To prove causal interactions of the features identified in this study, longitudinal data are needed. Poor educational achievement or the orientation toward deviant peers might also be a consequence of truancy. Second, the dimensions of cultural capital could only be assessed in a restricted way, since the national PISA study does not imply optimal indicators of embodied and institutionalized forms of cultural capital. However, one of the central points of this achievement was to show that using the Anomie Theory, when modified by other theoretical assumptions, leads to fruitful results in explaining deviant behavior, like truancy.

## NOTES

1. This algorithm is a parameter estimation method, which falls within the general framework of maximum likelihood estimation and is an iterative optimization algorithm.

2. Unfortunately, the term "reading literacy" could not be used as an indicator to measure school achievement, since the correlation between the term measuring the socioeconomic status and reading literacy is too high (0.40) and leads to multicollinearity using regression analysis.

# REFERENCES

Baumert, J., Artelt, C., Klieme, E., Neubrand, M., Prenzel, M., Schiefele, U., Schneider, W., Tillmann, J., & Weiss, M. (2002). *PISA 2000 – Die Länder der Bundesrepublik Deutschland im Vergleich [Comparison of the German federal States]*. Opladen: Leske + Budrich.

Bourdieu, P. (1983). Ökonomisches Kapital, kulturelles Kapital, soziales Kapital [Economical capital, cultural capital, social capital]. In: R. Kreckel (Ed.), *Soziale Ungleichheiten. Soziale Welt, Sonderband Nr. 2* (pp. 183–198). Göttingen: Schwartz.

Bourdieu, P. (1985). *Sozialer Raum und Klasse [Social area and class]. Lecon sur la Lecon.* Frankfurt am Main: Suhrkamp.

Broadwin, I. T. (1932). A contribution to the study of truancy. *American Journal of Orthopsychiatry, 2*, 253–259.

Burgess, S., Gardiner, K., & Propper, C. (2002). *The economic determinants of truancy. Centre for analysis of social exclusion.* London: London School of Economics.

Cohen, A. K. (1955). *Delinquent boys: The subculture of the gang.* London: Collier Mcmillan.

Coleman, J. S. (1988). Social capital in the creation of human capital. *American Journal of Sociology, 94*, 95–120.

Coleman, J. S., & Hoffer, T. (1987). *Public and private high schools.* New York: Basic Books.

Corville-Smith, J., Ryan, B. A., Adams, G. R., & Dalicandro, T. (1998). Distinguishing absentee students from regular attenders: The combined influence of personal, family, and school factors. *Journal of Youth and Adolescence, 27*, 629–640.

Durkheim, E. (1983 [1897]). Der Selbstmord [Suicide]. Frankfurt am Main: Suhrkamp.

Elliott, R. (1975). Some characteristics of school non-attenders at Lisnevin School. *Community Home School Gazette, 69*, 401–403.

Epstein, J. L. (1987). Toward a theory of family-school connections: Teacher practices and parent involvement. In: K. Hurrelmann, F. Kaufmann & F. Lösel (Eds), *Social interventions: Potential and constraints* (pp. 121–136). New York: Walter de Gruyter.

Estrada, P., Arsenio, W. F., Hess, R. D., & Holloway, S. (1987). Affective quality of the mother-child relationship: Longitudinal consequences for children's school-relevant cognitive functioning. *Developmental Psychology, 23*, 210–215.

Farrington, D. (1980). Truancy, delinquency, the home, and the school. In: L. Hersov & I. Berg (Eds), *Out of school: Modern perspectives in truancy and school refusal* (pp. 49–64). New York: Wiley.

Fergusson, D. M., Lynskey, M. T., & Horwood, L. J. (1995). Truancy in adolescence. *New Zealand Journal of Educational Studies, 30*, 25–38.

Ganzeboom, H. B. G., De Graaf, P. M., & Treiman, D. J. (1992). A standard international socio-economic index of occupational status. *Social Science Research, 21*, 1–56.

Glueck, S., & Glueck, E. (1950). *Unraveling juvenile delinquency.* Cambridge, MA: Harvard University Press.

Healy, W. (1915). *The individual delinquent.* Boston: Little, Brown.

Healy, W., & Bronner, A. F. (1926). *Delinquents and criminals. Their making and unmaking: Studies in two American cities.* New York: Macmillan.

Hess, R. D., & Handel, G. (1959). *Family worlds: A psychosocial approach to family life.* Chicago: University of Chicago Press.

Hirschi, T. (1969). *Causes of delinquency.* Berkeley: University of California Press.

Isreael, G. D., Beaulieu, L., & Hartless, G. (2001). The influence of family and community social capital on educational achievement. *Rural Sociology, 66*, 43–68.

Kline, L. W. (1898). The migratory impulse versus the love of home. *American Journal of Psychology, 10*, 1–81.

Lareau, A. (1996). Assessing parental involvement in schooling. In: A. Booth & J. F. Dunn (Eds), *Family school links: How do they affect educational outcomes* (pp. 57–69). New Jersey: Lawrence Erlbaum.

Lemert, E. M. (1964). Social structure, social control, and deviation. In: M. B. Clinard (Ed.), *Anomie and deviant behavior: A discussion and critique* (pp. 57–97). New York: The Free Press of Glencoe.

Loeber, R., & Farrington, D. P. (1998). *Serious and violent juvenile offenders: Risk factors and successful interventions.* Thousand Oaks, CA: Sage.

May, D. (1975). Truancy, school absenteeism and delinquency. *Scottish Educational Studies, 7*, 97–107.

McNeal, R. B. (1999). Parental involvement as social capital: Differential effectiveness on science achievement, truancy, and dropping out. *Social Forces, 78*, 117–144.

Merton, R. K. (1968). *Social theory and social structure.* New York: Free Press.

Ornstein, A. C., & Levine, D. U. (1985). *An introduction to the foundations of education.* Boston: Houghton Mifflin.

Rossides, D. W. (1990). *Social stratification: The American class system in comparative perspective.* Englewood Cliffs, NJ: Prentice-Hall.

Sampson, R. J., & Laub, J. H. (1993). *Crime in the making: Pathways and turning points through life.* Cambridge: Harvard University Press.

Schreiber-Kittl, M., & Schröpfer, H. (2002). *Abgeschrieben? Ergebnisse einer empirischen Untersuchung über Schulverweigerer [Resigned? Empirical results on a study about truants].* Munich: Westdeutscher Verlag.

Shaw, C. R., & McKay, H. D. (1942). *Juvenile delinquency and urban areas.* Chicago: University of Chicago Press.

Sommer, B. (1985). Truancy in early adolescence. *Journal of Early Adolescence, 5*, 145–160.

Tibbenham, A. (1977). Housing and truancy. *New Society, 39*, 501–502.

Toby, J. (1957). Social disorganization and stake in conformity: Complementary factors in the predatory behavior of young hoodlums. *Journal of Criminal Law, Criminology and Police Science, 48*, 12–17.

Tyerman, M. J. (1968). *Truancy.* London: University of London Press.

Van Petegem, P. (1994). Truancy as a social, educational and psychological problem: Causes and solutions. *Scientia Pedagogica Experimentalis, 31*, 271–286.

# REVISITING MERTON: CONTINUITIES IN THE THEORY OF ANOMIE-AND-OPPORTUNITY-STRUCTURES

Sanjay Marwah and Mathieu Deflem

## ABSTRACT

*Although the influence of Robert Merton's contributions in criminological sociology is widely acknowledged, there still remain misunderstandings about his theoretical project. In light of some of these ongoing ambiguities, this paper discusses recent criticisms of the Mertonian theory of deviant behavior and argues that a visionary sociological paradigm of anomie-and-opportunity-structures underlies Merton's contribution. The status of this paradigm, however, has often been misconstrued and has impaired the elaboration of a genuinely Mertonian theory of deviant behavior. We therefore clarify the various theoretically relevant elements of the Mertonian paradigm and offer suggestions as to its operationalization for crime and deviance research. We argue that future research should identify, examine, and test differentiated aspects of the anomie-and-opportunity-structures paradigm in order to arrive at a more consistent and substantiated conclusion on the validity of Merton's project. We conclude that properly conceptualized and operationalized, the paradigm still holds great promise for sociological theory and research on deviant behavior.*

Sociological Theory and Criminological Research: Views from Europe and the United States
Sociology of Crime, Law and Deviance, Volume 7, 57–76
ISSN: 1521-6136/doi:10.1016/S1521-6136(06)07004-7

# INTRODUCTION

The status of the late Robert K. Merton as a sociological giant on whose shoulders we all stand is undisputed. Among his lasting contributions to a plethora of sociological specialties, Merton's (1938) work in criminological sociology through his seminal paper on "Social Structure and Anomie" has provided an important sociological framework for the analysis of deviant behavior in American society. The influence of Merton's contribution to criminological sociology and other disciplinary perspectives in criminology is widespread (Braithwaite, 1980; Featherstone & Deflem, 2003; Rosenfeld, 1989). Yet, despite substantial modifications and revisions of Merton's original theory and recent attempts by Merton and others to provide reinterpretations and clarifications (Deflem, 1989; Merton, 1995, 1997; Messner, 1988), there still remain certain misunderstandings and unclarities about this theoretical project (Bernard, 1987, 1990, 1995; Martin, 2000; Menard, 1995; Passas, 1995). Ambiguities in the reception of Merton's paradigm in part stem from Merton being too abstract and unclear about the operationalization of his concepts for research purposes. However, owing to the powerful analytical insights of Merton's theoretical project, these shortcomings should not prevent the development and testing of a Mertonian theory of deviant behavior. On the contrary, we will argue that a visionary sociological paradigm of anomie-and-opportunity-structures underlies Merton's contribution to the study of deviance. As such, our effort also presents an attempt to think with, rather than about Merton, an endeavor which itself follows Mertonian aspirations (Merton, [1949]1968).

This paper discusses Merton's theoretical contribution to the sociological study of deviant behavior by linking a presentation of his original as well as his most recent contributions to the continually refined paradigm of anomie-and-opportunity-structures to some of the most prominent criticisms against and misunderstandings of Merton's perspective. A clear and thorough presentation of Merton's criminological paradigm is far from redundant, not only in light of certain misrepresentations of Merton's work (Featherstone & Deflem, 2003), but also because of the continually "evolving character" of the paradigm over the course of some 50 years (Merton, 1995, p. 5). A clarification of these revisions and extensions in the Mertonian tradition will enable to better respond to some of the major objections that have been made against Merton's theory and indicate the implications this has for the sociological study of crime and deviance. Based on this analysis, we argue that future research efforts should be directed at examining and testing different aspects of the anomie-and-opportunity-structures paradigm with explicit attention to the scope, domain, and falsification requirements of its concepts and theories. Without such work first being done, temptations to take the Mertonian paradigm out of context and prematurely dismiss it might otherwise unjustly continue to exist.

## THE ANOMIE-AND-OPPORTUNITY-STRUCTURES PARADIGM

Despite its enormous influence and popularity, Merton's theoretical work in the area of deviant behavior has received an ambiguous reception in terms of the paradigm's usefulness for research and the empirical validity of its propositions (Bernard, 1987; Gillis, 2004; Hilbert & Wright, 1979; Parnaby & Sacco, 2004; Piquero & Piquero, 1998; Pratt & Cullen, 2005; Rosenfeld, 1989). At a conceptual level, the notion of anomie has been praised as "useful and powerful" (Passas, 1995, p. 107) as well as condemned as "unnecessary and uncertain" (Besnard, 1990, p. 249). Much of the confusion in the secondary literature over the status and value of Merton's theoretical project is due to the fact that Merton presented not one but at least two theories in his original 1938 article and the related publications since (Merton, 1938, 1949a, 1957, 1964). On the one hand, Merton develops an anomie theory (of social organization), which postulates that an imbalance between cultural goals and socially acceptable means will result in a deinstitutionalization of means. On the other hand, Merton presents a strain theory (of deviant behavior) to suggest that social barriers can restrict people under certain socio-economic conditions (such as anomie) from having access to the legitimate means to achieve culturally valid goals, presenting a pressure toward the adoption of illegitimate means to pursue culturally accepted goals (Featherstone & Deflem, 2003). In the secondary literature, however, Merton's theory of anomie has often been mistaken for his theory of deviant behavior, a view that neglects that anomie and strain are two distinct concepts that refer to two different social realities, situated within an over-arching sociological paradigm. But Merton's theory of deviant behavior was in its original formulations not fully developed to any degree of satisfaction, especially for research purposes. Merton has acknowledged as much, particularly when he recently suggested the incorporation of opportunity structures theory in his criminological perspective, referring to "the theory of anomie-and-opportunity-structures" (Merton, 1995, 1997, p. 519).

It has been only recently in 1995 that Merton (1995) wrote an important retrospective piece on the evolution of the anomie-and-opportunity-structures paradigm. In this paper, Merton particularly sought to emphasize the importance of "opportunity structures" as the most neglected component of his original social structure and anomie article and the subsequent revisions to it:

> Central to the first, 1938, formulation of SS&A paradigm in print was the sociological idea of a continuing interplay and frequent tension between the cultural structure (the distribution and organization of values, norms, and interests) and the social structure (the distribution and organization of social positions or statuses). This, of course, has been generally recognized in the ensuing critical examination of the paradigm. However, a correlative structural idea has often been overlooked .... [T]he hypothesis of the social distribution of adaptations to the interaction between culturally defined goals and institutionally acceptable means is closely linked to the basic structural concept of differential access to opportunities among those variously located in the social structure (Merton, 1995, p. 6).

In Merton's paradigm, opportunity structures are distinct from both the cultural and the social structure. Merton was interested in how people's location in the social structure (their socio-economic status) relates to differential access to society's opportunity structures, defined as the interplay between structural context and individual modes of behavior (adaptation). The notion of opportunity structure, then, is introduced to explain the distribution of choices across individuals and groups located across the social structure:

> Opportunity structure designates the scale and distribution of conditions that provide various probabilities for acting individuals and groups to achieve specifiable outcomes. From time to time, the opportunity structure expands or contracts, as do segments of that structure. However, ... location in the social structure strongly influences, though it does not wholly determine, the extent of access to the opportunity structure. By concept, then, an expanding or contracting opportunity structure does not carry with it the uniform expansion or contraction of opportunities for all sectors of a socially stratified population, a familiar enough notion with diverse implications (Merton, 1995, p. 25).

Thus, importantly, the anomie-and-opportunity-structures paradigm does not imply a structuralist–deterministic perspective that neglects the role of human agency. Instead, perception of opportunities or expectations of particular roles will vary across individuals, demonstrating the importance of subjective and individual-level factors. Merton (1995) therefore recognizes that any sociological account of social behavior is incomplete and can be complemented by an analysis of individual-level processes. However, as a sociologist, Merton's interests are to explain deviance as a social phenomenon, that is, at the macro level, in particular in terms of the effects of various (cultural, social, and opportunity) structures on the patterning and distribution of choices and adaptations. It was this aspiration – to construct a distinctly sociological explanation of deviance against the attribution of social malfunctions to "imperious biological drives" – that lay at the very foundation of the development of Merton's project (Merton, 1938, p. 672).

In Merton's paradigm, opportunities and opportunity structures are generically understood and can be applied to various kinds of social phenomena, not only economic success (Merton, 1995, p. 30). Opportunity structures, also, are not necessarily fixed or immutable. Merton's theory underscores the importance of context, whereby some level of contingency is always operating and can influence outcomes or behaviors. Already in his original typology of individual adaptations in the 1938 article, Merton makes clear that countervailing forces, whether at the aggregate or individual level, exist to mitigate or, alternatively, accentuate existing individual-level or structural processes (Merton, 1938, p. 676).

Of special interest for the sociological study of deviance, Merton connects the anomie-and-opportunity-structures paradigm with complementary conceptions such as "the accumulation of advantage and disadvantage" and "structural constraints" (Merton, 1968, 1995, p. 17). The former concept highlights how socially based structures (especially the socio-economic structure) are created and maintained. Because the adaptation of innovation, for instance, tends to be more prevalent among the lower classes, Merton sees processes of disadvantage operating to stratify and distribute opportunities so that members of the lower classes have a more difficult time in achieving culturally accepted goals through legitimate means. As a result, the structural strain toward deviance will be more common for these disadvantaged groups (Merton, 1949a).

The embeddedness of the notion of structural constraints in the anomie-and-opportunity-structure paradigm makes theoretical sense inasmuch as strains and stresses at the structural level affect rates of deviant adaptations. In societies where socio-economic conditions constrain particular social categories more than others, the possibilities of alternative legitimate options and means to achieve culturally approved goals are limited and will influence deviant adaptations. Merton also discusses how motivations play a role in such behavior:

> Although the term structural constraint is often construed to mean that the social structure only places limitations upon individual choice, it was emphatically argued in the introduction to the 1949 extension of SS&A paradigm that this structural mode of "functional analysis conceives of the social structure as active, as producing fresh motivations which cannot be predicted on the basis of one's knowledge of man's native drives. *If the social structure restrains some dispositions to act, it creates others* ... [A]s Peter Blau has noted, in contrast to Durkheim's fundamental and strongly sociologistic

concept of "structural determinism," which puts aside such psychological concepts as motives as irrelevant, the mode of structural probabilism represented by the SS&A paradigm conceives of culturally and structurally induced "motivation as an intervening mechanism through which structural constraints usually become effective (with a) theoretical focus on the structural conditions as the crucial explanatory concept to account for social relations and conduct" (Merton, 1995, p. 17).

Consistent with Merton's emphasis on rates and aggregates of behavior, constraints and opportunities from various structural sources concentrate certain types of dispositions in certain social positions. Motivations as opportunities are still structural in nature and can be considered to have structural properties. The distribution of the effects of anomie in a Mertonian sense works through these processes so that the cultural structure is also implicated in emphasis of particular culturally accepted goals and approved institutional means in society at large.

The anomie theory in Merton's paradigm, although not discussed in detail in Merton's (1995) recent article, is also important to explain the presence and strength of cultural goals and the significance of the cultural structure. Thomas Bernard (1984, 1987) in this respect makes an important point in suggesting that Merton's theory comprises both structural and cultural propositions. The structural arguments (on differential access to legitimate means) could be tested within particular societies, while the cultural arguments (on the diffusion of cultural goals) are more appropriately tested cross-culturally or internationally. Also, Merton's concept of anomie cannot be tested at the individual level and is instead conceptually tied with (and explicitly based on) Durkheim's notion of social morality (Merton, 1938, pp. 672–673, 1964, pp. 214–215; see Bernard, 1995; Deflem, 1989), which has independently been influential for criminological research (Kim & Pridemore, 2005; Thorlindsson & Bernburg, 2004). Applying the Durkheimian paradigm, Merton chose to focus on American society where, he argued, anomie was widespread (in comparison to other nations) at a structural level, but its effects were not uniformly distributed across society.

Merton's concept of anomie, related to the American dream and the premium it places on monetary success, signifies that norms may lose their power differentially in distinct socio-economic strata. Despite the attempt to attribute culture as the source of strain and deviance in Merton's theory (Kornhauser, 1978), it is more appropriate to suggest that the cultural structure is where anomie is produced so that cultural goals and the norms to achieve them (institutional means) are given legitimacy and credence. These goals, means, and interests may be created and maintained through various processes, but they are always mediated through institutions, groups, and individuals. In any case, Merton's conception of widespread consensus on these cultural attributes throughout society is subject to empirical examination (as are alternative perspectives).

# (MIS)REPRESENTATIONS OF THE MERTONIAN PARADIGM

Given the wide scope and unfinished nature of the anomie-and-opportunity-structures paradigm, Merton's theories have been the subject of numerous criticisms and revisions over the years. In what follows we will aim to use our presentation of the Mertonian paradigm to evaluate some of these criticisms from the secondary literature. This analysis will serve to assess the validity of the anomie-and-opportunity-structures paradigm as a framework for research and analysis on deviant behavior. In particular, we will focus on the following criticisms and suggestions:

(a) Appropriation of Merton's theory for a micro, individual-level theory of deviance.
(b) Assertion that the cultural structure alone explains the rate and distribution of deviance.
(c) Identification of Merton as a structuralist who neglects human agency.
(d) Critique of Merton's theory as a one-sided structural model rather than an integrated cultural–structural model.

We will argue that many of these criticisms of Merton's theories have misinterpreted and even disregarded some of the central Mertonian formulations, mostly because critics have sought to defend alternative frameworks and models for the sociological study of deviant behavior.

*Appropriation of Merton's Sociological Theory at the Micro Level*

In criminology and criminological sociology, Merton's theories have particularly been challenged by social control and social disorganization theorists (Bernard, 1984). With regard to the validity of some of the propositions and applicability issues, critics have focused on: (1) a limited utility of Merton's notions of shared goals and their distribution across society; (2) a lack of clarity as to whether one is measuring aspirations or expectations; and (3) ambiguity as to whether strain and anomie refer to phenomena at the individual, group, or societal level.

With some exceptions (e.g., Messner & Rosenfeld, 1994), most of the direct empirical testing of Merton's strain theory has focused at the group and individual levels and the explanation of juvenile delinquency. Cloward and Ohlin (1960) and Cohen (1955), for instance, focused on strains for juveniles in gangs in lower-class areas and the resulting patterns of delinquency. Since many of the criticisms have come from social control theorists and, to a lesser degree, from social disorganization theorists, applicability questions focus on empirical testing and research at the individual level. Such a focus on individual behavior is problematic, not only given Merton's explicit sociological orientation, but also given the undisputable empirical significance of contextual effects on crime and deviance. However, one of the underlying assumptions of social control and social disorganization theorists (as well as newer routine activities/lifestyle victimization theories) is that individuals motivated toward deviance are spread throughout society, and any real explanation of crime and deviance must aim to explain conformity rather than deviance. Most social control theorists assume that differences in context are not primarily relevant in explaining deviant behavior and that individual-level factors play a more prominent role (Gottfredson & Hirschi, 1990; Hirschi, 1969; see Konty, 2005; Peter, LaGrange, & Silverman, 2003). Social disorganization theorists do recognize the importance of social contexts, but nevertheless work from the viewpoint that communities not organized to control its members are more prone to criminal and deviant behavior (Bursik & Grasmick, 1993). In the anomie tradition, Messner and Rosenfeld's (1994) institutional-anomie theory is consistent with social disorganization inasmuch as they also regard institutions as the master variable in explaining crime and deviance. In the institutional-anomie model, however, economic institutions dominate, while for social disorganization theories, a lack of institutions and low level of organization are the major reasons for deviance.

Critics of Merton coming from these theoretical camps miss out the important contribution made in the anomie-and-opportunity-structures framework, highlighting structural location and differential access to opportunities as important institutional parameters. The level of organization in communities or the importance of non-economic institutions is dependent on their competitiveness levels and relative access to resources. Furthermore, communities are not solely organized for the purpose of control of its members, but they also compete in the broader society and economy. For social disorganization theorists, competition is natural and involves distinct pathways and processes. Yet for Merton, competition is clearly social in terms of status and resources. The concept of opportunity structures highlights the importance of stratification of institutions and ability to organize and compete. Additionally, the concept of institutions in social disorganization theories seems more oriented toward internal organization and stability, but it does not adequately highlight the external sources of stability and organization. Therefore, as Merton (1976) himself has argued, the theories of social disorganization and strain can be complementary, focusing on different aspects of similar or related social phenomena, whereby unavoidably "each theory typically neglects other questions" (p. 32). Merton categorizes his own theory as one focused on deviant behavior, while he views social disorganization theories as examining "the defective arrangement or breakdown of systems of statuses and roles" (p. 28).

It is in our view a central misinterpretation of Merton's model to use it for the analysis of individual deviant behavior. More recent versions of criminological strain theories, such as general strain theory (Agnew, 1992; Paternoster & Mazerolle, 1994), rewrite Merton's theory in social–psychological terms to argue that strained individuals are frustrated and therefore more likely to commit crimes. While Merton has given some credence to the related notion of "anomia" as the individual expression of the social state of anomie (Merton, 1964), he is otherwise quite clear that he is interested in studying the rates of deviance, their distribution, and structural strain (Merton, 1959, 1995). Hence, since even the analytical scope and research domain of general strain theorists are different from Merton's original contribution, a dismissal of Merton's theory is premature on the grounds of these criticisms alone.

## The Cultural Structure as the Source of Strain

Ruth Kornhauser (1978) has popularized the notion that Merton's strain and anomie theories rely only on a notion of the cultural structure to explain the presence of strain and deviance. For Kornhauser, Merton's conception of strain derives from the broader culture, which Merton assumes to be largely uniform throughout society. Kornhauser maintains that this uniformity of culture implies that strain is constant and that most individuals are strained, so that strain cannot provide any real explanatory power at all. She also suggests that Merton actually uses a "control" variable to explain the concentration of the innovation mode of individual adaptation among the poor and lower classes. The prevalence of innovation in the lower socioeconomic strata of society would mainly come about because of defective socialization in the culturally accepted values of society. For Kornhauser, a strain toward deviance seems to be inherent in human nature, inasmuch as insatiable needs and their gratification exist for all human beings. A strain theory of deviant behavior would then be incomplete, as it would only look at the benefits of crime and deviance, not the costs.

Kornhauser focuses on culture in a fashion similar to cultural models of crime and deviance. But, ironically, a stable social structure preventing disorder and crime in Kornhauser's conception of social organization requires a strong culture, albeit grounded and embodied in the same social structure. As mentioned before, social disorganization theories accord prominence to the institutions of control, but the conception of such institutions is oriented toward a universal process of establishing structural stability. Stability and organization exist if members of communities are referenced to cultural differences between communities in terms of structural characteristics (Kornhauser, 1978, p. 75). People in poorer, more heterogeneous, and more mobile communities tend to have less controls and are more prone to deviance, because they lack the ability to realize common interests and values. Controls are primarily developed for the purpose of ensuring cooperative results and maintaining order. But as such outcomes often require a common morality and a specification of structural roles and obligations, the argument becomes circular and tautological.

Notions of cultural strain that are attributed to Merton's theory seem to be misguided and a priori motivated by a desire to dismiss Merton's criminological theory entirely. However, Merton never suggested that structural strain or anomie were equivalent to individual strain or anomia. Also, Merton argues that the characteristics of the cultural structure and the presence of anomie, but not the tendency toward strain, are widely spread in American society. Given this conception, Merton's primary interest had to be in explaining structural strain, for the cultural structure cannot be the source of any strains to deviance in particular groups. In societies where the cultural goals are overemphasized, Merton would foresee high levels of deviance across the board, but the form and concentration of deviation would always remain dependent on people's variable positioning in the social structure and their differential access to opportunity structures. Thus, Merton stresses distributional forces that in the anomie-and-opportunity-structures paradigm are mainly tied to the social and opportunity structures. Bernburg (2002) similarly argues that Merton's perspective incorporates stratification and distributional concerns. Merton's argument is that a society's culture reflects some level of consensus and sharing of values, but that anomic tendencies are created by the uneven distribution of means to reach the culturally emphasized goals. The attribution of cultural determinism to

Merton's paradigm is unfounded, given that the critics emphasizing the problem of the constancy of strain could be similarly accused of being structural (and surprisingly, even cultural) determinists.

## The Neglect of Human Agency

Another re-occurring criticism of the anomie-and-opportunity-structures theory focuses on the neglect of human agency and individual-level factors. Most clearly, Douglas Porpora (1989) has argued that macro-level models too exclusively concentrate on uncovering law-like generalizations about social facts at the expense of intervening, psychological processes involving human actors. For Porpora, a "sociological holist view" represents structures as external to individuals and operating in a mechanical and independent manner, divorced from human interests. Porpora does not cite Merton's theories, but the criticism matches those that have been developed against Merton in similar terms, most notably in self-control theory (Gottfredson & Hirschi, 1990).

Porpora's criticism highlights a critical aspect of the Mertonian paradigm, namely the significance it attributes to the purposive nature of human behavior. In the anomie-and-opportunity-structures paradigm, despite the importance given to structural strain, the specification of cultural goals and norms, and the structurally variable modes of adaptations, the impact of structures is clearly acknowledged as being mediated by human agents. Still, human behavior (actions and choices) involves structurally influenced (not determined) motivations to achieve goals and make choices for particular purposes. In the case of deviant behavior, as with other types of behavior, these purposes are located at the individual level, but they achieve the status of a structural property through the concentration of strain for similarly located individuals. Of course, people in similar positions and locations are bound to make similar choices, but only in a probabilistic sense. Once the structural property is achieved, the persistence of different structures only reflects the strength of the choices and adaptations of individuals within the society. Because human beings develop interests and give credence to values, the anomie-and-opportunity-structures paradigm is consistent with a conceptualization of structures as produced and reproduced through the actions and choices of individuals.

Porpora's non-deterministic conception of social structure, which holds that "people are motivated to act in the interests structurally built into their social positions," is actually not far removed from Merton's perspective (Porpora, 1989, p. 200). Specifically, Porpora's conception is similar to the anomie-and-opportunity-structures paradigm in its emphasis of structurally induced (cultural and social) motivations or interests as being critical in understanding structural strain. Porpora (1989) indeed argues that there is a "dialectical causal path that leads from structure to interests to motives to action and finally back to structure" (p. 200).

Yet, a crucial difference between Merton's theory of the social structure and Porpora's dialectics of structure and motivations is presented in the addition of the notion of opportunity structures in Merton's paradigm. Opportunities to achieve specific goals or outcomes are lacking in Porpora's conception, but it is precisely the opportunity structures component of the Mertonian paradigm that renders the deterministic critique mute. It is indeed through the interaction of all three kinds of structure (cultural, structural, and opportunity structures) that the anomie-and-opportunity-structures paradigm conceives of human behavior (including deviant behavior) as having structural properties and structural origins only in a probabilistic sense at the aggregate level. Aspects of human agency intervene in the actualization and perception of structural opportunities to shape the process through which certain structures will more or less likely produce certain kinds of behavior at the aggregate level (see also Cohen, 1985; Messner & Rosenfeld, 1994).

Merton (1949) has himself acknowledged that his work "has largely neglected but not denied the relevance of the social–psychological processes" that link social structure and modes of adaptation (p. 312). Merton (1959) has also admitted that his efforts to distinguish between socially generated pressures and vulnerabilities to these pressures were lacking and that it would still be "necessary to identify other sociological variables that intervene between structurally induced pressure for deviant behavior and actual rates of deviant behavior" (p. 188). Among the extensions of Merton's paradigm, Albert Cohen's (1965) attempt to integrate Merton's perspective with a Meadian role theory is among the most influential bridge-building constructs in this respect. Likewise, Richard Cloward and Lloyd Ohlin (1960) extended the Mertonian framework to account for the differential nature of the illegitimate opportunity structure. Merton (1995) acknowledges that Cloward and Ohlin provided a necessary addition to his theory, although his own theory focuses primarily on legitimate opportunities (see Marwah, 2001). Merton has generally responded favorably to the efforts to integrate his framework with related theoretical perspectives (Merton, 1968, pp. 231–233, 1995, pp. 33–44). Most recently, for instance, Merton received the criminology of Edwin Sutherland as a theoretical complement to his strain theory (Merton, 1997; see also Bernburg, 2002; Cullen, 1988).

Conversely, as Merton (1995, pp. 38–44) observes, the notion of opportunity has been acknowledged by other criminologists like Sutherland and Cohen, although codification of the concept was not accomplished consciously and explicitly in their theories.

### A One-Sided Structural Model?

Although Merton's paradigm is less deterministic than most structural models, there still exists the view that structural sociology can never adequately stress the importance of culture in human behavior. Rubinstein (1992, 1993, 1994) uses Merton's anomie-and-opportunity-structures model as an exemplary of such tendencies in structural sociology. In Rubinstein's view, structuralist perspectives like Merton's not only neglect human agency, but also ignore the role of culture at the individual level. Both sociologists and economists would share this tendency of using structure to explain human behavior. As both fields in Rubinstein's characterization tend to ignore how human actors have cultural predispositions and a will to make choices (moral or otherwise), these scientific disciplines would deterministically favor structural or exogenous explanations. The difference between economists and sociologists is that the later view social order on the basis of competing groups and collectivities, while the former view order as composed of disaggregated and competing individuals. For Rubinstein (1993, 1994), sociological and economic efforts to make human actors featureless downplay the importance of human will and human culture. For Rubinstein, both will and culture are individual properties and as such his model of human behavior and action is closer to the rational actor models of the economists. Further, Rubinstein views any structural level properties as wholly incomplete and ideological in their convictions of the influence of opportunity structures on individual outcomes. Also, he does not accept the existence of a cultural structure as the notion is used in the anomie-and-opportunity-structures paradigm.

Based on these considerations, Rubinstein (2001) provides a reconceptualization of structuralist perspectives, in which he suggests that culture emerges and is articulated in practical contexts. According to his argument, culture and structures of opportunity are intimately linked. Rubinstein contrasts this approach with structural sociology by emphasizing that culture is only partly instrumentally devised and that its content is indeterminate and open to opportunistic reading by actors. Actors' personality traits, decisions, and choices are considered as more important than structural and larger cultural institutional factors in explaining individual behaviors including criminal behaviors. Therefore, Rubinstein (2001) characterizes Merton's theory as explaining crime in terms of blocked opportunity, while providing "no 'rational' reason for class and ethnic-based exclusion from the legitimate opportunity structure" (p. 49). Rubinstein sees both access to opportunity structures and cultural resources as individually determined.

Reviewing these criticisms, it is clear that Rubinstein does not sufficiently explore Merton's integrated cultural and social opportunity structural model, which does not exclude the importance of agency and actor choices and decisions. While there is clearly a difference in emphasis between Merton's (structural strain) and Rubinstein's (individual interpretations) models, the individual cultural model can pose a limitation to the Merton's paradigm only in bringing out that the sociological paradigm does not offer a psychological analysis (Rosenfeld, 1989, p. 455). The individual (subjective) element of opportunity structures (relative to the cultural and structural levels) suggests that the paradigm can only be conceived as a probabilistic model at the level of individual behavior, a point that has been stated explicitly by Merton (1995) himself. Since Durkheim sociology defines itself by uncovering the causes and outcomes of such social facts at an aggregate level. However, if different individuals select the opportunities they are confronted with in different ways, the persistence of structural effects suggested in the Mertonian paradigm may perhaps limit the explanatory power of the paradigm to exclude the determinants of individual choices. Individual attributes and personality characteristics can still override similar choices being made by individuals in the same structural locations.

Aside from the need to empirically determine which factors are important, the anomie-and-opportunity-structures paradigm does have the advantage of not being dependent – as individual-level models are – in trying to explain motives and actions based on psychological and mental processes. Measures for these later processes are not easily available. More importantly, an essentialist perspective that conceives of behavior only at the individual level would lead to deny that human actors can be influenced through their interactions with other actors and their shared structural locations (Fuchs, 2001). What instead should be proposed, and what is offered in the Mertonian paradigm, is a social-realist theory, which acknowledges the interplay between structure and culture, on the one hand, and human agency, on the other hand. Any separation among these relevant components is always analytical. As Cruickshank (2000) argues, "while structure, culture, and agency are always intertwined in reality, to study their interplay, it is necessary to use a theoretical abstraction to separate the different factors" (p. 83).

## THE CENTRALITY OF OPPORTUNITY STRUCTURES

An explicitation of Merton's matured version of the anomie-and-opportunity-structures theory, with which we started this article, clarifies the strength of the paradigm relative to its most common criticisms. Especially with the elaboration of the notion of opportunity structure, Merton (1995) has now clarified that the social structure is defined as the organization and distribution of status positions, not institutionalized means. Compared to the earliest versions of the paradigm, this version separates positions from means and locates the production of these means in a differential structure. Merton now clearly recognizes the necessity of including the production and distribution of means into separate realms, each subject to different dynamics. In the older versions of the paradigm, the distribution of means was awkwardly mixed with the production of means and related with the social structure in unclear ways.

Merton (1995) also provides more specific guidelines on applying the anomie-and-opportunity-structures paradigm, which has distinct consequences for theorizing and research in structural sociology. A first guideline is that access to opportunities does not necessarily entail actual utilization of those opportunities (Merton, 1995, p. 8). Acting individuals and their definitions of the situation (e.g., the opportunities perceived and used by them) are important to predict ultimate outcomes such as deviant behavior. Merton has chosen to give individuals and their motivations a place in his paradigm, despite its emphasis on structural factors and extra-individual environments. Merton recognizes that structures are analytical abstractions that are unable to operate without actors. These abstractions are useful to help understand the organization and relationships between actors and the creation of objective situations and contexts in which actions occur.

An additional guideline suggested by Merton (1995, p. 8) relates to how differential access to opportunity is a probabilistic, not a deterministic concept. The role of structures of any kind in Merton's paradigm are in shaping and influencing actor behavior and choices. For example, the existence of anomie in the broader society only increases the likelihood of certain adaptations under specified conditions. The paradigm is thus fully probabilistic in its ability to explain social phenomena such as deviant behavior.

Further specifying the original model of individual adaptations, Merton now differentiates rebellion, called non-conformist behavior, from innovation, ritualism, and retreatism, termed aberrant behavior. The aberrant types of adaptations involve more self-interested conduct, as "aberrants try to hide their violations of social norms even as they regard the norms they violate as legitimate ... As a result, their rule-breaking is socially defined simply as an effort to satisfy their personal interests in normatively unacceptable ways" (Merton, 1995, p. 12). Aberrants, unlike rebels, do not challenge the existing values and goals of a society or group's culture, but rather seek to satisfy their own personal needs. These are precisely the types of persons who are innovators accepting the broader goals, but using illegitimate means to achieve these goals.

Finally, the differentiation of non-conformist and aberrant behavior also shows that Merton's model incorporates the societal reactions toward deviant behavior, a point that has occasionally been overlooked in discussions of Merton's theory (Heckert & Heckert, 2004). Merton's recognition of the reactions by society and its definitional power to turn deviance to crime (or not) is most clear in the case of ritualism, a mode of adaptation which is "not generally considered to present a 'social problem'" (Merton, 1957, p. 240), but which Merton describes as a case of overconformity (Merton, 1957, pp. 236, 238–241). In fact, Merton additionally makes the stronger claim that deviant behavior is not necessarily dysfunctional, but that some "degree of deviation from current norms is probably functional for the basic goals of all groups" (Merton, 1957, p. 236). In this respect, then, Merton's theory can make a considerable advance in criminological theorizing by its attempt at integrating a causation perspective of deviance in a constructionist perspective of crime. A problematization of the nexus between deviance and crime is at the heart of Merton's theory of anomie-and-opportunity-structures.

# CONCLUSION

In this paper, we have provided an analysis of Robert Merton's anomie-and-opportunity-structures theory in view of ongoing developments in the elaboration and refinement of the Mertonian paradigm. Particularly relying on Merton's (1995) recent retrospective piece on the paradigm, we have argued for the centrality of the notion of opportunity structure in the Mertonian framework. Taking this important recent development into account, our discussion revealed that the Mertonian paradigm may continue to hold great promise in current theory and research examining deviant behavior, an insight that has already spawned a renewed interest in empirical research in the anomie-and-opportunity-structures tradition (e.g., Hagan & McCarthy, 1998; Passas, 1990, 2000). While further empirical research is surely needed complimentary to our analysis, it is clearly unfortunate that the theory of deviant behavior in the Mertonian paradigm has in some of the secondary literature been subject to unjust criticisms and misinterpretations. Upon more careful examination, the paradigm can hold strong because it incorporates many of the concerns of social scientists to develop an integrated cultural–structural model of human behavior and include both structural and human agency elements in such a model.

Many of the misattributions leveled against Merton by researchers who are theoretically positioned outside the anomie-and-opportunity-structures paradigm in reality demonstrate the objectives and limitations of their own approaches. Social control and social disorganization theorists, for instance, give overriding importance to institutional factors. The former criminologists ignore contextual factors, such as socio-economic conditions, whereas the latter tend to be structural determinists and, surprisingly, move toward being cultural determinists. The realist–Marxist conception of social structure that is adopted by Porpora has a certain similarity with the one used in the anomie-and-opportunity-structures paradigm, except that the latter paradigm incorporates cultural and opportunity structures as well. Given that the anomie-and-opportunity-structures paradigm incorporates or at least acknowledges the importance of human agency in social science behavior, future models using this paradigm will have to acknowledge the probabilistic nature of any structural modeling. Nevertheless, structural properties of behavior exist and the anomie-and-opportunity-structures paradigm goes further than most existing models in describing the parameters making up such structures.

Finally, the criticisms against a Mertonian structural model as ignoring voluntaristic, individual-level variables have their own limitations, mainly arising from a downplaying of the existence of supra-individual structures and, especially, the existence of cultural and opportunity structures. Such approaches explore the psychological and mental processes of individuals but are subject to problems of making any generalizations across individuals. It is clear that scholars adhering to such absolute criticisms about structural sociology do not approve of any research showing the importance of structural effects on human behavior, particularly the role of power and stratification underlying conceptions of cultural, social, and opportunity structures. If Merton's *oeuvre* is to have any meaningful impact in the future of our discipline, it should at least be its legacy that it is a truly sociological contribution.

# REFERENCES

Agnew, R. (1992). Foundation for a general strain theory of crime and delinquency. *Criminology, 30,* 47–87.

Bernard, T. J. (1984). Control criticisms of strain theories: An assessment of theoretical and empirical adequacy. *Journal of Research in Crime and Delinquency, 21,* 353–372.
Bernard, T. J. (1987). Testing structural strain theories. *Journal of Research in Crime and Delinquency, 24,* 262–280.
Bernard, T. J. (1990). Twenty years of testing theories: What have we learned and why? *Journal of Research in Crime and Delinquency, 27,* 325–347.
Bernard, T. J. (1995). Merton versus Hirschi: Who is faithful to Durkheim's heritage? In: F. Alder & W. S. Laufer (Eds), *The legacy of anomie theory. Advances in criminological research* (Vol. 6, pp. 81–90). New Brunswick, NJ: Transaction.
Bernburg, J. G. (2002). Anomie, social change and crime: A theoretical examination of institutional-anomie theory. *British Journal of Criminology, 42,* 729–742.
Besnard, P. (1990). Merton in search of anomie. In: J. Clark, C. Modgil & S. Modgil (Eds), *Robert K. Merton: Consensus and controversy* (pp. 243–254). London: Falmer Press.
Braithwaite, J. (1980). Merton's theory of crime and differential class symbols of success. *Crime and/et Justice, 7,* 90–94.
Bursik, R. J., Jr., & Grasmick, H. G. (1993). Economic deprivation and neighborhood crime rates, 1960–1980. *Law & Society Review, 27,* 263–283.
Cloward, R., & Ohlin, L. E. (1960). *Delinquency and opportunity: A theory of delinquent gangs.* New York: Free Press.
Cohen, A. K. (1955). *Delinquent boys.* New York: Free Press.
Cohen, A. K. (1965). The sociology of the deviant act: Anomie theory and beyond. *American Sociological Review, 30,* 5–14.
Cohen, A. K. (1985). The assumption that crime is a product of environments: Sociological approaches. In: R. F. Meier (Ed.), *Theoretical methods in criminology* (pp. 223–243). Beverly Hills, CA: Sage Publications.
Cruickshank, J. (2000). Social theory and the underclass: Social realism or rational choice individualism. In: M. S. Archer & J. Q. Tritter (Eds), *Rational choice theory: Resisting colonization* (pp. 75–92). London: Routledge.
Cullen, F. T. (1988). Were Cloward and Ohlin strain theorists?' 'Delinquency and opportunity' revisited. *Journal of Research in Crime and Delinquency, 25,* 214–241.
Deflem, M. (1989). From anomie to anomia and anomic depression. *Social Science and Medicine, 29,* 627–634.
Featherstone, R., & Deflem, M. (2003). Anomie and strain: Merton's two theories. *Sociological Inquiry, 73,* 471–489.
Fuchs, S. (2001). *Against essentialism: A theory of culture and society.* Cambridge, MA: Harvard University Press.
Gillis, A. R. (2004). Institutional dynamics and dangerous classes: Reading, writing, and arrest in nineteenth-century France. *Social Forces, 82,* 1303–1331.
Gottfredson, M. R., & Hirschi, T. (1990). *A general theory of crime.* Stanford, CA: Stanford University Press.
Hagan, J., & McCarthy, B. (1998). Social capital theory and the renewal of a strain-and-opportunity paradigm in sociological criminology. *Sociologie et Societies, 30,* 133–145.
Heckert, A., & Heckert, D. M. (2004). Using an integrated typology of deviance to expand Merton's anomie theory. *Criminal Justice Studies, 17,* 75–90.
Hilbert, R. E., & Wright, C. W. (1979). Representations of Merton's theory of anomie. *The American Sociologist, 14,* 150–156.

Hirschi, T. (1969). *Causes of delinquency*. Berkeley, CA: University of California Press.

Kim, S.-W., & Pridemore, W. A. (2005). Social change, institutional anomie and serious property crime in transitional Russia. *British Journal of Criminology, 45*, 81–97.

Konty, M. (2005). Microanomie: The cognitive foundations of the relationship between anomie and deviance. *Criminology, 43*, 107–132.

Kornhauser, R. (1978). *Social structures of delinquency: An appraisal of analytic models*. Chicago: University of Chicago Press.

Martin, R. (2000). Anomie, spirituality, and crime. *Journal of Contemporary Criminal Justice, 16*, 75–98.

Marwah, S. (2001). Contrasting notions of opportunity in crime and violence theory and research. Paper presented at the annual meeting of the Society for the Study of Social Problems, Anaheim, CA, August 2001.

Menard, S. (1995). A developmental test of Mertonian anomie theory. *Journal of Research in Crime and Delinquency, 32*, 136–174.

Merton, R. K. (1938). Social structure and anomie. *American Sociological Review, 3*, 672–682.

Merton, R. K. (1949a). Social structure and anomie: Revisions and extensions. In: R. N. Anshen (Ed.), *The family: Its functions and destiny* (pp. 226–257). New York: Harper.

Merton, R. K. ([1949]1968). On the history and systematics of sociological theory. In: *Social theory and social structure* (pp. 1–38). New York: Free Press.

Merton, R. K. ([1957]1968). Continuities in the theory of social structure and anomie. In: *Social theory and social structure* (pp. 215–248). New York: Free Press.

Merton, R. K. (1959). Social conformity, deviation and opportunity structures: A comment on the contributions of Dubin and Cloward. *American Sociological Review, 24*, 177–189.

Merton, R. K. (1964). Anomie, anomia, and social interaction: Contexts of deviant behavior. In: R. M. Clinard (Ed.), *Anomie and deviant behavior* (pp. 213–242). New York: Free Press.

Merton, R. K. (1968). The Matthew effect in science. *Science, 159*, 56–63.

Merton, R. K. (1976). Social problems and sociological theory. In: R. K. Merton & R. Nisbet (Eds), *Contemporary social problems* (4th ed., pp. 1–43). New York: Harcourt Brace Jovanovich.

Merton, R. K. (1995). Opportunity structure: The emergence, diffusion, and differentiation of a sociological concept. In: F. Adler & W. S. Laufer (Eds), *The legacy of anomie theory. Advances in criminological research* (Vol. 6, pp. 3–78). New Brunswick, NJ: Transaction.

Merton, R. K. (1997). On the evolving synthesis of differential association and anomie theory: A perspective from the sociology of science. *Criminology, 35*, 517–525.

Messner, S. F. (1988). Merton's social structure and anomie: The road not taken. *Deviant Behavior, 9*, 33–53.

Messner, S. F., & Rosenfeld, R. (1994). *Crime and the American dream.* (2nd ed.). Belmont, CA: Wadsworth Publishing Company.

Parnaby, P. F., & Sacco, V. F. (2004). Fame and strain: The contributions of Mertonian deviance theory to an understanding of the relationship between celebrity and deviant behavior. *Deviant Behavior, 25*, 1–26.

Passas, N. (1990). Anomie and corporate deviance. *Contemporary Crises, 14*, 157–178.

Passas, N. (1995). Continuities in the anomie tradition. In: F. Adler & W. S. Laufer (Eds), *The legacy of anomie theory. Advances in criminological research* (Vol. 6, pp. 91–112). New Brunswick, NJ: Transaction.

Passas, N. (2000). Global anomie, dysnomie, and economic crime: Hidden consequences of neoliberalism and globalization in Russia and around the world. *Social Justice, 27*, 16–44.

Paternoster, R., & Mazerolle, P. (1994). General strain theory and delinquency: A replication and extension. *Journal of Research in Crime and Delinquency, 31*, 235–263.

Peter, T., LaGrange, T. C., & Silverman, R. A. (2003). Investigating the interdependence of strain and self-control. *Canadian Journal of Criminology and Criminal Justice, 45*, 431–464.

Piquero, A., & Piquero, N. L. (1998). On testing institutional anomie theory with varying specifications. *Studies on Crime and Crime Prevention, 7*, 61–84.

Porpora, D. V. (1989). Four concepts of social structure. *Journal for the Theory of Social Behavior, 19*, 195–211.

Pratt, T. C., & Cullen, F. T. (2005). Assessing macro-level predictors and theories of crime: A meta-analysis. *Crime and Justice, 32*, 373–450.

Rosenfeld, R. (1989). Robert Merton's contributions to the sociology of deviance. *Sociological Inquiry, 59*, 453–466.

Rubinstein, D. (1992). Structural explanation in sociology: The egalitarian imperative. *The American Sociologist, 23*, 5–19.

Rubinstein, D. (1993). Opportunity and structural sociology. *Journal for the Theory of Social Behavior, 23*, 266–283.

Rubinstein, D. (1994). The social construction of opportunity. *The Journal of Socio-Economics, 23*, 61–78.

Rubinstein, D. (2001). *Culture, structure & agency: Towards a multidimensional society.* Thousand Oaks, CA: Sage Publications.

Thorlindsson, T., & Bernburg, J. G. (2004). Durkheim's theory of social order and deviance: A multi-level test. *European Sociological Review, 20*, 271–285.

# CRIMINOLOGICAL IMPLICATIONS OF THE THOUGHT OF GEORGE HERBERT MEAD

Ross L. Matsueda

## ABSTRACT

*The ideas of George Herbert Mead have received renewed interest in philosophy and the social sciences on both sides of the Atlantic. This chapter reviews recent developments and interpretations of Mead's thought and discusses their implications for criminological theory. Four theoretical issues are addressed. First, how is the concept of identity conceived and related to social outcomes? Second, how is human agency theorized within a unified theoretical framework? Third, what role do societal reactions play in shaping social action, such as law violation? Fourth, how are features of the life course socially constituted, and what are the theoretical mechanisms by which life course events shape future behavioral outcomes? The discussion is illustrated with classical and contemporary empirical studies. The chapter closes by discussing the role of qualitative and quantitative methods for advancing criminological research from a Meadian standpoint.*

Sociological Theory and Criminological Research: Views from Europe and the United States
Sociology of Crime, Law and Deviance, Volume 7, 77–108
Copyright © 2006 by Elsevier Ltd.
All rights of reproduction in any form reserved
ISSN: 1521-6136/doi:10.1016/S1521-6136(06)07005-9

Sociology and philosophy have witnessed a resurgence of interest in prag-matist philosophy and social thought. Through the seminal work of Hans Joas (1985, 1993, 1996), this interest in an essentially American philosoph-ical tradition has recently spread to Europe. In sociology, the writings of John Dewey, Charles Peirce, and George Herbert Mead have received renewed attention as theorists grapple with problems of human agency, creativity of action, complex social relations, rational choice, and social values. In criminology, George Herbert Mead's writings about social proc-esses from the standpoint of a social pragmatist have had an influence on many of the classical theories of crime. They may have had an indirect influence, through the writings of W. I. Thomas, on the general approach of Sutherland's differential association theory, and clearly were the inspiration for Cohen's (1955) social psychological mechanism by which delinquent subcultures are innovated. Blumer's (1969) symbolic interactionist interpre-tation of Mead's ideas, which stress the ways in which negotiated meanings are built up through collective action, directly underlay the labeling ap-proach to deviance of Tannenbaum, Lemert, and Becker. The Iowa School of symbolic interaction, most notably Kuhn (1964), influenced the struc-tural version of symbolic interactionism of Stryker (1980) and McCall and Simmons (1978) and indirectly influenced Schwartz and Stryker's (1970) and Matsueda and Heimer's (1997) theories of deviance and crime. This paper draws on recent reinterpretations and extensions of Mead's social pragma-tism to address key theoretical questions facing criminologists, including human agency and creativity, identity and the self, differential association and social learning, rational choice and deterrence, and temporality and the life course.

## KEY ISSUES IN THE SOCIOLOGICAL UNDERSTANDING OF CRIME

Theorizing about criminal behavior has historically been dominated by sociological theory, perhaps because crime is generally recognized to be a social construction, constituted by socially organized actors in specific con-junctions of historical periods, societies, and groups within society. Socio-logical theories of crime have enjoyed a rich and varied history, including classical theories of social disorganization and cultural transmission (Shaw & McKay, 1969), anomie (Merton, 1938), differential association (Sutherland, 1947), labeling (Tannenbaum, 1938; Becker, 1963), subculture (Cohen, 1955; Cloward & Ohlin, 1960; Short & Strodtbeck, 1965), and social control

(Matza, 1964; Hirschi, 1969; Kornhauser, 1978). More recently, such theories have been extended to social learning (Akers, 1998), control in the life course (Sampson & Laub, 1993), and control-balance (Tittle, 1995). These criminological theories have drawn liberally from the broader sociological theories of their time, and addressed key debates taking place among sociological theorists. For example, Merton drew heavily from Durkheim to explain class differentials in deviance rates, Shaw and McKay drew from Park and Burgess's human ecology perspective and applied it to delinquency rates in urban areas, Sutherland drew from W. I. Thomas, Louis Wirth, and other early interactionists in specifying that crime is learned in interaction and rooted in culture conflict, and Tannenbaum, and later Becker, drew from Blumer's (1969) symbolic interactionism to specify that deviance is a socially constructed label, which has consequences for the labeled person.

Recent literature in sociological theory has been grappling with four theoretical questions important for theorizing about crime. First, how is the concept of identity conceived and related to social outcomes? Second, how is human agency theorized and why is it important? Third, what role do societal reactions play in shaping social actions such as law violation? Fourth, how are features of the life course socially constituted and what are the theoretical mechanisms by which life course events shape later criminality? The answers to those questions go far in distinguishing among major perspectives. For example, Giddens' (1984) structuration approach posits a duality between structure and culture in which agency plays a prominent role; Coleman's (1990) social capital theory emphasizes a rational actor individual, but ties rationality to social structure through the concept of social capital; and post-modern perspectives reject the assumption of objective reality and emphasize multiple, fractured identities in modernity and the importance of deconstructing social phenomena.

This paper addresses these questions from the standpoint of a theory of crime based on Mead's social pragmatism. It builds on some of my earlier writings, with Karen Heimer, on a symbolic interactionist theory of crime, and focuses on the question of crime causation, rather than on the societal reaction to crime – except to note that the writings on labeling from the standpoint of symbolic interactionism are compatible with the perspective developed here, and that labeling and crime causation are a part of the same process. This paper argues that we can draw on Mead's theory of temporality, which helps unify his theories of the self, social control, and cognition to shed new light on questions of agency and creativity, identity and the self, structure and culture, process and life course, and rationality and decision making.

# MEAD'S THEORY OF SOCIAL CONTROL

At the heart of Mead's social psychology and his theory of social control lies the concept of taking the role of the other. I will describe this concept in detail, apply it to the social control of crime, and use it to illustrate other features of Mead's perspective, including his theory of temporality, cognition, agency, and rationality. Mead begins with three assumptions. First is a methodological holism, in which "the whole (society) is prior to the part (the individual), not the part to the whole; and the part is explained in terms of the whole, not the whole in terms of the part or parts" (Mead, 1934, p. 7). Second is a social process model within which society, selves, and cognition, arise, and which can be studied by using the abstract concept of a social act, a cooperative act between two or more individuals. Third, is an organic or functionalist social psychology, in which social acts are viewed as a "dynamic whole" (rather than as aggregations of stimulus–response sets), and the component elements are analyzed in terms of their functions (Mead, 1934, p. 7).

## Mead's Temporally Ordered Phases of the Act

As a preliminary, note that Mead begins his analysis of the act by dividing it into four functional and temporally ordered phases: impulse, perception, manipulation, and consummation. Impulses, which are ultimately rooted in physiology, but are also subject to social conditioning, initiate the act, seeking stimuli (physical objects) for their expression. The consummation stage sees the impulse expressed or frustrated, and objects infused with meaning – meanings are socially constituted in a process that spans the entire act. Between impulse and consummation are the mediating stages of perception and manipulation. Perhaps the key phase is manipulation, in which objects are observed with vision and, more importantly, manipulated with the hand. Objects provide resistance to the hand or body – they "push back" – and in this sense manipulation is social. As Miller (1973, p. 121) states concisely, "The inside of the object is involved in manipulation, and we cannot handle or manipulate an object unless it offers resistance and thereby cooperates with us." Physical objects are socially constituted in manipulation – we apprehend its hardness, brittleness or sharpness – and we do so instrumentally for the purpose of reaching consummation. For example, a burglar manipulates a doorknob in the dark as a phase in stealing valuables from a home.

Perception allows us to approach objects at a distance in terms of hypothetical manipulation and consummation. Perception is an active process of searching for objects that would lead to consummation of an impulse, anticipating their physical characteristics – how they would feel if we touched them. For this reason Mead termed perception a "collapsed act," which includes all stages of the act (impulse, manipulation, and consummation) (Mead, 1938, p. 128). Whether or not the anticipations are correct are determined in the manipulation phase. Moreover, in the stage of manipulation, perception and contact are nearly simultaneous, or as Cook (1993, p. 172) puts it, the "temporal passage that normally intervenes between seeing (distance perception) and bodily contact is at a minimum; such passage can therefore be ignored by the acting organism." Here, in the present, human beings can delay consummation of the act, consider the anticipated resistance of objects at a distance, constitute objects through reflection, and thereby consider alternative lines of action in the present. At this point, there is an "enduring fabric as a basis for alternative courses of action, a world of things that have identical dates, namely, the date of the manipulatory area" (Mead, 1938). Thus, human beings' ability to delay consummation of an act enables them to engage in cognitive processes, in which alternative solutions to problematic situations are considered in the present in the manipulatory phase. Here we see Mead's theory of temporality in the stages of the act.

## Taking the Role of the Other

The key concept in Mead's social psychological writings is role-taking, which occurs in social acts.[1] Within an ongoing social process, social acts are built up by participants adjusting their responses to each other within an ongoing social process. When adjustments are smooth and routine, situations are non-problematic, and behavior non-reflective. When, however, an ongoing response or impulse is temporarily blocked, the situation becomes problematic, and individuals engage in role-taking, seeking solutions to the problematic situation by taking the role of others, viewing themselves as objects from the standpoint of others, and considering alternative lines of action from the standpoint of others (Mead, 1934).

Specifically, when an impulse is blocked by a physical or social barrier, an emotion – such as anger, fear, sadness, or happiness – is released, and the impulse is transformed into an image, which includes a plan of action and the anticipated reactions of others to the plan. The impulse is reacted to by another impulse, which follows the plan to overt behavior, combines the plan with another, or blocks the plan, causing the situation to remain problematic – in which case, the individual again takes the role of the other, forms a self as an object, and considers new alternatives from the standpoint of others. This process – the serial process of cognition – continues until the problem is solved or the social act fades. Mead (1934) termed the image the "me" and the impulse the "I," and specified them as two phases of the self – the self as an object drawn from the past, and the acting self responding in the present. By "solution," Mead meant not that the problem is resolved in an optimal way, but rather that it is solved for the practical purposes at hand, which means the blocked or conflicting impulses are freed and the social act is allowed to resume. Moreover, when similar problematic situations are repeatedly solved in functionally equivalent ways, they become less problematic, and behavior becomes habitual or non-reflective. In highly institutionalized settings, with strong norms, most behaviors are non-reflective, actors are not self-conscious, and stimuli lead directly to responses; at times, however, even normative behavior is interrupted by unanticipated or unconventional exigencies, and behaviors become reflective, actors take themselves as objects, and stimuli are mediated or interpreted by cognitive processes.

Mead's (1934) theory of cognition consists of this dialectical inner-dialogue of the "I" and the "me," which, in form and substance, resembles the "conversation of gestures" occurring between two individuals, except that it occurs between the phases of the self in the mind. Role-taking is possible by the use of language – or "significant symbols" to use Mead's term – which calls out functionally identical responses in oneself as well as in others (Miller, 1973). The universal character of language allows us to isolate, hold onto, and manipulate or reconstruct alternate responses, anticipating how others might respond, before carrying them out in overt behavior. Here we glimpse Mead's theory of temporality: role-taking occurs in the present, in adjusting to a problematic situation in the present, and applies past experiences to anticipated future outcomes (Mead, 1932). From an indefinite past, a specific depiction of the past (the "me") is called up to solve a problem in the present in the context of a future goal with anticipated consequences. The response of the "I" occurs in the present, but only insofar as it has been called out by the "me" (a past) in terms of a specific anticipated future. Moreover, the "I" – or more specifically, the dialectical unfolding of the "I" and the "me" – contains an element of novelty or emergence, which stems from being in multiple perspectives simultaneously. Mead used the term "sociality" to refer to the ability to be in multiple spatio-temporal perspectives, simultaneously – a prerequisite for role-taking.

Because the reaction of the "I" to the "me," always entails some element of emergence and novelty, the response of the "I" can never be perfectly predicted or known in advance. We constantly surprise ourselves. Indeed, the "I" is knowable only in the future as another "me" – a depiction of the past – within another problematic situation. In Mead's (1964, p. 141) terms, "The self-conscious, actual self in social intercourse is the objective 'me' or 'me's' with the process of response continually going on and implying a fictitious 'I' always out of sight of himself." Moreover, the "I" can suggest new alternatives ("me's") and vice-versa. This parallels Dewey's (1958) theory of "ends in view," in which ends are always in the present and are reciprocally related to means (Joas, 1994). Once a problematic situation is solved, and conflicting impulses are resolved through role-taking, a reconstruction of the situation has occurred, and a new self emerges from the old self: "Solution is reached by the construction of a new world harmonizing the conflicting interests into which enters the new self" (Mead, 1964, p. 149).

For Mead, emergence and reconstruction are key elements of human experience, and arise through role-taking. The past and future are hypothetical representations in experience and can be reconstructed in the present to resolve a problem. As one present passes into another, novelty emerges, which allows us to experience continuity. For Mead (1964, p. 350), "pure continuity could not be experienced," but "as present passes into present, there is always some break in continuity," and "the break reveals the continuity, and continuity is the background for the novelty." Only by experiencing novelty in the context of continuity does one experience passage. Moreover, once novelty emerges, we create continuity by reconstructing the past so as to "transform the unexpected emergent into something that should have been expected" all along (Cook, 1993, p. 149). Novelty and emergence bring about social reconstruction in the perceptual field of objects, allowing for new meanings to arise, and providing for new, reconstructed, changed selves.

In sum, Mead's concept of role-taking has three key functions for the social act: anticipatory, reflexive, and appropriative functions (Cook, 1993; see also Lauer & Boardman, 1971). The anticipatory function allows individuals to anticipate how others will react to their responses before responding overtly. The reflexive function allows individuals to become self-conscious, to see themselves, and to grasp the meaning of their behavior. The appropriative function allows individuals to incorporate responses, attitudes, and values of others into one's own line of conduct, adjusting to others into coordinated behavior.

## The Social Structure of the Self

The self, then, arises in social interaction as an object, and thus, is socially constituted (given meaning) as an object in the same way other physical objects are constituted. For Mead (1964, p. 141), the organized society is prior to the individual, and the self has a definite social structure, which derives from the larger society in which the individual participates: "Inner consciousness is socially organized by the importation of the social organization of the outer world." That structure is revealed in Mead's well-known analogy of "play" and "the game," which describes the developmental process of acquiring a mature self. Early in life, children learn to play roles by taking the role of concrete others independently: they play policeman and arrest themselves; they play parent and scold themselves (Mead, 1934, p. 150). During this period, the child becomes aware of his or her body, learns to identify with the body (that is, draw a connection between the self and the body), and differentiate the body from the rest of the world. Later, having developed a sense of the body, and a rudimentary or compartmentalized self, children diversify the self by learning the game, in which they take the role of the entire group or "generalized other," including the norms, rules, and expectations governing various positions and roles of the group, community, or society. They learn to relate the rules, expectations, and obligations of their own roles to those of others within the organized system. This process of taking the role of the generalized other is the most effective form of social control because organized groups and institutionalized norms enter individual behavior (Heimer & Matsueda, 1994).

Moreover, if we begin with the organized group or institution, with its differentiated roles, expectations, values, and norms, and then explain individual selves, minds, and social activities, we see that the structure of individual selves reflect the larger social structure of the groups in which individuals participate. A key question is which attitudes or organized roles will be invoked to solve a particular problematic situation? The answer is simple: the one that is most relevant, and offers, from the standpoint of the unfolding self, the best chance of freeing the impulse and solving the problem. If it fails, another "me" is called out. The relationship between the structure of the group and action is not a simple deterministic function, however, for three reasons. First, individuals participate in a plethora of distinct and overlapping groups, and their participation varies from superficial association to deep commitments.[2] Second, the specific groups, or generalized others, that will be invoked in a problematic situation depend on the exigencies of that specific situation. That is, the specific formulation of the past arising in the "me" depends on the problem at hand. Third, the specific response of the "I" to the "me" is not deterministic, but rather involves a dialectic, in which there is an element of novelty, creativity, and emergence. It may be useful to contrast, on the one hand, a *stable self*, derived from previous stable participation in certain organized groups, with, on the other hand, a *situational self*, arising in the present (as the dialectic between the "I" and the "me") through role-taking to solve problematic situations. In other words, we can contrast stable identities with situational identities (Alexander & Rudd, 1984).

## IDENTITIES AND CRIME

Clearly, for Mead, the locus of social control lies in the genesis of the self as an object from the standpoint of the generalized other. In other words, social control lies in the ways identities are formed from the standpoint of reference groups, and invoked to solve problematic situations. Thus, we can describe the self from two vantage points. First is a situational or acting self, operating self-consciously in the present, emerging between old and new selves by adjusting to conflicting impulses, and knowable only in the future as a past acting self, now incorporated in the stable self. This is the realm of human agency, emergence, and novelty. Second is the stable self, which gives behavior continuity. We can conceive of such a self by summing across a person's biographical history, including past social selves, social acts, and most importantly, past solutions to problematic situations. This self has a structure, which lies in the past, and corresponds to the structure of the generalized other – that aspect of society in which the individual has participated. The stable self is the realm of structure, constraint, and habit. The relationship between the two components of the self illustrates Mead's theory of temporality: the stable self lies in the past, but is called up in the present as a certain depiction of that stable self as the "me," which is responded to by the "I" to solve a present problem in light of anticipated future consequences. The situational self then becomes incorporated in the stable self, ready to be called up to solve future problems.

Because the self is multidimensional and as complex as the temporal and spatial organization of groups within which the individual participates, any study of the self must restrict focus on a single domain or dimension. Criminological research has examined the implications of both stable and situational selves for criminal and moral action. Research on stable selves or identities has used quantitative methods to unearth patterned views of the self. For example, early work by Schwartz and Stryker (1970) hypothesized that, compared to boys labeled "good boys" by teachers, those labeled "bad boys" would have poor and uncertain self-concepts, have difficulty with masculine identities, and have few conventional significant others such as teachers. Research by Kaplan and his colleagues has examined how self-derogating attitudes – self rejection – affect delinquent behavior directly, and indirectly through delinquent peers (Kaplan, Johnson, & Bailey, 1987). In my own work on youth crime, I have tried to specify a conception of the self as a reflected appraisal of how others appraise one in interaction (Matsueda, 1992). Applied to delinquency, I find that parents' actual appraisals of youth as a rule violator leads to youth reflected appraisals as a rule violator from the standpoint of parents, teachers, and peers, which in turn, is associated with future delinquent acts (see also Triplett & Jarjoura, 1994). Bartusch and Matsueda (1996) showed how this process explains delinquency for both males and females, but has stronger effects for females, presumably because adolescent girls are more concerned with the opinions of others. Finally, Heimer and Matsueda (1994) have shown that reflected appraisals as a rule violator is one aspect of role-taking producing delinquency, along with delinquent peers, anticipated reactions of significant others to delinquency, and delinquent attitudes. They term the process as one of "differential social control" (see also Heimer, 1996).

Criminological research on situational selves has used qualitative methods to reconstruct situations in which – using the terms adopted here – individuals have engaged in role-taking to solve problematic situations in illicit ways. I will mention a few classical examples from criminology. Cressey (1953) developed a theory of the criminal violation of financial trust – defined as taking a position of financial trust in good faith, but then violating that faith – based on interviews with convicted embezzlers, who reconstructed the circumstances of their offenses. Cressey argued that a three-stage sequence led to violations of trust: (1) the offender realized he had a serious financial problem that could not be shared with others; (2) he perceived that he could solve the problem by violating financial trust; and (3) he was able to use vocabularies of motive to adjust his conception of self as an upstanding moral person with a conception of self as one who absconded with entrusted money. Those rationalizations or definitions of the situation, included "I was just borrowing the money and planned to pay it back," "I was entrusted with the money, and can do with it what I please," and "It's not really a crime."[3] Some offenders found themselves "in too deep," and unable to repay their debt and turned themselves in, thereby maintaining a self-image as an honest person. Others repented when caught, and again maintained their moral self-image. In a minority of cases, upon being caught, the offender changed their self-image from an upstanding member of the community to that of a criminal.

Becker's (1963, p. 42) study of marijuana smoking showed how "deviant motives actually develop in the course of experience with the deviant activity," or in other words, how means and ends evolve reciprocally within a social act. Thus, novice smokers take the role of experienced users to learn to smoke marijuana, including how to inhale and hold the smoke in the lungs, how to recognize the effects of being high, and how to define the effects as pleasurable. In this way, an inherently ambiguous physiological experience – dizzy, nauseous, euphoric, or comical – is transformed and redefined into a social object defined as being "high," and more importantly, being pleasurable. Such definitions are built up through role-taking in groups, as other experienced members help demonstrate how to smoke properly, how to recognize the feeling of being high (including having the "munchies"), and how to interpret the high feeling as pleasurable and even euphoric. Thus, "marihuana acquires meaning for the user as an object which can be used for pleasure" and with repeated experiences of this sort, "there grows a stable set of categories for experiencing the drug's effects" (Becker, 1963, p. 56). Moreover, because marijuana is illegal, whether one progresses from a beginning user to occasional user and then to a regular user depends on how one adapts to social control attempts to limit supply of the drug, detect drug users, and define the behavior as immoral. Through role-taking, regular users have developed contacts with drug dealers, have learned verbalizations that neutralize definitions of the behavior as immoral, and have dealt with the possibility of being caught by segregating acquaintances into users versus nonusers, by withdrawing into groups who condone marijuana, or by realizing that detection would not be so bad. Through these processes, regular users adopt a stable conception of self as a marijuana smoker from the standpoint of their generalized other.

Luckenbill (1977) found that homicides are often situated transactions that escalate from a minor dispute to violence because actors seek to maintain a favorable self-image, stand strong rather than backing down, and thereby jointly construct a violent definition of the situation. Analyzing reconstructed descriptions of homicide transactions, Luckenbill developed a sequential process model of homicide. One actor issues a challenge or insult, the second actor perceives it as such and accordingly as a threat to his self-image. Rather than backing down and losing face, the second responds by standing his ground and insulting, threatening, or challenging in kind. In turn, the first actor perceives a threat to self and responds in kind, followed by the second actor responding to this response, and so on, in a spiraling escalation of violence. Often bystanders encourage, agitate, or cheer on the combatants. Luckenbill concludes that such transactions are often a character contest unfolding in stages, as each interactant seeks to show strong character and avoid losing face by standing strong and not backing down, until the interaction spirals into a murderous definition of the situation (see also Felson, 1978).

Katz (1988, p. 5) examines the "the range of sensual dynamics" operating within the immediate situation of a criminal event, finding that criminals are often seduced into crime by the prospect of excitement and kicks, or what he terms "sneaky thrills." Sneak thieves are often preoccupied with "getting over" and the "excitement and thrill" from succeeding in their thefts. When caught or arrested, they typically express shock, subsequently treat their theft as "real crime," and typically end their deviant careers to avoid commitment to a deviant identity. Professional shoplifters, in contrast, see themselves as members of a criminal subculture and as "real thieves," and therefore see arrest as just another "cost of doing business" (Katz, 1988, p. 66). Katz also writes about violence committed by street youth. Such youth work at developing a reputation as a "badass," demonstrating a "superiority of their being" by dominating and forcing their will on others. They start a fight or "force a humiliating show of deference" by accidentally bumping another male, challenging them with eye contact and the opening line, "Whatcuhlookinat?" (Katz, 1988, p. 110).

Anderson (1999) goes beyond this analysis of inner city violence by identifying a "code of the street" operating on the streets of Philadelphia, which he argues is rooted in the local circumstances of ghetto poverty as described by Wilson's (1987) underclass thesis. Cut off from gaining success in mainstream institutions, alienated African–American youth come to distrust the legal system for resolving their disputes, and turn to violence and an emphasis on "manhood" to resolve disputes and gain status. Status and a sense of self is derived from developing a reputation based on showing toughness, nerve, and physical prowess and adhering to the code of the street: never backing down from a fight, always coming to the defense of one's crew, and exacting revenge or "payback" when one or one's loved one is disrespected. Moreover, Anderson's work shows how, within the backdrop of a broader socioeconomic urban context, organized groups structure individual selves, and therefore, solutions to problematic situations. His ideal types of "decent families" and "street families" illustrates the ways in which conflicting groups give rise to conflicting impulses that are solved through taking the role of the other.

These studies of the acting or situational self suggest that behavior is not strictly determined by outside forces, but rather include a volitional component, or human agency. Moreover, within Mead's perspective is an implicit theory of agency, which can link structure to action, stable selves to situational selves, habit to emergence, and stability to change.

## HUMAN AGENCY IN CRIMINOLOGICAL THEORY

Although the question of human agency can be traced to moral philosophers of the Enlightenment, including forefathers of criminology, Bentham and Beccaria, sociological interest in human agency has stimulated Wrong's (1961, p. 183) critique of sociological theorists' "oversocialized conception of man," in which "man 'internalizes social norms' and seeks a favorable self-image by conforming to the 'expectations' of others." Wrong argued for a dialectical conception, which has been developed in theories of Giddens (1984), Bourdieu (1977), Sewell (1992), and others. In criminology, Kornhauser (1978) applied Wrong's critique to "cultural deviance theory," her term for her caricature of differential association and subcultural theories, arguing that such theories are deterministic and eschew notions of human agency (see Matsueda, 1988, 1997). More recently, Sampson and Laub (1993) and Laub and Sampson (2003) have raised the question of agency in their theory of informal social ties across the life course. Elsewhere, in the context of specifying a theory of crime, Karen Heimer and I have argued that Mead's perspective includes a theory of agency, which resolves the deterministic critique of structuralism (Matsueda & Heimer, 1996). Here, I briefly summarize the work of Emirbayer and Mische (1998), who draw on Mead's theory of temporality to specify a complete theory of agency.

There are at least four theoretical reasons to be concerned about human agency for a theory of crime. First, a conception of human agency allows us to break free of a completely deterministic model and oversocialized conception of behavior. Second, agency provides a mechanism for change in individual criminal behavior – a crucial concept for translating theory into policy and for accounting for criminal trajectories across the life course. Third, it provides a mechanism by which individual actors can effect change in macro-level outcomes, such as institutions, cultures, and subcultures, which in turn act back on crime. Finally, a theoretical conception of agency is compatible with theorizing about legal concepts, such as moral responsibility and legal culpability. Unfortunately, much of the discussion of human agency is not rooted in observable behavior, but rather degenerates into a metaphysical discussion of concepts of "will," (e.g., Matza, 1964) which is demonstrated empirically in case studies in which actors claim they were acting on their will. Other conceptions of agency simply treat it as a residual category, in which all that cannot be explained by variables of a social theory is attributed to "agency." A more satisfying solution would be to develop a conception of human agency from within the general theoretical framework explaining criminality.

In their remarkably complex and free-ranging treatise on human agency, Emirbayer and Mische (1998, p. 970) draw on Mead's theory of temporality to specify a conception of agency as "the temporally constructed engagement by actors of different structural environments – the temporal-relational contexts of action – which, through the interplay of habit, imagination, and judgment, both reproduces and transforms those structures in interactive response to the problems posed by changing historical situations." To emphasize the temporal orientation of agency, they identify three elements of role-taking that constitute sequential phases of agency. The "iterational element" refers to the process of calling up the past through the structure of the me –"actors selectively recognize, locate, and implement such schemas" – which gives continuity to behavior and identities (Emirbayer & Mische, 1998, p. 975). The "projective element" refers to the cognitive process of considering alternate lines of action and creatively combining or reconfiguring them in light of "actors' hopes, fears, and desires for the future." The "practical-evaluative element" refers to recognizing a situation as problematic, characterizing the problem in terms of a specific past, and deliberating among alternatives to arrive at a decision to be executed in overt behavior to attain a future objective. Although they do not use the term, Emirbayer and Mische (1998) are referring to Mead's concept of role-taking, and identifying human agency in the process of taking the role of the generalized other, being in multiple temporal and spatial perspectives in the present (by considering alternative lines of action from the standpoint of others), and adopting a practical solution to the problem using a specific depiction of the past. Stated simply, human agency emerges in problematic situations via the dialectical conversation between the "I" and the "me."

Closely aligned with the concept of agency in Mead's thought are notions of creativity, spontaneity, and novelty. This arises in the impulsive, spontaneous response of the "I" to the structured, normative, group-based image of the "me," which explains why "we surprise ourselves by our own actions" (Mead, 1934, p. 174). Thus, there is an element of creativity in every act of role-taking, solving a problem using reflective intelligence: "The resulting action is always a little different from anything he could anticipate" (Mead,

1934, p. 177). The degree of creativity, of course, varies in degree from slight differences to wholesale transformations. This notion is so crucial to Mead's thought that Joas (1996) has used it to develop a theory of the "creativity of action."

Embedded in Mead's perspective, then, is a theoretical mechanism for innovation, which can be used to address a critical problem in criminology: where does crime come from? That is, where do the ideas, justifications, and motives for new crimes originate? Such an explanation, which is beyond the scope of this chapter, would begin with a situation of social disorganization, in which conventional organization is undermined by conflicting attitudes giving rise to rule violation. For example, male minority youth in disadvantaged inner city neighborhoods face social disorganization, frustration, and alienation, as family, education, and labor market institutions fail to meet their needs and inculcate conventional commitments. Such a situation calls for social reorganization, in which new rules for behavior provides expression of the new attitudes (Thomas & Znaniecki, [1918] 1958). Here a key element is played by indigenous leaders, who use their prestige, efficiency, and ability to motivate through fear and hope to build cooperation and new schemes of behavior, corresponding to new norms and institutions, which increases social cohesion (Thomas & Znaniecki, [1918] 1958). Those new schemes of behavior, such as codes of honor or the code of the street, provide ways of attaining respect and honor on the streets, often through illegal behavior. In fact, however, such honor codes have a long history in the U.S. (e.g., Ayers, 1984), and therefore, the problem is one of transforming existing rules and status systems to fit a particular problematic situation facing inner city, disadvantaged, minority youth. The important point is that indigenous leaders, who correspond to "organizational entrepreneurs" in the neo-institutional organizations literature (e.g., Powell & DiMaggio, 1991), use their agency to solve a problematic situation in creative ways, suggesting new schemes of behavior for obtaining status. Through role-taking, they jointly innovate new schemes of behavior and systems of status, and succeed in persuading a critical mass of similarly disadvantaged youth to participate in such a system (e.g., Cohen, 1955). Once the system is in place, other disadvantaged youth can gain status in the eyes of other participants in the system by adhering to the code – never backing down from a fight, watching one's back, responding with violence when one's girlfriend is disrespected, and exacting revenge when violence strikes a member of a crew (e.g., Anderson, 1999). That is, by exercising their human agency, and taking the role of the generalized other (including the rules and sanctions of the status system), members can use the tenets of the system strategically for their own personal gain.

More generally, this conception of human agency is important for theorizing about criminal acts because it (1) derives agency from the underlying
mechanisms of the theory, rather than simply adding on a residual term or a
metaphysical concept of will in an ad hoc way to an otherwise deterministic
theory; (2) moves beyond the tired free-will-determinism debate by positing
a dialectic between individual and society; (3) supplies a theoretical mechanism by which individual and group change can occur; and (4) provides a
temporal framework compatible with a life span approach, from which the
specific mechanisms explaining turning points flow naturally. Mead's theory
of agency and social control can be applied to Sutherland's (1947) classical
theory of differential association and free the theory of its statement of
determinism, address some criticisms of the theory raised by Sutherland
himself, and provide a stronger link between differential association and
differential social organization (see Matsueda, 2006). Moreover, it can provide the theoretical mechanism by which labeling can amplify crime or lead
to desistance through the life course.

## LABELING, DEVIANCE AMPLIFICATION, AND DESISTANCE

The perspective on deviance most closely associated with symbolic interaction is labeling theory, which traditionally has ignored the etiology of
crime and deviance, and focused on the process of labeling deviance. Indeed,
some versions of labeling theory have defined crime and deviance not as
objective behaviors, but rather as a mere label conferred by a social audience
(e.g., Becker, 1963). Here, I will reject this definition and assume that, while
crime is socially constituted in interaction, there are objective behaviors that
violate laws for which a strong consensus can usually be found among
members of society. Nevertheless, labeling theory provides a framework,
consistent with Mead, for specifying the consequences of societal reactions
to crime.[4] The concept of labeling can be traced to Tannenbaum's (1938)
discussion of the "dramatization of evil," which arises from conflict between
the community and its youth over the definition of the situation. From the
perspective of youth, acts of breaking windows, climbing over roofs, and
stealing from street vendors are forms of play, adventure, and fun. From the
standpoint of the community, these acts are forms of evil, nuisance, and
delinquency, which call for control (Tannenbaum, 1938, p. 17). Repeated
conflict between youth and community sets in motion a process of escalating

conflict, in which adults label the youth as increasingly "bad" and "evil" and the youth respond with more resistance to the adults. Their resistance elicits increased negative labeling, as adults seek to control the increasingly serious behavior of youth.

The community, then, gradually shifts from defining the youthful acts as evil to defining the youth themselves as evil persons. Soon the youth's speech, companions, and hangouts come to be regarded with suspicion, the youth recognizes that he or she is being defined as evil, and the youth comes to see herself as a delinquent. Thus, at times, the "person becomes the thing he is described as being" (Tannenbaum, 1938, p. 20). The youth responds to negative labeling in different ways, sometimes resisting aggressively, sometimes conforming, and sometimes fleeing. Such youth are particularly vulnerable to the influence of older more experienced delinquents. Moreover, society's attempts at control, through deterrence and rehabilitation at times exacerbate the problem. Arrest and incarceration can intensify the hardening process, opening up their worlds to formal institutions of control, and exposing them to increasingly hardened criminals.

Lemert (1951) used the term, "secondary deviance," to describe deviant acts which are explicit responses to societal reactions to deviance. Secondary deviance occurs when society's response to initial or "primary" deviance, including stigmatization, punishment, and segregation, causes fundamentally changes in a person's social roles, self-identity, and personality, resulting in additional deviance. Whereas the primary deviant's life and identity are organized around conventional activities, "the secondary deviant's life and identity are organized around the facts of deviance" (Lemert, 1967, p. 41). Becker (1963) expanded labeling to include the process by which moral entrepreneurs marshal support from various interest groups to outlaw a behavior in the first place, and the process by which rule enforcers – police, prison guards, and security – enforce those laws, typically by attending more to bureaucratic imperatives of enforcement than the substantive content of the laws. Moreover, law creation and enforcement, for Becker, typically work against the interests of the powerless in society, who are more likely to be labeled as deviant or criminal.

Labeling theory points to a theoretical mechanism by which negative reactions to crime can increase future criminality, and by inference, positive reactions can reduce future crime (for a review of empirical evidence, see Paternoster & Iovanni, 1989). Braithwaite's (1989) theory of reintegrative shaming seeks to identify the conditions under which labeling will lead to stigmatization and secondary deviance. For Braithwaite, severe punishment, such as incarceration, stigmatizes the offender as an outcast, cuts the

individual off from conventional society, and forces the person into affiliation with subcultural groups – if she has the opportunities and tastes for
such affiliations. In contrast, when community disapproval – particularly
public shaming – is followed by reacceptance into the community of law
abiding citizens, the offender is likely to desist from crime. This reintegrative
shaming effects desistance by embedding social disapproval in the broader
context of social acceptance, minimizing stigmatization and subcultural
affiliation, and building a person's conscience through shaming and repent-
ance. Reintegrative shaming is more effective in communitarian societies
with high social capital – mutual obligations, trust, and loyalties embedded
in interdependencies – because the shamed individual is more intertwined in
the lives of others. Finally, shaming begins in early child socialization within
the family, as parents punish children while expressing love, rather than
rejecting the child.

These ideas were presaged by Mead (1918) in an essay on the psychology
of punitive justice. Mead argued that punishment allows members of society
to express impulses of outrage and hostility at the criminal – impulses that
are normally restrained by social norms. This expression creates a strong
emotional identification with conventional society and a feeling of anger
at the criminal. Despite this human tendency, Mead felt that such expression of hostility, eventuating in the effective segregation of criminals from
society, would be less effective than integrating the criminal. For Mead,
the solution was to expand the scope of the generalized others for both
the criminal and conventional elements. That is, through role-taking and
deliberation, the criminal would come to appreciate the perspective of
the conventional society, while at the same time, conventional members
would come to understand the perspective and situation of the criminal. By
incorporating each others' perspectives into their own, each would move
toward a more universal understanding of the problem, and be capable of
forging a creative solution that took all roles into account. This is consistent
with W. I. Thomas's concept of reorganization and with Shaw's Chicago
Area Project, which attempted to translate social disorganization-cultural
transmission theory into practice.

Clearly, law creation, rule enforcement, primary deviance, labeling, and
secondary deviance are all intertwined within the organization of society.
Labeling theory and reintegrative shaming point to specific problems of prisoner reentry into society – stigmatization from conventional society increases
problems of obtaining jobs, refraining from street life and affiliating with
criminals, and maintaining or developing strong ties to family and conventional others (e.g., Petersilia, 2003). For example, using a quasi-experimental

audit study, in which pairs of job applicants matched on job credentials applied for real entry-level jobs, Pager (2003) found that felons and blacks were less likely to get callbacks for interviews than similar non-felon and white applicants. Moreover, race and felon status interacted: black applicants with a criminal record were least likely to get a callback. Pager concluded that the "mark of a criminal record" results in stigmatization and negative labeling, presenting a barrier for criminals to reenter society. Thus, the process of negative labeling can transform the experience of incarceration from a way of paying one's debt to society (or deterring the criminal from future crimes) to a way of increasing the likelihood of future crime – reducing the rate of desistance. The effect of incarceration, a life course role-transition, then, depends on the meaning of the role, which is constituted through social interaction.

## CRIME IN THE LIFE COURSE

Elsewhere, Karen Heimer and I have discussed the relevance of symbolic interactionism for a life course theory of crime (Matsueda & Heimer, 1997). There we made three principal points: (1) Mead's theory of temporality and role-taking explains how the life course is constituted, and provides a basis for theorizing about state dependence (change) versus heterogeneity (stability); (2) Mead's biosocial conception of human beings provides a framework for addressing how genes interact with environments; (3) role-taking provides a theory of the meaning of role-transitions, an explanation of role-selection, and a mechanism by which role transitions alter trajectories of behavior. Here we expand on that discussion by discussing the role of human agency, and of Giordano, Cernkovich, and Rudolph's (2002) concept of "hooks for change."

### *Temporality, the Life Course, and Life History Narratives*

Mead's theory of temporality provides a theoretical framework for conceptualizing aging, the passage of time, and the life course, and is compatible with Dannefer's critique of an ontogenetic development model rooted in biology in favor of a sociogenic model rooted in symbolic interaction. Rather than treating the life course as a series of ontogenetically determined age-graded life stages, and analyzing departures from age as abnormal, one can treat the life course as sociogenetically determined by

"symbolic knowledge and intentionality mediating development," as a malleable human organism interacts with a structurally diverse social environment (Dannefer, 1984).

Moreover, Mead's theory of temporality applies to the constitution of the
life course itself. Objective features of a life course are indefinite and exist
independently of consciousness; what is important is the specific meaning
of features of the life course, which are constituted in interaction. Thus,
when individuals consider a problematic situation in the present, and call
up aspects of their biographical history – which includes organized roles,
role-transitions, and trajectories – in light of a future trajectory, they are
constituting features of the life course by taking those features into self-
conscious consideration. In this way, the temporal dimensions of the life
course emerge in the present, in the same way that spatial or relational
dimensions emerge in constituting space or relationships in interaction.

This conception of temporality applies to the use of life history narratives
to reconstruct an individual's biographical history. Such narratives are attempts to reconstruct a conception of the past in terms of a present problem
(e.g., the researcher's attempt to link criminal acts to stages of the life
course) in light of future consequences (e.g., accurately depicting the life
history of the subject for use in contributing to scientific knowledge).
Clearly, the way in which the researcher frames the terms of the narrative,
queries the subject, and probes certain topics is essential to the success of the
enterprise, which is a joint social act between researcher and subject. The
trick, presumably, is to determine if the subject can mirror his or her reconstruction of the life course within the researcher's various (perhaps
competing) theoretical conceptualization of the unfolding of the life course.

## Human Agency and the Life Course

Because life course theories of crime seek to explain changes (as well as
stability) in criminality over the life span, a concept of human agency is
crucial. This point was made originally in life course criminology by Sampson
and Laub (1993). Laub and Sampson (2003), in their excellent extension
of their analysis of the Glueck data to age 70, return to the concept of
agency and cite Emirbeyer and Mische's (1998) theory of agency – which is
explicitly based on Mead's writings. They do not, however, develop a theory
of human agency themselves. Consequently, their empirical illustrations of
agency, while illuminating, are not framed theoretically, and thus, are just as
consistent with a conception of agency reduced to a residual term or a

metaphysical concept such as "will," as they are to a more theoretically nuanced conception of agency. What is needed is a theory of agency, consistent with the theory of crime and desistance, that provides the mechanism by which "a subjective reconstruction of the self is especially likely at times of transition" (Laub & Sampson, 2003). Mead's theory of temporality and role-taking can specify such a mechanism.[5] Most behavior is habitual, guided unreflectively by habits built up in the past; here agency is fairly dormant or indirect, lying in the past as legacies of prior acting selves, which serve to guide present habitual behavior. In problematic situations, however, agency comes to the forefront as the unfolding dialectic phases of the self constitute the past in terms of the future. Agency is particularly apparent when the problematic situation involves major life course changes or transitions. Here the individual engages in role-taking, activating relevant aspects of his or her biographical history to constitute a life course transition to realize a future goal, such as earning more money, gaining status, or avoiding arrest.

Applying a conception of human agency based on Mead to crime in the life course also would free Laub and Sampson's (2003) theory of informal control from the questionable tenets of control theories. Influenced by Kornhauser's (1978) writings on social disorganization, and Hirschi's (1969) writings on social control (see also Gottfredson & Hirschi, 1990), Sampson and Laub (1993) have maintained the control argument that crime is not learned, subcultures are not important in the genesis of crime, and delinquent peers do not cause delinquency. A Meadian perspective provides a mechanism by which organized groups influence behavior, a mechanism that applies equally to all groups, regardless of the *form* of their organization or the *content* of their influence. Thus, organized delinquent groups, such as delinquent gangs, may increase the likelihood of crime by providing criminal role-expectations, values, and norms, as well as objective opportunities, which are *in part selected* through peer processes. These role-expectations, values, and norms at times crystallize into subcultures, which call for delinquent or criminal behavior in certain situations. The subcultures rarely float autonomously, cut off from conventional culture, but are interwoven into the very fabric of conventional society – albeit as pockets, rather than smooth continuous threads.[6]

## The Aging Body, Cognitive Transformation, and Desistance

Criminal acts, like other forms of action, entails physiological action by the body, whether that action entails overt physical effort or the cognitive planning that precedes the act. The body plays an important role here, at times being used instrumentally (and illegally) to solve a problematic situation, as when a male street youth uses his physical prowess to gain status by physically dominating a rival, when a burglar uses manual dexterity to enter buildings undetected, and when an insider trader uses his or her computer keyboard to buy and sell stocks illicitly based on insider information. Therefore, the functioning of the body plays a part in social action and crime over the life course.

At the risk of oversimplification, we can state this hypothesis in three stages of individual physiological development. During childhood, the body has yet to mature, complex thought is still being learned, and habits have yet to stabilize. Forms of impulsive acts are more likely than acts requiring complex information processing. Acts requiring strength or sexual prowess are limited. In adolescence and young adulthood, a transition to sexual maturation, including hormonal changes stimulates risky impulsive behaviors and inhibits cautious, careful acts. At the same time, physical maturation allows greater flexibility in behavior, including acts requiring strength, such as violence, planning, and skill. The transition to old age witnesses physiological breakdowns in the body and once again inhibits complex cognitive and physical behaviors, in particular, risky behaviors such as crime. Consequently, most behaviors, including crime, fertility, athletic prowess, and career productivity tend to follow a familiar age curve: a sharp increase from childhood to adolescence, followed by a slow decline throughout the adult years (Hirschi & Gottfredson, 1983). But just as important as the physiological capacity of the body is the way in which individuals constitute an image of the body in interaction (Joas, 1985). That image does not correspond perfectly to the physiological capacity of the body, which is not definite, but rather arises through role-taking. For example, one's image of one's body arises in problematic situations, when the body as an object is constituted from the standpoint of others' evaluations. Similarly, one's image of the physical capacity of the body is constituted in interaction through role-taking, as when an athlete is able to exceed conventional expectations from his or her body, and when an aging criminal realizes that he or she is too old to participate in gang fights, pull off stick-up robberies, or continue with burglaries (Shover, 1985). Such events involve an evaluation of the self from the standpoint of others.

The concept of role-taking provides a theoretical mechanism to explain how role-transitions may lead to changes in delinquent trajectories, such as speeding or slowing desistance from crime. The process of making a transition into a new life course role, such as a student, employee, or gang member, entails taking the role of the generalized other within which the new role is embedded, leaving behind an old self, and initiating the embracement of a new self, corresponding to the new role. Drawing on Mead's theories of agency and the self, Giordano et al. (2002) use the term "cognitive transformations" to emphasize instances of role-taking in which creativity moves an individual to a different trajectory, and "hooks for change" to emphasize the actors' role in latching on to an opportunity and to stress that hooks or key phrases often appear in life history narratives. They specify four types of cognitive transformations: (1) a shift to openness to change; (2) exposure to a hook for change; (3) ability to envision an appealing "replacement self" that can supplement the old identity; and (4) transformation in views of the deviant behavior or lifestyle (as no longer appealing or viable). Using quantitative analyses of survey data and qualitative analyses of narratives of a subsample of desisters, they find evidence of cognitive transformations leading to desistance for both men and women. Such findings are important because they get at the *theoretical mechanisms* by which role-transitions speed or slow the desistance process. Thus, for example, they explain how stable employment and marital attachments increase desistance from crime. That is, it is not merely the utility derived from work and marriage, but rather also a process of changing identities derived from organized groups.

## METHODOLOGICAL ISSUES AND DIRECTIONS FOR RESEARCH

In presenting the criminological implications of recent reinterpretations and extensions of Mead's thought, this discussion has remained at a very abstract theoretical, and at times even meta-theoretical, level. Many of Mead's ideas provide promising answers to challenging problems facing contemporary sociological theory. That promise, however, requires research and theorizing at a more concrete level, showing exactly what structural aspects of concrete organizations and groups are relevant to criminality and how they arise as selves through role-taking to influence the direction of ongoing social interaction. Some of the examples I have cited, such as Anderson's work on code of the streets and Giordano et al.'s (2002) work on cognitive transformations, are doing precisely that, and there are many more. Such directions for research requires both inductive qualitative research identifying the ways in which social organization is constituted in social interaction through role-taking, and deductive quantitative research measuring the patterned and structured outcomes of role-taking (e.g., norms, identities, and habits) and relating them to causes and consequences of criminal acts.

## Levels of Explanation and Methods of Research

Mead did not develop a methodological strategy for studying social phenomena from his perspective. We can, however, sketch some recommendations. My argument, that research is needed at both macro- and micro-levels, and using both qualitative and quantitative methods, may appear prosaic and faddish, but I will at least try to be specific in my prosaic and faddish recommendations. As noted above, Mead clearly argued for starting analyses with the organization of the society or group, and then to identify social interaction, role-taking, and joint action with reference to that organization. Methodologically, this implies that one cannot hope to understand social action without first understanding the structure of the larger groups within which that action takes place. One cannot hope to understand the actions of a numbers banker without understanding the structure of the organized crime family – as well as the structure of demand of potential customers – in which the actions are embedded. One cannot hope to understand the actions of a gang member without understanding the organization of the gang and the gang's role in within the structure of the community. One cannot hope to understand the obstruction of justice behavior of government officials without understanding the political organization of the office in relation to the situation.

To identify the ways in which individuals negotiate or interpret meanings, adjust to each other's conduct, and thereby coordinate their conduct into joint action, one must directly observe or reconstruct the interaction process. This is the methodological emphasis of Blumer's (1969) symbolic interaction, which argues for using naturalistic inquiry, sensitizing concepts, and exploration of social phenomena to refine concepts and construct explanations, rather than being imprisoned by rigid theoretical concepts and mindless testing of hypotheses derived from such concepts. In criminology, a number of classical studies have born fruit, including the classical studies of Becker's (1963) *Outsiders*, Matza's (1964) *Delinquency and Drift*, Luckenbill's (1977) *Homicide as a Situated Transaction*, and Katz's (1988) *Seductions of Crime*. In terms of our above discussion, such studies focus on the social act, emphasizing the emergent properties of social interaction, which are irreducible to the biographical histories of the individual participants. From the standpoint of the individual, emergence arises via the "I"'s response to the "me." Such direct observation and inductive reasoning is particularly powerful when examining a phenomenon about which we lack strong theories – e.g., the process of becoming a marijuana smoker, the group processes and structures operating within gangs, the dynamics of homicide transactions, and the immediate, momentary, emotional experience of enacting a crime.

But in contrast to Blumer's (1956) followers, who take literally the polemical arguments of his essay, "Sociological Analysis and the Variable," and reject the use of statistical analysis of variables to study social phenomena, I argue that such analyses – or at least the careful use of the results of such analyses – is essential to the study of role-taking and crime. Because individuals are embedded in organized groups and social institutions, they develop consistent reference groups or generalized others. Although complex, overlapping, and ever changing, such embeddedness accounts for stability in reference groups and therefore, the self, which in turn, explains continuity in behavior. Individuals, then, are distributed in social groups in ways structured in part by social networks, which cannot be revealed in case studies or studies of interaction sequences. One must use variables measuring the features of certain organized groups, such as commitments to lawful activities or views of self as a "badass," relevant to the social action investigated. This is consistent with Blumer's (1969, p. 139) largely ignored conclusion that "in the area of interpretative life, variable analysis can be an effective means of unearthing stabilized patterns of interpretation, which are not likely to be detected through the direct study of the experience of people."[7] Of course, studies that combine quantitative and qualitative approaches have the *potential* of maximizing benefits of each (for example, see Pearce, 2002). Examples in criminology include Short and Strodtbeck (1965), Giordano et al. (2002), and Laub and Sampson (2003). Although such mixed-method approaches are in some ways ideal, it is not necessary that every study employs a mix of methods, so long as they are informed by all relevant research findings regardless of method.

These arguments, I believe, are generally consistent with Mead's appraisal of Cooley's writings – one of the few places where his methodological views are revealed. There, Mead (1930, p. 706) praises Cooley for treating selves and others on the same "plane of reality of experience," and demonstrating that society is "an outgrowth of the association and co-operation of the primary group in face-to-face organization." Mead also admonishes Cooley for treating selves and others as "ideas in people's minds" (rather than arising from concrete social interaction), which renders the question of human agency sociologically meaningless. Moreover, Mead (1930, p. 705) argues that while Cooley did recognize the "importance of statistical methods" and "community surveys," he nevertheless is uninterested in "the application of the scientific method to the study of society," the economic history of society, or the development of society from earlier forms, and instead adopts a "psychological" method of introspection to get at selves which exist as a psychical phase. In contrast, Mead (1930, p. 705) advocates treating selves as belonging to objective experience, and a "society of selves in advance of inner experiences," which allows for sociological analyses such as "those of W. I. Thomas, Park and Burgess, and Faris."

This argument suggests that the symbolic interactionist traditions of the Chicago school, led by Blumer and his followers, and the Iowa school, led by Kuhn and his followers, both conduct research consistent with Mead. The Chicago school emphasizes the use of naturalistic inquiry, direct observation, and in-depth interviews to examine the situational self, nego-tiated meanings, and cooperative action. The Iowa school uses surveys and quantitative methods to examine patterned selves, stable meanings, and institutionalized behavior. Other research, such as by Cottrell (1971), a student of Mead, uses experimental methods (analyzed using statistical methods) to test the mechanism of role-taking. My point is that research using all three methods – naturalistic inquiry, quantitative analyses of sur-vey data, and experiments, are essential for testing, extending, and applying Mead's ideas to criminal behavior.

## Directions for Future Research

The general theme of this chapter has been that patterned selves, which remain relatively stable, arise because stable generalized others are rooted in social organization. Thus, we can speak of views of self from the standpoint of others as a "badass," "sneak thief" (or an upstanding "athlete"), which entails role-relationships to other badasses, sneak thieves (upstanding athletes), potential victims of violence or theft, and the larger conventional society. Such views of self also encompass norms and vocabularies of motive that govern and motivate role behavior. At the same time, however, situ-ational or acting selves arise in problematic situations, giving rise to human agency, creativity, and practical intersubjectivity – all of which is condi-tioned by a specific depiction of the past. The situational self entails taking the role of the other, and thus, is rooted in organized groups, and accounts for change in the self.

Future research on social forms of crime at particular conjunctions of historical period and special context should examine four questions relevant to a perspective based on Mead. First, what are the crucial organized groups relevant to the criminal behavior under study? As noted above, the most important group is the concrete group present within the interaction, but beyond this, other groups, such as families, peers, fellow workers, and neighbors are often relevant generalized others guiding habitual behavior and offering solutions to problematic situations. For example, Becker (1963) identifies the marijuana using group as the primary generalized other for becoming a marijuana user, but also identifies conventional groups as important for moving from occasional to regular user. Cressey (1953) identifies the inability of embezzlers to share their financial problem with conventional groups as a key step in the criminal violation of financial trust. Anderson (1999) finds that for street youth, failure in conventional society, isolation from decent families, and affiliation with street culture led to espousing the code of the street.

Second, how are complex role-relationships, role-expectations, norms, and values organized within groups such that they control the behavior of its members? Anderson (1999) finds that the role of the "badass" is inversely related to conventional roles, and governed by the code of the street, which at times calls for violent behavior, and at other times calls for artful and nuanced acts of avoiding violence while still maintaining respect. How do group roles, norms, and values operate with respect to other crimes, and how do they relate to the self?

Third, how can we develop quantitative measures of the self, role-relationships, norms, and values to get at the stable self and stable patterns of interaction? Survey data have helped measure broad conceptions of the self as reflected appraisals, vocabularies of motive, and criminal values (e.g., Heimer & Matsueda, 1994; Heimer, 1996, 1997). But we need to be more specific in our operationalizations, link them more directly to the organization of groups, and specify the interactions among the various aspects of the self.

Fourth, what is the relationship between a conception of decision making based on role-taking and one based on rational choice? And as a corollary, what is the role of deterrence from the standpoint of Mead? Clearly, role-taking, as a mechanism for solving problematic situations, has an instrumental character. But the model entails that the alternatives within the choice set, as well as the criterion for adoption, are built up in interaction, rather than imposed externally. Therefore, a utility maximization model likely distorts the general process of making decisions about crime, but that under certain circumstances – institutional contexts – actors will act rationally.

From this standpoint, much criminological research from traditional perspectives will reveal incomplete portraits of processes producing crime. Research on conventional social bonds from a social control standpoint will ignore the role of criminal organization, and the rich micro-organization of situations leading to crime. Research on labeling and secondary deviance will ignore the processes by which identities lead to primary deviance. Research on learning definitions of crime from the standpoint of differential association theory will ignore the role of the self, situational interaction, and agency. Research from individual strain theories will ignore the ways in which strains or stressors are constituted in interaction and are reciprocally related to coping mechanisms. Research on rational choice and deterrence, will assume that ends and means can be identified before the fact, and miss out on the ways in which preferences are formed in interaction in groups, cognition operates in situations, and means and ends (preferences) interact within situations.

# NOTES

1. Elsewhere, Karen Heimer and I have described Mead's concept of role-taking and social control and applied it to delinquency; here I draw liberally from that discussion (see Matsueda & Heimer, 1997, pp. 169–170).

2. Structural symbolic interactionists use the term "identity salience" to hypothesize that certain aspects of the self (from the standpoint of generalized others) will be called up to solve a certain class of problematic situations (e.g., McCall & Simmons, 1978; Stryker, 1980).

3. Sykes and Matza (1957) later systematized such verbalizations, drawing on Fritz and Weineman's psychoanalytic typology of rationalizations, and termed them "techniques of neutralization."

4. This section draws from Matsueda (2000), in which I discuss the historical roots and current status of labeling theory.

5. Laub and Sampson (2003) note that their perspective is compatible with symbolic interactionist theories of desistance of Matsueda and Heimer (1997) and Giordano et al. (2002). Here we seek to make this point more explicit.

6. This contrasts sharply with Kornhauser's (1978) depiction of "cultural deviance theories" – a caricature of subcultural theories – in which she argues that subcultures are not only autonomous, but perfectly socialize its members to autonomous subcultural values (see Matsueda, 1988).

7. For a provocative but, in the end, unsatisfying discussion of these methodological issues, see Hammersley (1989). Also see McPhail and Rexroat (1979) for a more extreme claim of divergence between the methodology of Mead and Blumer.

## ACKNOWLEDGMENT

A portion of this chapter was presented at the Annual Meetings of the American Society of Criminology, Toronto, Canada, November 16–19. The research upon which this paper was based was supported in part by grants from the National Science Foundation (SES-0004323) and the National Institute on Drug Abuse (R01DA18148). The author was an Honorary Fellow at the University of Wisconsin, which provided office space, computing, and administrative support. The funding agencies bear no responsibility for the analyses and interpretations drawn here. James F. Short, Jr. provided comments on an earlier draft.

## REFERENCES

Akers, R. L. (1998). *Social learning and social structure: A general theory of crime and deviance.* Boston: Northeastern University Press.

Alexander, C. A., & Rudd, J. (1984). Predicting behaviors from situated identities. *Social Psychology Quarterly, 47,* 172–177.

Anderson, E. (1999). *Code of the street: Decency, violence and the moral life of the inner city.* New York: Norton.

Ayers, E. L. (1984). *Vengeance and justice: Crime and punishment in the 19th-century American South.* New York: Oxford University Press.

Bartusch, D. J., & Matsueda, R. L. (1996). Gender, reflected appraisals, and labeling: A cross-group test of an interactionist theory of delinquency. *Social Forces, 75,* 145–177.

Becker, H. S. (1963). *Outsiders: Studies in the sociology of deviance.* New York: Macmillan.

Blumer, H. (1956). Sociological analysis and the "variable". *American Sociological Review, 32,* 683–690.

Blumer, H. (1969). *Symbolic interactionism: Perspective and method.* Englewood Cliffs, NJ: Prentice-Hall.

Bourdieu, P. (1977). In: R. Nice (Trans.), *Outline of a theory of practice.* Cambridge, UK: Cambridge University Press.

Braithwaite, J. (1989). *Crime, shame, and reintegration.* Cambridge: Cambridge University Press.

Cloward, R. A., & Ohlin, L. E. (1960). *Delinquency and opportunity.* New York: Free Press.

Cohen, A. K. (1955). *Delinquent boys.* Chicago: University of Chicago Press.

Coleman, J. C. (1990). *Foundations of social theory.* Cambridge, MA: Harvard University Press.

Cook, G. A. (1993). *George Herbert Mead: The making of a social pragmatist.* Urbana: University of Illinois Press.

Cottrell, L. S., Jr. (1971). Covert behavior in interpersonal interaction. *Proceedings of the American Philosophical Society, 115,* 462–469.

Cressey, D. R. (1953). *Other people's money.* Glencoe, IL: Free Press.

Dannefer, D. (1984). Adult development and social theory: A paradigmatic reappraisal. *American Sociological Review, 49,* 100–116.

Dewey, J. (1958). *Experience and nature*. New York: Dover Publications.
Emirbayer, M., & Mische, A. (1998). What is agency? *American Journal of Sociology, 103,* 962–1023.
Felson, R. B. (1978). Aggression as impression management. *Social Psychology Quarterly, 41,* 204–213.
Giddens, A. (1984). *The constitution of society.* Cambridge: Polity Press.
Giordano, P. C., Cernkovich, S. A., & Rudolph, J. L. (2002). Gender, crime, and desistance: Toward a theory of cognitive transformation. *American Journal of Sociology, 107,* 990–1064.
Gottfredson, M. R., & Hirschi, T. (1990). *A general theory of crime.* Stanford, CA: Stanford University Press.
Hammersley, M. (1989). *The dilemma of qualitative method: Herbert Blumer and the Chicago tradition.* London: Routledge.
Heimer, K. (1996). Gender, interaction, and delinquency: Testing a theory of differential social control. *Social Psychology Quarterly, 59,* 39–61.
Heimer, K. (1997). Socioeconomic status and violent delinquency. *Social Forces, 75,* 799–833.
Heimer, K., & Matsueda, R. L. (1994). Role-taking, role-commitment, and delinquency: A theory of differential social control. *American Sociological Review, 59,* 365–390.
Hirschi, T. (1969). *Causes of delinquency.* Berkeley: University of California Press.
Hirschi, T., & Gottfredson, M. R. (1983). Age and the explanation of crime. *American Journal of Sociology, 89,* 552–584.
Joas, H. (1985). In: R. Meyer, (Trans.), *George Herbert Mead: A contemporary reexamination of his thought.* Cambridge: Polity Press.
Joas, H. (1993). J. Gaines, R. Meyer & S. Minner (Trans.), *Pragmatism and social theory.* Chicago: University of Chicago Press.
Joas, H. (1994). The creativity of action: Pragmatism and the critique of the rational action model. In: I. Carlgren, G. Handal & S. Vaage (Eds), *Teachers' minds and actions* (pp. 62–73). London: Falmer Press.
Joas, H. (1996). In: J. Gaines & P. Keast (Trans.), *The creativity of action.* Chicago: University of Chicago Press.
Kaplan, H. B., Johnson, R. J., & Bailey, C. A. (1987). Deviant peers and deviant behavior: Further elaboration of a model. *Social Psychology Quarterly, 50,* 277–284.
Katz, J. (1988). *Seductions of crime.* New York: Basic Books.
Kornhauser, R. R. (1978). *Social sources of delinquency.* Chicago: University of Chicago Press.
Kuhn, M. (1964). Major trends in symbolic interaction theory in the past twenty-five years. *Sociological Quarterly, 5,* 61–84.
Laub, J. H., & Sampson, R. J. (2003). *Shared beginnings, divergent lives.* Cambridge, MA: Harvard University Press.
Lauer, R. H., & Boardman, L. (1971). Role-taking: Theory, typology and propositions. *Sociology and Social Research, 55,* 137–148.
Lemert, E. M. (1951). *Social pathology: A systematic approach to the theory of sociopathic behavior.* New York: McGraw-Hill.
Lemert, E. M. (1967). *Human deviance, social problems, and social control.* Englewood Cliffs, NJ: Prentice-Hall.
Luckenbill, D. F. (1977). Homicide as a situated transaction. *Social Problems, 25,* 176–186.
Matsueda, R. L. (1988). The current state of differential association theory. *Crime and Delinquency, 34,* 277–306.

Matsueda, R. L. (1992). Reflected appraisals, parental labeling, and delinquent behavior: Specifying a symbolic interactionist theory. *American Journal of Sociology, 97,* 1577–1611.

Matsueda, R. L. (1997). "Cultural deviance theory": The remarkable persistence of a flawed term. *Theoretical Criminology, 1,* 429–452.

Matsueda, R. L. (2000). Labeling theory: Historical roots, implications, and recent developments. In: R. Paternoster & R. Bachman (Eds), *Explaining criminals and crime: Essays in contemporary criminological theory* (pp. 223–241). Los Angeles, CA: Roxbury Press.

Matsueda, R. L. (2006). *Reflections on the Sutherland tradition.* Unpublished paper presented at the Annual Meetings of the American Society of Criminology, Toronto, Canada.

Matsueda, R. L., & Heimer, K. (1996). *Symbolic interaction, the Chicago School, and beyond.* Unpublished paper presented at the Annual Meetings of the American Society of Criminology, Chicago.

Matsueda, R. L., & Heimer, K. (1997). A symbolic interactionist theory of role transitions, role commitments, and delinquency. In: T. Thornberry (Ed.), *Advances in criminological theory: Developmental theories of crime and delinquency,* (Vol. 7, pp. 163–214). New Brunswick, NJ: Transaction.

Matza, D. (1964). *Delinquency and drift.* New York: Free Press.

McPhail, C., & Rexroat, C. (1979). Mead vs. Blumer: The divergent methodological perspective of social behaviorism and symbolic interactionism. *American Sociological Review, 44,* 449–467.

McCall, G., & Simmons, J. L. (1978). *Identities and interaction.* New York: Free Press.

Mead, G. H. (1918). The psychology of punitive justice. *American Journal of Sociology, 23,* 577–602.

Mead, G. H. (1930). Cooley's contribution to American social thought. *American Journal of Sociology, 35,* 693–706.

Mead, G. H. (1932). *The philosophy of the present.* Chicago: Open Court Publishing.

Mead, G. H. (1934). *Mind, self, and society.* Chicago: University of Chicago Press.

Mead, G. H. (1938). *The philosophy of the act.* Chicago: University of Chicago Press.

Mead, G.H. (1964). In: A. J. Reck (Ed.), *Selected writings.* Chicago: University of Chicago Press.

Merton, R. K. (1938). Social structure and anomie. *American Sociological Review, 3,* 672–682.

Miller, D. L. (1973). *George Herbert Mead: Self, language, and the world.* Austin, TX: University of Texas.

Pager, D. (2003). The mark of a criminal record. *American Journal of Sociology, 108,* 937–975.

Paternoster, R., & Iovanni, L. (1989). The labeling perspective and delinquency: An elaboration of the theory and assessment of the evidence. *Justice Quarterly, 6,* 359–394.

Pearce, L. D. (2002). Integrating survey and ethnographic methods for systematic anomalous case analysis. *Sociological Methodology, 32,* 103–132.

Petersilia, J. (2003). *When prisoners come home: Parole and prisoner reentry.* New York: Oxford University Press.

Powell, W. W., & DiMaggio, P. J. (1991). *The new institutionalism in organizational analysis.* Chicago: University of Chicago Press.

Sampson, R. J., & Laub, J. H. (1993). *Crime in the making.* Cambridge, MA: Harvard University Press.

Schwartz, M., & Stryker, S. (1970). *Deviance, selves, and others.* Washington, DC: American Sociological Association.

Sewell, W. H., Jr. (1992). A theory of structure: Duality, agency, and transformation. *American Journal of Sociology, 98*, 1–29.

Shaw, C., & McKay, H. D. (1969). *Juvenile delinquency and urban areas* (Revised Edition). Chicago: University of Chicago Press.

Short, J. F., Jr., & Strodtbeck, F. L. (1965). *Group process and gang delinquency.* Chicago: University of Chicago Press.

Shover, N. (1985). *Aging criminals.* Beverly Hills, CA: Sage.

Sutherland, E. H. (1947). *Principles of criminology* (4th Ed.). Philadelphia: Lippincott.

Stryker, S. (1980). *Symbolic interactionism.* Menlo Park, CA: Benjamin/Cummings.

Sykes, G., & Matza, D. (1957). Techniques of neutralization: A theory of delinquency. *American Sociological Review, 22*, 664–670.

Tannenbaum, F. (1938). *Crime and the community.* Boston: Ginn and Co..

Thomas, W. I., & Znaniecki, F. ([1918] 1958). *The Polish peasant in Europe and America*, Vol. 2. New York: Dover Publications.

Tittle, C. R. (1995). *Control balance: Toward a general theory of deviance.* Boulder, CO: Westview Press.

Triplett, R. A., & Jarjoura, G. R. (1994). Theoretical and empirical specification of informal labeling. *Journal of Quantitative Criminology, 10*, 241–276.

Wilson, W. J. (1987). *The truly disadvantaged.* Chicago: University of Chicago Press.

Wrong, D. H. (1961). The oversocialized conception of man in modern sociology. *American Sociological Review, 26*, 183–193.

# OPENING THE BLACK BOX: THE SOCIAL PSYCHOLOGY OF GENDER AND DELINQUENCY

Karen Heimer, Stacy De Coster and Halime Ünal

## ABSTRACT

*This paper shows how sociological feminist perspectives on gender inform our understanding of gender and juvenile delinquency. We draw on theory and research on hegemonic definitions of gender and show how these shape the development of gender across the major social contexts experienced by children. We then draw on sociological and psychological research to suggest how these contexts give rise to social psychological mechanisms underlying differences across and within gender in delinquency.*

The gender gap in delinquency is a central fact of criminology. However, despite increasing attention to the role of gender, the development of theories to explain gender differences in offending still lags far behind theories of other important issues in criminology. To be sure, research on gender, crime, and delinquency has advanced in several important ways since the publication of the now classic critiques of criminology as male centered (e.g. Smart, 1976). Yet, when we step back and take stock of the literature on gender and delinquency, we see surprisingly few attempts to build explicit theories of the gendering of illegal behavior. Rather, too much research in criminology still takes the "add gender and stir" approach. Too many

Sociological Theory and Criminological Research: Views from Europe and the United States
Sociology of Crime, Law and Deviance, Volume 7, 109–135
ISSN: 1521-6136/doi:10.1016/S1521-6136(06)07006-0

empirical studies in criminology continue to treat "sex" as a (nuisance) variable to be controlled, or simply try to mediate the "sex effect" using traditional criminological constructs that have little to do with gender, per se. It
has become commonplace to lament this situation. But, even so, its consequences are sometimes not appreciated fully. One of these is that the empirical literature often seems to be a collection of findings – sometimes
contradictory – that are difficult to assimilate. Indeed, a casual reading of the
literature on gender and delinquency can lead to more confusion than clarity.

   The alternative, of course, is to treat gender as a construct that is worthy
of theoretical attention in its own right. There have been a handful of
attempts to do this within criminology. Several feminist scholars have
offered explanations of gender differences in criminal justice outcomes and
their impact on women's subsequent offending, which are informed by
feminist theory (Daly, 1994; Chesney-Lind, 1997). Messerschmidt (1993)
proposed a theoretical framework focusing largely on the relationship between masculinity, social class, and crime. Hagan, Gillis, and Simpson
(1985, 1987) developed a power-control theory that proposes that social
class locations of families and power structures within families are the root
causes of gender differences in common, non-serious delinquency. All of
these lines of work push forward our understanding of the gender gap in
offending. Nevertheless, the focus of each has been more on structural
concerns than on social psychological factors. Such structural explanations
are clearly important and in need of continued development. Yet, we also
need to devote further attention to the social psychological processes.

   Many studies examine social psychological constructs suggested by traditional theories of crime, which focus mainly on explaining male behavior
(e.g. family attachments, attitudes, and values about law violation). However, criminologists infrequently venture beyond the traditional use of these
constructs. Rather, most research tends to examine whether the unmodified
constructs from traditional theories can account for gender differences in
offending, instead of reconceptualizing these constructs in light of the feminist theory and research on gender, more generally (see Miller & Mullins,
2005, for an excellent discussion of this issue). In short, despite some advances in recent decades, we still have a poor understanding of the "black
box" of gender and offending. Feminist scholars argue that what is needed is
a theory that addresses the differentiated experiences of females and males
within patriarchal societies (Daly & Chesney-Lind, 1988; Chesney-Lind,
1997).

   The goal of our paper is to suggest a road map for developing a theory of
the differentiated social psychological experiences of females and males that

have implications for delinquency. We do not propose a full-blown theory here, but rather offer an orientating framework with discussion of key constructs that are likely to be important for the development of a complete social psychological theory of gender and delinquency. We draw on sociological feminist theory and research on gender. Our focus is limited to the social psychological mechanisms linked to gender socialization and law violation during childhood and adolescence, and does not address social structural factors. Social structural factors, such as poverty and racial segregation, clearly influence the gendering of delinquency, and we have addressed some possible mechanisms recently in other work (De Coster & Heimer, forthcoming). In the present paper, however, we bracket the social structural constraints of race and class to focus exclusively on social psychological mechanisms so that the scope of this paper is more manageable.

The paper proceeds as follows: First, we discuss sociological feminist perspectives and research on hegemonic definitions of gender – the widely accepted beliefs about the nature of the genders. Next, we address how definitions of gender emerge in the major social arenas of childhood and adolescence. We then use existing sociological and psychological research to build a road map of some major social psychological processes that arise from the gender-differentiated experiences within these social contexts.

## GENDER DEFINITIONS UNDER PATRIARCHY

An important component of socialization during childhood and adolescence is learning about the meaning of being female or male in our society or the *meaning of gender*. This includes learning about how others in our social worlds view femaleness or maleness, as well as the behavioral expectations associated with gender. Feminist scholars point out that the socialization processes that create gender both support and are perpetuated by the powerful system of social control known as patriarchy (e.g. Ferree, Lorber, & Hess, 1999; Ridgeway & Smith-Lovin, 1999; Lorber, 2005). This system of social control subordinates females to males and is characterized by a core cultural belief that females and males are inherently different socially, as well as biologically. This core belief gives rise to accompanying beliefs and attitudes about the characteristics typical of each sex, norms about the "proper" social arrangements between females and males, and gendered behavioral expectations of each sex (Goffman, 1977). In our previous work on delinquency, we have referred to these beliefs, attitudes, and norms as *gender definitions* (Heimer, 1995, 1996; Heimer & De Coster, 1999). Miller

(1998, 2001) has addressed these issues as well, when discussing the meaning of gender and girls' delinquency (see also Miller & Mullins, 2005).

Feminist scholars have noted that these gender definitions tend to exaggerate differences and downplay similarities between the sexes (Ferree et al., 1999; Ridgeway & Smith-Lovin, 1999; Lorber, 2005). For example, research shows that femaleness or "femininity" often is equated with a high capacity for nurturance, a tendency toward passivity rather than aggressiveness, and physical and emotional weakness; by contrast, maleness or "masculinity" tends to be equated with competitiveness, independence, rationality, and strength (e.g. Burke, 1989; Jackman, 1994). The reason that gender definitions are so consequential is that they are hegemonic – they are pervasive and dominant in patriarchal societies (Connell, 1995). More specifically, these definitions are built into major institutions, permeate most social interactions, are extolled at the symbolic level, and are influential in the judgments of most types of behavior by both females and males (Goffman, 1977; West & Zimmerman, 1987; Connell, 1995). It is for this reason that some feminist scholars have identified this aspect of culture as an important site of the reproduction of male dominance and patriarchal relations (e.g. Walby, 1990). In this paper, we use the term *hegemonic gender definitions* to refer to this aspect of culture.

In the remainder of this paper, we explore key ways in which hegemonic gender definitions are relevant for understanding the social psychology of gender and delinquency. We propose that these definitions influence socialization practices in several contexts, including the family, peer groups, school, and mass media. Gendered socialization in these contexts, in turn, promotes very different ways of thinking, feeling, and responding to situations among males versus females, which may be quite consequential for the gendering of delinquency.

## GENDER DEFINITIONS ACROSS SOCIAL CONTEXTS

### The Family

The family is the first context in which most children learn about gender. We have identified two major areas of sociological research that help to understand how gender is shaped within families – parental reactions to children's behavior and the division of household labor by gender.

First, research clearly indicates that most parents encourage their children to behave in ways that are consistent with hegemonic gender definitions. For example, parents are more likely to encourage their boys to be independent, autonomous, self-reliant, physically active, and independent, whereas they are more likely to encourage their girls to be nice, well-behaved, unselfish, physically attractive, and dependent (see Block, 1984). Observational studies find that parents tend to reward children for "gender-appropriate" behaviors and sanction cross-gender behaviors, even in very young children (e.g. Snow, Jacklin, & Maccoby, 1983; Fagot & Hagan, 1991). Girls are reinforced for playing with dolls and engaging in submissive and dependent behaviors, like help-seeking, whereas boys receive negative responses when they engage in female-typical play or dependent behaviors and are reinforced when they behave in assertive ways. This, then, is a mechanism through which children are taught hegemonic definitions of gender, beginning at very young ages.

Second, children learn gender definitions from their participation in co-operative family life, specifically in the sharing of household chores. Research reports that children's chores tend to be divided according to traditional male and female roles (Gager, Cooney, & Call, 1999; Mortimer, 2003). Girls work in the kitchen and care for younger children, boys take out garbage and cut grass. Another way to think about gender and children's responsibility for domestic labor is to distinguish between responsibility for work involved in taking care of or cleaning up after oneself – self-care work – and responsibility for taking care of or cleaning up after family members – family care work (White & Brinkerhoff, 1981). For example, Brannen (1995) reports that girls are more likely to engage in tasks that benefit others, and the differences between girls and boys are greatest with respect to family care tasks that are stereotypically feminine, such as dusting, ironing, and setting the table. These patterns vary across families, of course. Parents who divide their own labor according to traditional gender roles also do so for their children's work (Crouter, Manke, & McHale, 1995). Moreover, research demonstrates that when parents endorse traditional gender definitions, their children tend to accept them (Starrels, 1992; Moen, Erickson, & Dempster-McClain, 1997). The mechanisms through which congruence between parents' and children's gender definitions are produced likely involve the two processes discussed above – parents' encouragement of gendered behaviors and assignment of household chores. However, this intergenerational transmission of gender definitions is by no means perfect (Moen et al., 1997), in part because gender socialization occurs also in contexts other than the family, including peer groups, schools, and the media.

## The Peer Group

Children's peer cultures reflect the dominant adult culture (Corsaro & Eder, 1995). The peer group therefore is another important agent in the transmission and reproduction of hegemonic gender definitions. Gender socialization in peer groups begins in the preschool years and continues throughout childhood and adolescence (Maccoby & Jacklin, 1987; Eder, 1995). Much of this socialization appears to occur within gender-segregated play groups, within which children reinforce gender appropriate activities and punish and criticize activities that are inconsistent with hegemonic gender definitions, even at very young ages (Lamb, Easterbrooks, & Holden, 1980; Maccoby & Jacklin, 1987; Thorne, 1993).

In addition, the games children play in peer groups are likely an important vehicle through which they learn the behavioral expectations associated with hegemonic definitions of gender. Studies show that boys play mostly in large, competitive, organized groups, enact more physically aggressive play, and engage in more large-scale rule violation and risk-taking than girls (Lever, 1976, 1978; McGuffey & Rich, 1999). They shun intimate physical contact, like holding hands; instead, physical contact involves mainly mock violence or poking (Thorne & Luria, 1986; Thorne, 1993). In general, boys encourage each other to be tough, aggressive, and competitive in their play and es-tablish clear boundaries of acceptable masculinity (Lever, 1976; Thorne, 1993). Messerschmidt's (2000) case study of nine adolescent boys supports a similar pattern and emphasis on displaying masculinity in male peer groups. By contrast, girls tend to play in small, intimate groups in which play focuses more on turn-taking games than is the case with boys (Lever, 1976, 1978; Thorne, 1993). Girls also tend to seek out intimate physical contact more so than boys; they touch, hold hands, and comb one another's hair in their play, even at early ages (Thorne & Luria, 1986). In addition, girls report having more disclosing friendships in which they expect and receive kindness and empathy (see McCarthy, Felmlee, & Hagan, 2004). In general, girls' play encourages concern with relationship to others, appearances, emotional skills, and nurturance, consistent with hegemonic definitions of femininity. As would be expected, research shows that status or popularity within peer groups is based on how well youngsters uphold these values and achieve success in gendered activities (e.g. Kessler, Ashenden, Connell, & Dowsett, 1985; Eder & Parker, 1987; Adler, Kless, & Adler, 1992).

## The School

Children and adolescents also are bombarded with hegemonic gender definitions in schools. Research shows that texts and teaching materials tend to depict females more as passive, dependent, and nurturant, whereas they tend to portray males as strong, active, aggressive, and independent (see Sadker & Sadker, 1994; Evans & Davies, 2000). In addition, studies show that perceptions of abilities vary with gender of the student, even in recent years (Jacobs, Lanza, Osgood, Eccles, & Wigfield, 2002; Jacobs & Eccles, 1992; Sadker & Sadker, 1994). Science, math, and computer science still tend to be viewed as the terrain of boys, whereas clerical, secretarial, and home economics classes are more likely to be viewed as appropriate for girls. Moreover, research reveals that teachers react somewhat differently to female and male students. As early as preschool, teachers criticize boys when they engage in feminine behaviors, and criticize girls when they engage in masculine activities (Fagot, 1984). In both primary and secondary school, teachers give greater attention and encouragement to boys than girls, regardless of the subject material, and are more apt to view boys' poor performance as due to lack of effort rather than intellectual competence (Sadker & Sadker, 1994). In addition, teachers are more likely to provide instructions so that boys can do tasks on their own, and are more likely to do things for girls, reinforcing the view of females as inherently more dependent than males (Sadker & Sadker, 1994).

Youths also learn gender definitions through extracurricular activities and peer culture in school. Studies show that extracurricular activities tend to promote gender definitions that equate masculinity with toughness, aggression, competition, and achievement, on the one hand, and equate femininity with physical attractiveness, on the other hand (Eder, 1985; Kessler et al., 1985; Eder & Parker, 1987; Adler et al., 1992). For example, certain athletic activities (e.g. football) reinforce the link between masculinity and toughness, competitiveness, and aggression, whereas activities like cheerleading reinforce the cultural emphasis on physical appearance that corresponds to hegemonic definitions of femininity. These gender definitions permeate peer culture in the school context. To "fit in" with peer groups at school, boys and girls are encouraged to express values and behaviors consistent with these gender definitions (Eder, 1985; Eder & Parker, 1987; Adler et al., 1992). For boys, athletic prowess is an important determinant of acceptance and status. Indeed, Messerschmidt (2000) shows that boys who are not athletic and do not match hegemonic definitions of masculinity as tall, strong, and athletic are more apt to be insulted by their peers, and consequently, feel threatened and inadequate.

## Media

A fourth important domain in which children are exposed to hegemonic gender definitions is the media, including children's books, cartoons, magazines, television, movies, radio, and video games. Studies of children's picture books show that the depictions of females and males tend to fit gender stereotypes consistent with dominant gender definitions (e.g. Grauerholz & Pescosolido, 1989; Crabb & Bielawski, 1994). Male characters are more likely than female characters to be aggressive, independent, and rational; the female characters are more likely to be passive, emotional, and nurturing. Male characters also are more likely to be depicted in non-domestic activities; whereas, females are shown engaging in domestic activities. These themes also pervade children's and adolescents' magazines (Peirce, 1993; Willemsen, 1995; Schlenker, Caron, & Halteman, 1998). Magazines targeting audiences of young girls emphasize beauty and appearance, romantic relationships, and expectations for domestic work and caring for others in the future. Numerous studies document that youth also are bombarded with similar messages about the meaning of gender in television programing (Signorielli, 1991), commercials (Johnson & Young, 2002), radio (Furnham & Thomson, 1999), cartoons (Thompson & Zerbinos, 1997), and video games (Dietz, 1998). Across these media, females are typically portrayed as young, attractive, romantic, warm, emotional, passive, insecure, dependent on others, altruistic, and concerned about social relationships and the needs of others, especially family members. They often are depicted as subordinate to and supportive of males. They are less aggressive and violent than males, and are more likely to be cast as victims and in need of help (see Signorielli, 1991). By stark contrast, males are depicted as active, powerful, independent, rational, and dominant. When depicted in the domestic arena, they often are engaged in traditionally male-typed tasks, such as emptying garbage or defending their families against threats (Pierce, 1989). Yet, much of the violence and aggression by males in these media is antisocial, rather than defensive, and is sometimes directed against females (Signorielli, 1991).

*Summary*

Across the major social arenas in which they participate, children and adolescents are encouraged to accept and abide by hegemonic definitions of gender. Of course, there is variation across youths in exposure to these definitions because of variation across families, schools, peer groups, and attention to the media. Yet, the overarching picture is one in which most children are continually exposed to hegemonic definitions of gender. In sum, these ideas about gender are pervasive in the lives of children and adolescents.

This pervasiveness across social contexts creates significant implications for the social psychological processes that link gender and delinquency. But, the precise nature of these processes has been poorly explicated to date, constituting the "black box" of gender and delinquency. In the remainder of this paper, we begin to illuminate some of the social psychological processes that may help us to better understand the gendering of delinquency.

## SOCIAL PSYCHOLOGICAL DIMENSIONS OF GENDER SOCIALIZATION AND DELINQUENCY

There are two types of questions that need to be addressed to understand the social psychological processes linking gender with delinquency. Unfortunately, this distinction very often has been obscured in the literature on gender, crime, and delinquency. The first type of question focuses on the mechanisms that lead to differences across gender in *levels of delinquency* (i.e. the gender gap). These mechanisms include *differential exposure* across gender to conditions that make delinquency more or less likely, such as levels of parental supervision, styles of discipline, emotional attachments to others, or the inculcation of taste for risk. But the mechanisms leading to the gender gap in delinquency also may include *differential impact* across gender of some of these conditions, such as the stronger influence of emotional attachments to others on girls' than boys' behavior, even among girls and boys who are similar in their attachments to others. The second type of question concerns *variation within gender* in law violation. For example, individual differences in acceptance of hegemonic gender definitions or definitions favoring law violation may help to understand differences among girls (and among boys) in delinquent behavior. We address each of these types of questions below.

In the sections below, we draw on existing research in sociology, criminology, gender studies, and psychology to identify some key social psychological mechanisms that can help us understand the link between gender and delinquency. Of course, there are other potentially important mechanisms that we do not address. But, we consider the sections below to be a first step in developing a road map of important social psychological constructs and processes producing differences within and across gender in delinquency.

### The Internalization of Hegemonic Gender Definitions

One major implication of our above discussion of hegemonic gender definitions is that individuals internalize these definitions and attempt to match their behavior to them in an attempt to negotiate gender identity in daily interactions. Indeed, research shows that when people internalize traditional gender definitions, they are motivated to act in accordance with them (Burke, 1989). Through this process, the "social control of gender-relevant behavior is translated into self-control" (Heimer, 1996, p. 42).

These arguments have clear implications for the gender gap in law violation, largely because acceptance of hegemonic gender definitions can be expected to have a different impact on behavior among females than among males. As we have maintained throughout, these definitions depict a feminine ideal that includes high capacity for nurturance, passivity, connectedness to others, and physical weakness; such characteristics are inconsistent with victimizing others physically or taking their property. By contrast, the masculine ideal emphasizes competitiveness, aggressiveness, independence, and strength; hegemonic definitions of masculinity, therefore, are less inconsistent with most forms of delinquency. This has led some criminologists to argue that acceptance of hegemonic gender definitions is a key contributor to the gender gap in law violation (e.g. Messerschmidt, 1993; Simpson & Ellis, 1995; Heimer, 1995, 1996; Heimer & De Coster, 1999).

In addition to the fact females and males likely are self-motivated to conform to hegemonic gender definitions as a way to claim gender through their daily interactions, it is also the case that departures from commonly accepted gender definitions are likely to draw social sanctions. Owing to the inconsistency between hegemonic definitions of femininity and delinquency, some scholars have argued that there is a pervasive tendency to view females who engage in crime and delinquency as more deviant than their male counterparts (see Schur, 1984), and in effect, as "doubly deviant" – departing from the law as well as from definitions of appropriate behavior for females (e.g. Heimer, 1996; Heimer & De Coster, 1999). Thus, girls may anticipate stronger social sanctions than boys for the same acts of deviance.

Beyond this, we may also expect that individual differences among females and males in acceptance of gender definitions will be associated with individual differences in offending within gender. Indeed, this is the focus of Messerschmidt's (2000) recent case studies of masculinity and violence. However, quantitative studies do not find that higher levels of acceptance of hegemonic gender definitions increase delinquency among males (Simpson & Ellis, 1995; Heimer, 1995, 1996; Heimer & De Coster, 1999). This could be due, of course, to the ways that gender definitions are measured in these studies.[1] It is notable that these quantitative studies show that girls who have internalized higher levels of gender definitions are less likely than other girls to commit delinquency. In a qualitative study, Miller (2001) reports that gang girls sometimes called upon hegemonic gender definitions to avoid involvement in some of the riskiest criminal behaviors. Doing this, however, is somewhat of a double-edged sword, as it feeds into perceptions of female gang members as weak and/or subordinate to males.

In sum, the internalization of hegemonic gender definitions is consequential for the gender gap in delinquency, as well individual differences in delinquency among females and among males. As we highlighted in the Section "Gender definitions across social contexts", broad societal acceptance of these definitions likely shapes the treatment of female and male youth within families, peer groups, and schools, reproducing acceptance of gender definitions in subsequent generations.

In the next section, we focus specifically on uncovering differences in the treatment of boys and girls within the family context and how boys and girls respond differently to similar treatment in families. With this discussion, we demonstrate the complexity of the operation of hegemonic gender definitions – they simultaneously shape the treatment of males and females by parents and other family members, as well as the differential responses of girls and boys to similar treatments.

## Familial Controls and Emotional Bonds

Much of the existing literature on the gender gap in juvenile delinquency focuses on the differential treatment of girls and boys within families (often to the unfortunate exclusion of other important socialization contexts, such as the peer group and school). Most studies focus on gender differences in exposure to direct familial controls, such as supervision, monitoring, and styles of discipline. Some studies also examine gender differences in exposure to indirect controls, namely, levels of emotional attachments. Most of this research on direct and indirect controls, however, has focused exclusively on gender differences in exposure or levels of control, and has ignored the possibility that the impact of these controls may vary across gender.

This line of research most often examines gender differences in levels of monitoring or supervision within families. Research shows that girls are more closely supervised than boys during late childhood and adolescence (e.g. Jensen & Eve, 1976; Hagan et al., 1985). Based on this kind of evidence, control theorists have argued that girls are less delinquent than boys because they are monitored and supervised more closely than boys.

Some research has gone beyond this "main effects" argument to show that even similar levels of supervision can have a *differential impact* on girls and boys. Specifically, research finds that even though girls are more closely supervised, boys are somewhat more responsive to these direct controls (e.g. Heimer, 1996), and the gender gap in delinquency reflects *both* the difference in exposure to direct controls as well as the difference in impact of the controls (Heimer & De Coster, 1999). In other words, when boys and girls are exposed to similar levels of supervision, these direct controls appear to have a stronger impact on boys' than girls' delinquency. So, when we statistically partition the sources of variance in the gender gap in delinquency, we find that both the gender difference in exposure to direct controls and the gender difference in the impact of direct controls are important (Heimer & De Coster, 1999).

The finding that direct controls have a greater impact on boys' than girls' delinquency may seem somewhat counterintuitive at first, and at odds with much of the delinquency literature. We argue that this is because delinquency research too often has taken an oversimplified view of parental control, considering only mean differences across gender and ignoring potential differences in the meaning of different *types* of social controls, given hegemonic definitions of gender. Indeed, whereas direct parental controls like supervision and monitoring may be more consequential for controlling boys' illegal behavior, emotional bonds to parents may serve as a stronger source of control over girls' delinquency (Heimer & De Coster, 1999). Perhaps because hegemonic gender definitions encourage girls more than boys to be concerned with emotional connections to others, parents can control daughters largely via the threat of damage to emotional bonds (see also Hagan et al., 1985). By contrast, because hegemonic masculinities encourage greater independence among boys, direct controls like supervision may be more useful for controlling boys' behavior. This means that for females, monitoring or supervision may be important mainly because of what it communicates about the parent–child bond; thus, the effects of direct controls net of emotional bonds may be less important for girls than for boys. By contrast, direct controls should be important for males net of emotional bonds, because they include tangible outcomes such as rewards and punishments. Our point here is that the finding of a gender difference in impact of direct and emotional social controls can be viewed as part and parcel of the process of youngsters responding to similar parental treatment in ways that are consistent with hegemonic gender definitions.

Beyond these mechanisms underlying the gender gap in delinquency, it is also the case that variation in direct parental controls and emotional bonding can explain variation in delinquency *within* gender. Indeed, this has been a primary focus of the literature on delinquency by males for most of this century (e.g. Glueck & Glueck, 1950; Hirschi, 1969). Research that examines female and male delinquency separately has found support for these relationships, for the most part (Canter, 1982; Cernkovich & Giordano, 1987; Heimer, 1996; Heimer & De Coster, 1999).

This research clearly pushes forward our understanding of the relationship between family processes, gender, and the gender gap in delinquency. However, this line of research neglects the other social contexts discussed above, in the Section "Gender definitions across social contexts". Clearly, patterns of parental control reflect and reproduce hegemonic gender definitions. But, hegemonic gender definitions have implications for other dimensions of the social psychological process underlying the gendering of delinquency.

### Delinquent Definitions

Social psychological research on male delinquency often has emphasized the role of delinquent definitions, or the attitudes, beliefs, values, and rationalizations that normalize and motivate law violation (Sutherland, 1947; Akers, Krohn, Lanza-Kaduce, & Radosevich, 1979). We maintain that differences in the treatment of girls and boys across social contexts produce important gender differences in the learning of delinquent definitions. In our previous work, we have combined this concept with arguments about the internalization of gender definitions and family and peer influences to develop and test hypotheses about the learning processes contributing to gender differences in delinquency (Heimer, 1996; Heimer & De Coster, 1999). Unlike some other social psychological constructs that have been addressed by research on gender and delinquency (e.g. family controls), delinquent definitions are presumed to be learned and reinforced in almost all social contexts. Based on the research discussed in the Section "Gender definitions across social contexts", we suggest some specific ways in which the learning and reinforcement of delinquent definitions may be gendered across the major social arenas occupied by children.

For example, the research on peer groups and peer culture in schools discussed above suggests that the games and relationships that emerge in same-sex peer groups expose boys more so than girls to aggressive behavior and rule violation. Indeed, being tough and breaking rules in groups is one avenue for accomplishing masculinity (e.g. Thorne, 1993; Messerschmidt, 2000). Even extracurricular school activities reinforce the definition of masculinity in terms of aggressiveness, competitiveness, and physical strength (e.g. Kessler et al., 1985; Adler et al., 1992). We argue that such ideals about maleness encourage boys to be receptive to and internalize definitions that favor breaking rules, including the law. By contrast, because female peer groups encourage behavior consistent with hegemonic definitions of femininity, which emphasizes interpersonal intimacy and concern with managing relationships to others (e.g. Lever, 1976, 1978; Thorne, 1993), play with peers can be expected to expose girls to lower levels of definitions favoring law violation and victimizing others (either physically or financially), and to negatively sanction such definitions should they arise. In short, boys are more likely than girls to be exposed to aggressive and law-violating models within their peer groups, and thus, should be less likely to learn delinquent definitions. Moreover, peer-group culture can influence even those youths who are excluded from it. Messerschmidt (2000) has recently shown that some boys who are rejected by peers (often for not being masculine enough or being too feminine) attempt to cope by engaging in extreme forms of violence (e.g. physical and sexual abuse of weaker others) as a way to display an exaggerated masculinity.

Gender differences in the internalization of delinquent definitions also are likely influenced by media portrayals of females and males. Because the media tends to portray females as passive, as weak, and as victims (e.g. Signorielli, 1991), it encouraged girls to learn definitions favorable to conformity to the law and to define violence and victimization as potentially harmful to themselves and others and thus, as aversive. Similarly, because the media portrays males as more active, powerful, and at times, as victimizers, it is more likely to encourage boys than girls to internalize definitions that favor violence and law violation.

There is good reason to expect, therefore, that boys will be more likely than girls to internalize definitions that favor property and violent delinquency. Empirical research has documented this difference across gender in the internalization of violent definitions (Huesmann, Guerra, Zelli, & Miller, 1992; Heimer & De Coster, 1999). Nevertheless, our research indicates that once violent definitions are learned, they appear to influence boys and girls similarly (Heimer & De Coster, 1999). In other words, in cases where girls and boys hold identical beliefs and values about aggression and violence, they are equally likely to behave in aggressive, antisocial ways.

### Moralities of Justice and Moralities of Care

Some feminist scholarship highlights another aspect of morality that may be important for understanding the link between gender and delinquency, which has not been addressed to date. Specifically, Gilligan (1993) maintains that there are two distinctive types of moral orientations – the morality of justice and morality of care – which color the ways in which individuals perceive and respond to moral dilemmas. Each of these moral orientations reflects different concerns about social relationships (Gilligan & Attanucci, 1988a). On the one hand, individuals who adopt a morality of justice orientation tend to focus on fairness or equality in relationships between people; they therefore are likely to emphasize justice and the determination of right versus wrong. On the other hand, individuals who prefer a morality of care orientation tend to focus on whether and how people's needs are met in relationships; they consequently are likely to emphasize care and responsiveness to others. Gilligan and Attanucci (1988a) demonstrate that although people may consider both the morality of justice and morality of care when they think about the real-life moral dilemmas, they tend to maximize one and minimize the other of these moral orientations. These moralities could be viewed as special instances of definitions favoring law violation, as will become more apparent below. However, we treat them as distinct because they have very special relevance for the link between gender and delinquency, and yet, have received only passing mention in the sociological literature on gender and law violation.

Research on these divergent moralities indicates that males are more likely to maximize the morality of justice orientation and females are more likely to maximize the morality of care viewpoint when confronted with moral dilemmas (Gilligan & Attanucci, 1988b). Gilligan (1993) maintains that these gender differences in moral development can be traced to gender differences in self-definition. More specifically, the ways that children perceive their relations to others during early childhood are structured by gender, thus creating gender differences in self-definition that have consequences for moral development. Early on, boys are encouraged to view themselves as separate and different from their mothers as a way of developing masculine identity (see Chodorow, 1978). Gilligan and Wiggins (1988) argue that even though boys may be attached strongly to their mothers, they are encouraged to identify themselves with their fathers. However, their views of fathers emphasize authority and power. Consequently, in comparing themselves with fathers, boys experience inequality and powerlessness, which they begin to try to overcome. This leads boys to be more likely than girls to define their roles in terms of obligations and rules. In addition, the themes of separation and independence become more important to boys' definitions of self. Gilligan (1988) argues that when an individual sees him or herself as a separate object, they become more concerned with protecting their own self-fulfillment and thus, emphasize the problems of inequality and oppression and focus on the ideals of equality and justice.

By contrast, girls are encouraged from an early age to see themselves as intimately connected to others (Gilligan, 1993). Chodorow (1978) maintains that because mothers are more likely the primary caregivers to children, girls focus on ties between their mothers and themselves when they begin to form their gender identities. According to Gilligan and Wiggins (1988), this mitigates the experience of inequality in relations between girls and their parental role models (Gilligan & Wiggins, 1988). Consequently, the focus on attachments to others – rather than a focus on power and inequality – becomes crucial to girls' self-definition. The focus on attachment, rather than separation from others, leads children to become more aware of having an effect on others, and at the same time, being affected by others, which teaches the child the importance of others' feelings and how people care for one another and harm one another. This translates into the greater emphasis on the morality of care in girls' than boys' perceptions of moral dilemmas.

Because girls' preference to adopt an ethic of care emphasizes the feelings of others, we would expect them to choose behavioral pathways that avoid harm to others when they encounter problematic situations. Indeed, some research is suggestive of this relationship, reporting that females are less susceptible than males to peer influence when they evaluate behaviors as morally wrong; males and females are equally susceptible to peer influence when behaviors are not evaluated as morally wrong (Mears, Ploeger, & Warr, 1998). However, this may be the tip of the iceberg and further research on gender and delinquency targeting moralities of justice and care more specifically is needed. We also expect that individual girls who are oriented more toward justice than care to be more likely to break the law than girls who are oriented more toward care than justice in their moral decision making. The same should hold true among boys. So, gender differences in average levels of orientations toward justice and care can help us to understand the gender gap in delinquency, and individual variation in these moral orientations can help to explain individual differences in delinquency within gender. But, as in the case of delinquent definitions, there is no reason to expect a difference across gender in the impact of these orientations under circumstances where boys and girls give similar emphasis to moralities of justice versus care.

### Empathic Expressiveness

One common preconception about gender differences in social psychological functioning is that females are more empathic and sympathetic toward others than are males. Indeed, this fits with classical sociological theorizing about the emotional/expressive versus instrumental roles of women and men (e.g. Parsons & Bales, 1955). However, reviews of empirical research in developmental psychology do not find a consistent and clear gender difference in empathic responding, when various types of empathy and sympathy are considered together (see Maccoby & Jacklin, 1974; Block, 1984). Rather, as a detailed review and meta-analysis of research reveals, the size of the gender difference is strongly associated with the type of measurement technique employed (Eisenberg & Lennon, 1983). Specifically, trivial gender differences are found when the measurement techniques are most unobtrusive and presumably tap natural inclinations, such as measures of physiological arousal and facial responses or gestures. By contrast, the largest gender differences emerge when females and males rate their own empathetic and/or sympathetic responses, and under conditions where individuals clearly perceive that they are being observed.

From our perspective, this research is consistent with the feminist argument that hegemonic gender definitions magnify any inherent sex differences, and that these definitions are so pervasive across social settings and interactions that individuals try to conform to these stereotypical images in an attempt to manage impressions and create gender in their daily interactions. Because gender definitions portray the feminine ideal in terms of emotional connectedness to others and high capacity for nurturance, we might expect that females would display higher levels of empathy than males under conditions where the salience of their responses is high (such as in situations of self-rating or clear observation by others). Given that claiming gender is an important aspect of most social interactions (Goffman, 1977; West & Zimmerman, 1987), it seems likely that gender differences in the expression of empathy would arise across most social situations.

Consequently, even if females do not experience higher levels of empathic response on an innate, biological level, they do appear to *express* higher levels of empathy and sympathy than males in circumstances in which the response is more salient to them (Eisenberg & Lennon, 1983). It is the expression of empathy, consistent with hegemonic definitions of femininity, which becomes a potentially important piece of the puzzle linking gender and delinquency, although this has not been addressed in the delinquency literature to date. To the extent that females claim gender through expressing empathy and emotional concern for others in their daily interactions, we would expect that they would be less likely than males to engage in the inconsistent behavior of victimizing others and breaking the law.

Within gender, research shows that individuals who express high levels of empathy are more likely to engage in prosocial and cooperative behavior toward others (for review, see Eisenberg & Miller, 1987; also Eisenberg & Strayer, 1987) and are less likely to engage in aggressive and antisocial behavior (Miller & Eisenberg, 1988). These patterns hold for both females and males. In addition, there does not appear to be much of a gender difference in the magnitude of the effect of empathic response on aggressive, antisocial behavior (Miller & Eisenberg, 1988). In short, it appears that both females and males who express high levels of empathy are equally likely to help others and inhibit aggression toward others.

However, if we consider together the findings that (a) high levels of empathic expression are associated with low levels of antisocial behavior and high levels of prosocial behavior and (b) that females are more likely than males on average to express empathy, we can see support for our argument linking empathy and the gender gap in delinquency. Simply put, the greater tendency of females than males to express empathy may explain why they are less likely to victimize others.

Of course, among both females and males, there are individuals who are lacking in empathic expression. Studies show that, regardless of gender, individuals who reside in highly cohesive families are most likely to display empathic responding in laboratory settings (Eisenberg et al., 1991). In addition, among females but not males, there is a significant positive relationship between empathic responding and family's emotional expressivity, especially mothers' expressions of sympathy and role-taking the perspectives of others (Fabes, Eisenberg, & Miller, 1990; Eisenberg et al., 1991). Other research reports a positive correlation between girls' capacity for empathy and maternal tolerance, affection, and permissiveness, but a negative correlation between girls' empathy and maternal conflict, rejection, punishment, and excessive control (Feshbach, 1982). These findings suggest the following conclusions: Both boys and girls from families lacking strong bonds will be less likely to express empathy and more likely to commit delinquency. Moreover, among girls the expressive behavior modeled by the same-sex parent is crucial, so that when mothers are lacking in empathic expressiveness, their daughters will respond to others with less empathy and thus, may be more likely to become involved in antisocial behaviors, like delinquency.

*Shame*

Shame is another social psychological outcome that appears to be gendered, and also has particular relevance for law violation (Braithwaite, 1989). Feeling shame involves the perception that one has failed to live up to the ideals of oneself or others, and thus cannot present oneself to others in a desirable light (Ferguson & Crowley, 1997). Scheff (1988) argues that shame is a major linchpin of social control, and increases when individuals are aware that their rule or norm infractions may damage relationships to others. Empirical research supports this argument, finding that the threat of shame inhibits crime (Grasmick & Bursik, 1990). Because hegemonic gender definitions encourage females to focus on connectedness to others, girls may be more likely than boys to experience shame when they violate rules and norms. Consistent with this, research finds that, on average, females express more shame than males (Ferguson & Crowley, 1997; see also Abell and Gecas, 1997). Criminological research shows that females report greater shame than males when they violate the law (Finley & Grasmick, 1985; Grasmick & Bursik, 1993). Thus, the gender gap in delinquency may be explained in part by greater average levels of experiences of shame among females than males. Consistent with this, Svensson (2004) reports that a sample of Swedish female adolescents feel more shame in the face of significant others than do males. Moreover, shame proves to be more important for females than for males both in deterring delinquency and in mediating the relationship between family interactions and delinquency (see also Hay 2003; see also Blackwell, 2000). Although these studies are suggestive, there is a need for more systematic study of the complex dynamics linking gender, shame, and delinquency before we can develop convincing arguments about the differential impact of shame on law violation across gender.

*Anger*

Anger also is likely important for the relationship between gender and delinquency. In the development of general strain theory, Agnews (1985, 1992) posited anger to be the most important emotion for understanding the link between strain and delinquency. The logic he uses in developing this argument is that anger – more than other emotions – energizes individuals for action, increases feelings that one has been injured, and leads to the desire for retaliation or corrective action. However, the extent to which anger functions in this way may be gendered, with the logic of the argument applying to the experience of anger among males but perhaps not among females.

Although there is a common assumption that males experience anger more often and more intensely than females, research on anger finds that females report becoming angry as often and as intensely as men (see Biaggio,

1989). However, there is evidence that the expression of anger varies across gender in ways that might be related to delinquency. Specifically, males are more likely to express their anger through outward, aggressive channels, whereas females are more likely to express anger through crying or other less aggressive means (Eagly & Steffen, 1986). In other words, anger may serve to energize and lead to the desire for corrective action among males, but not among females. These differences are expected given the operation of he-gemonic gender definitions and the gender-differentiated experiences and socialization patterns that accompany these. Specifically, gender definitions depict the feminine ideal as concerned with preserving interpersonal rela-tionships and opting for passive rather than hostile, aggressive responses. Overall, then, hostile expressions of anger and aggression are more likely among males than females, and this may well contribute to the gender gap in delinquency (see Broidy & Agnew, 1997, for a similar argument). Some research on the link between anger, gender, and delinquency in sociology has supported this gendered argument. Specifically, research documents that both males and females respond to stress with anger; however, anger is more likely to lead to property and violent delinquency among males than among females (Sigfusdottir, Farkas, & Silver, 2004). Alternatively, studies of drug use report very different findings – anger is more likely to lead to drug use among females than among males (Colder & Stice, 1998; Swaim, Oetting, Edwards, & Beauvais, 1989). This, of course, is consistent with the proposition that females are less likely to act aggressively in response to anger. Again, research on the link between this social psychological out-come, gender, and delinquency has not advanced far enough to allow for definitive predictions about whether the impact of feelings of anger on delinquency may vary across gender. However, one would expect, as with the other processes discussed above, that *within* gender, more anger – especially hostile anger – is associated with higher levels of delinquency, all else constant.

### Orientations toward Risk

Recent research on the gender gap on delinquency has emphasized gender differences in preferences for risk-taking, as a result of socialization proc-esses that prepare males for success in a capitalist market economy (e.g. Hagan et al., 1987). Other research indicates that males are more likely than females to prefer risk-taking, even when it is clear that no benefits can re-sult from taking a risk (see review by Byrnes, Miller, & Schafer, 1999). In addition, research shows that peer groups model risk-taking behavior and enhance tendencies to take risks among boys (Miller & Byrnes, 1997), and male peer groups encourage risk-taking in the form of rule infractions (Lever, 1976, 1978; Thorne & Luria, 1986).

As power-control theory argues, taste for risk increases the chances of common delinquency, and thus the gender difference in preferences for risk-taking is likely one source of the gender gap in delinquency (Hagan et al., 1985, 1987). However, there is some suggestion in the delinquency literature that preferences for risk-taking have different consequences for delinquency among girls than boys, and this may have a more substantial impact on delinquency than mean differences across gender in levels of preference for risk. Indeed, one study using a large nationally representative sample reports that among boys, preferences for risk are more strongly associated with delinquency than is the case among girls, and that this difference in the magnitudes of effects is more consequential for the gender gap than is the gender difference in levels of preference for risk (Heimer, 1995). It may be that because delinquency is so inconsistent with hegemonic definitions of femininity and is viewed as "doubly deviant" for females, girls who do have strong preferences favoring risk-taking are more likely than similar males to channel these tastes into other forms of risky behavior and avoid delinquent lines of action (e.g. sports, skydiving). This gender difference aside, however, it is also the case that girls who have acquired strong tastes for risk are more likely to be delinquent than girls with little preference for risk-taking, just as in the case of boys (Heimer, 1995).

## CONCLUSION

Our goal in this paper has been to suggest a road map for future work on the social psychology of gender and delinquency. We view hegemonic definitions of gender as central in the socialization of gender and argue that this has critical implications for the experiences of females and males, which in turn are key for understanding the link between gender and delinquency. We also identified social psychological mechanisms that are produced in these various social contexts, including individuals' internalization of hegemonic gender definitions, delinquent definitions, moralities of care versus moralities of justice, as well as responses to parental controls, feelings of empathy, shame, and anger, and orientations toward risk-taking. All of these are potentially important for the social psychology of gender and delinquency. We hope that future research will explore further the mechanisms identified here, thus illuminating "the black box" of gender and delinquency research.

Moreover, future research on gender and crime must pay more heed to distinctions between questions about the sources of the gender gap in offending versus questions about differences in criminal involvement within gender (i.e. among females and among males). Currently, the distinction is too often blurred. Both types of questions are critical for any comprehensive theory of gender and delinquency. In addition, research targeting the gender gap must recognize two very distinct sources of this gap – stemming from gender differences in exposure (i.e. mean differences in levels explanatory constructs across gender) and gender differences in impact (i.e. differences in the effect of the construct across gender). In other words, we need to know not only whether girls experience less shame and anger, but also whether these experiences influence delinquency differently across gender. The development of clear and coherent social psychological theories of gender and delinquency will have to be attuned to these distinctions.

## NOTES

1. As we have noted in our previous work (Heimer, 1996; Heimer & De Coster, 1999), the notion of the internalization of pervasive gender definitions departs from other treatments of masculinity and femininity in the delinquency literature, which has sometimes focused on traits and sometimes on roles, producing some inconsistent findings.

## REFERENCES

Abell, E., & Gecas, V. (1997). Guilt, shame and family socialization: A retrospective study. *Journal of Family Issues, 18*, 99–123.
Adler, P. A., Kless, S. J., & Adler, P. (1992). Socialization to gender roles: Popularity among elementary school boys and girls. *Sociology of Education, 65*, 169–198.
Agnew, R. (1985). A revised strain theory of delinquency. *Social Forces, 64*, 151–167.
Agnew, R. (1992). Foundation for a general strain theory of crime and delinquency. *Criminology, 30*, 47–87.
Akers, R. L., Krohn, M. D., Lanza-Kaduce, L., & Radosevich, M. (1979). Social learning and deviant behavior: A general test of a specific theory. *American Sociological Review, 44*, 635–655.
Biaggio, M. K. (1989). Sex differences in behavioral reactions to provocation of anger. *Psychological Reports, 64*, 23–26.
Blackwell, B. S. (2000). Perceived sanction threats, gender, and crime: A test and elaboration of power-control theory. *Criminology, 38*, 439–488.
Block, J. H. (1984). *Sex role identity and ego development*. San Francisco: Jossey-Bass.
Braithwaite, J. (1989). *Crime, shame and reintegration*. Melbourne: Cambridge University Press.

Brannen, J. (1995). Young people and their contribution to household work. *Sociology, 29*, 317–338.
Broidy, L., & Agnew, R. (1997). Gender and crime: A general strain theory perspective. *Journal of Research in Crime and Delinquency, 34*, 275–306.
Burke, P. J. (1989). Gender identity, sex and school performance. *Social Psychological Quarterly, 44*, 83–92.
Byrnes, J. P., Miller, D. C., & Schafer, W. D. (1999). Gender differences in risk taking: A meta-analysis. *Psychological Bulletin, 7*, 367–383.
Canter, R. J. (1982). Family correlates of male and female delinquency. *Criminology, 20*, 149–168.
Cernkovich, S. A., & Giordano, P. C. (1987). Family relationships and delinquency. *Criminology, 25*, 295–322.
Chesney-Lind, M. (1997). *The female offender: Girls, women and crime*. Thousand Oaks, California: Sage.
Chodorow, N. (1978). *The reproduction of mothering*. Berkeley: University of California.
Colder, C. R., & Stice, E. (1998). A longitudinal study of the interactive effects of impulsivity and anger on adolescent problem behavior. *Journal of Youth and Adolescence, 27*, 255–274.
Connell, R. W. (1995). *Masculinities*. Berkeley: University of California.
Corsaro, W. A., & Eder, D. (1995). Children's peer culture. *Annual Review of Sociology, 16*, 197–220.
Crabb, P. B., & Bielawski, D. (1994). The social representation of material culture and gender in children's books. *Sex Roles, 30*, 69–79.
Crouter, A. C., Manke, B. A., & McHale, S. M. (1995). The family context of gender intensification in early adolescence. *Child Development, 66*, 317–329.
Daly, K. (1994). *Gender, crime, and punishment*. New Haven, CT: Yale University.
Daly, K., & Chesney-Lind, M. (1988). Feminism and criminology. *Justice Quarterly, 5*, 497–538.
De Coster, S., & Heimer, K. (forthcoming). Crime at the intersections: Race, gender, and offending. In: R. D. Peterson, L. J. Krivo & J. Hagan (Eds), *The many colors of crime: Inequalities of race, ethnicity, and crime in America*. New York: New York University.
Dietz, T. L. (1998). An examination of violence and gender role portrayals in video games: Implications for gender socialization and aggressive behavior. *Sex Roles, 38*, 425–442.
Eagly, A. H., & Steffen, V. J. (1986). Gender and aggressive behavior: A meta-analytic review of the social psychological literature. *Psychological Bulletin, 100*, 303–330.
Eder, D. (1985). The cycle of popularity: Interpersonal relations among female adolescents. *Sociology of Education, 58*, 154–165.
Eder, D. (with C. C. Evans and S. Parker). (1995). *School talk: Gender and adolescent culture*. New Brunswick, NJ: Rutgers University.
Eder, D., & Parker, S. (1987). The cultural production and reproduction of gender: The effect of extracurricular activities on peer-group culture. *Sociology of Education, 60*, 200–213.
Eisenberg, N., Fabes, R. A., Schaller, M., Miller, P., Carlo, G., Poulin, R., Shea, C., & Shell, R. (1991). Personality and socialization correlates of vicarious emotional responding. *Journal of Personality and Social Psychology, 61*, 459–470.
Eisenberg, N., & Lennon, R. (1983). Sex differences in empathy and related capacities. *Psychological Bulletin, 94*, 100–131.
Eisenberg, N., & Miller, P. M. (1987). The relation of empathy to prosocial and related behavior. *Psychological Bulletin, 101*, 91–119.

Eisenberg, N., & Strayer, J. (1987). *Empathy and its development*. New York: Cambridge University Press.

Evans, L., & Davies, K. (2000). No sissy boy here: A content analysis of the representation of masculinity in elementary reading textbooks. *Sex Roles, 42*, 255–270.

Fabes, R. A., Eisenberg, N., & Miller, P. (1990). Maternal correlates of children's vicarious emotional responsiveness. *Developmental Psychology, 26*, 639–648.

Fagot, B. I. (1984). Teacher and peer reaction to boys' and girls' play styles. *Sex Roles, 11*, 691–702.

Fagot, B. I., & Hagan, R. (1991). Observations of parent reactions to sex-stereotyped behaviors: Age and sex effects. *Child Development, 62*, 617–628.

Ferguson, T. J., & Crowley, S. L. (1997). Gender differences in organization of guilt and shame. *Sex Roles, 37*, 19–43.

Ferree, M. M., Lorber, J., & Hess, B. B. (1999). Introduction. In: M. M. Ferree, J. Lorber & B. B. Hess (Eds), *Revisioning gender* (pp. xv–xxxvi). Thousand Oaks, CA: Sage.

Feshbach, N. D. (1982). Sex differences in empathy and social behavior in children. In: N. Eisenberg (Ed.), *The development of prosocial behavior* (pp. 315–338). New York: Academic Press.

Finley, N. J., & Grasmick, H. G. (1985). Gender roles and social control. *Sociological Spectrum, 5*, 317–330.

Furnham, A., & Thomson, L. (1999). Gender role stereotyping in advertisements on two British radio stations. *Sex Roles, 40*, 153–165.

Gager, C. T., Cooney, T. M., & Call, K. T. (1999). The effects of family characteristics on time use in teenagers' household labor. *Journal of Marriage and Family, 61*, 982–994.

Gilligan, C. (1988). Remapping the moral domain: New images of self in relationship. In: C. Gilligan, J. V. Ward, J. M. Taylor & B. Bardige (Eds), *Mapping the moral domain: A contribution of women's thinking to psychology theory and education* (pp. 3–19). Cambridge: Harvard University Press.

Gilligan, C. (1993). *In a different voice*. Cambridge: Harvard University Press.

Gilligan, C., & Attanucci, J. (1988a). Two moral orientations. In: C. Gilligan, J. V. Ward, J. M. Taylor & B. Bardige (Eds), *Mapping the moral domain: A contribution of women's thinking to psychology theory and education* (pp. 73–86). Cambridge: Harvard University.

Gilligan, C., & Attanucci, J. (1988b). Two moral oientations: Gender differences and similarities. *Merrill-Palmer Quarterly, 34*, 223–237.

Gilligan, C., & Wiggins, G. (1988). The origins of morality in early childhood relationship. In: C. Gilligan, J. V. Ward, & J. M. Taylor with B. Bardige (Eds), *Mapping the moral domain: A contribution of women's thinking to psychology theory and education* (pp. 111–137). Cambridge: Harvard University Press.

Glueck, S., & Glueck, E. T. (1950). *Unraveling juvenile delinquency*. Cambridge: Harvard University Press.

Goffman, E. (1977). The arrangement between the sexes. *Theory and Society, 4*, 301–331.

Grasmick, H. G., & Bursik, R. J., Jr. (1990). Conscience, significant others, and rational choice: Extending the deterrence model. *Law and Society Review, 24*, 837–862.

Grasmick, H. G., & Bursik, R. J., Jr. (1993). Changes in the sex patterning of perceived threats of sanctions. *Law and Society Review, 27*, 679–705.

Grauerholz, E., & Pescosolido, B. A. (1989). Gender representation in children's literature: 1900–1984. *Gender and Society, 39*, 113–125.

Hay, C. (2003). Family strain, gender, and delinquency. *Sociological Perspectives, 46*, 107–135.

Hagan, J., Gillis, A. R., & Simpson, J. H. (1985). The class structure of gender delinquency: Toward power control theory of common delinquent behavior. *American Journal of Sociology, 90,* 1151–1179.

Hagan, J., Simpson, J. H., & Gillis, A. R. (1987). Class in the household: A power control theory of gender delinquency. *American Journal of Sociology, 92,* 788–816.

Heimer, K. (1995). Gender, race and the pathways to delinquency: An interactionist analysis. In: J. Hagan & R. D. Peterson (Eds), *Crime and inequality* (pp. 140–173). Stanford, CA: Stanford University.

Heimer, K. (1996). Gender interaction and delinquency. Testing a theory of differential social control. *Social Psychological Quarterly, 59,* 39–61.

Heimer, K., & De Coster, S. (1999). The gendering of violent delinquency. *Criminology, 37,* 277–318.

Hirschi, T. (1969). *Causes of delinquency.* Berkeley: Free Press.

Huesmann, L. R., Guerra, N. G., Zelli, A., & Miller, L. (1992). Differing normative beliefs about aggression for boys and girls. In: K. Bjorkqvist & P. Niemela (Eds), *Of mice and women* (pp. 77–88). San Diego: Academic Press.

Jackman, M. R. (1994). *The velvet glove: Paternalism and conflict in gender, class and race relations.* Berkeley: University of California.

Jacobs, J. E., & Eccles, J. S. (1992). The impact of mothers' gender-role stereotypic beliefs on mothers and children's ability perceptions. *Journal of Personality and Social Psychology, 63,* 932–944.

Jacobs, J. E., Lanza, S., Osgood, D. W., Eccles, J. S., & Wigfield, A. (2002). Changes in children's self-competence and values: Gender and domain differences across grades one through twelve. *Child Development, 73,* 509–527.

Jensen, G. F., & Eve, R. (1976). Sex differences in delinquency: An examination of popular sociological explanation. *Criminology, 13,* 427–448.

Johnson, F. L., & Young, K. (2002). Gendered voices in children's television advertising. *Critical Studies in Media Communication, 19,* 461–480.

Kessler, S., Ashenden, D. J., Connell, R. W., & Dowsett, G. W. (1985). Gender relations in secondary schooling. *Sociology of Education, 58,* 34–48.

Lamb, M. E., Easterbrooks, M. A., & Holden, G. W. (1980). Reinforcement and punishment among preschoolers: Characteristics, effects and correlates. *Child Development, 51,* 1230–1236.

Lever, J. (1976). Sex differences in the games children play. *Social Problems, 23,* 478–487.

Lever, J. (1978). Sex differences in the complexity of children's play and games. *American Sociological Review, 43,* 471–483.

Lorber, J. (2005). *Breaking the bowls: Degendering and feminist change.* New York: W.W. Norton.

Maccoby, E. E., & Jacklin, C. N. (1974). *The psychology of sex differences.* Stanford, CA: Stanford University Press.

Maccoby, E. E., & Jacklin, C. N. (1987). Gender segregation in childhood. *Advances in Child Development and Behavior, 20,* 239–387.

McCarthy, B., Felmlee, D., & Hagan, J. (2004). Girl friends are better: Gender, friends, and crime among school and street youth. *Criminology, 42,* 5–35.

McGuffey, C. S., & Rich, B. L. (1999). Playing in the gender transgression zone: Race, class, and hegemonic masculinity in middle childhood. *Gender and Society, 13,* 608–627.

Mears, D. P., Ploeger, M., & Warr, M. (1998). Explaining the gender gap in delinquency: Peer influence and moral evaluations of behavior. *Journal of Research in Crime and Delinquency, 35,* 251–256.

Messerschmidt, J. W. (1993). *Masculinities and crime: Critique and reconceptualization of theory.* Lanham, MD: Rowman and Littlefield.

Messerschmidt, J. W. (2000). *Nine lives: Adolescent masculinities, the body and violence.* Colorado: Westview Press.

Miller, J. (1998). Up it up: Gender and the accomplishment of street robbery. *Criminology, 36,* 37–68.

Miller, J. (2001). *One of the guys: Girls, gangs, and gender.* New York: Oxford University Press.

Miller, D. C., & Byrnes, J. P. (1997). The role of contextual and personal factors in children's risk taking. *Developmental Psychology, 33,* 814–823.

Miller, P. A., & Eisenberg, N. (1988). The relation of empathy to aggressive and externalizing/ antisocial behavior. *Psychological Bulletin, 103,* 324–344.

Miller, J., & Mullins, C. W. (2005). Stuck up, telling lies and talking too much: The gendered context of young women's violence. In: K. Heimer & C. Kruttschnitt (Ed.), *Gender and crime: Patterns of victimization and offending* (pp. 41–66). New York: New York University.

Moen, P., Erickson, M. A., & Dempster-McClain, D. (1997). Their mothers' daughters? The intergenerational transmission of gender attitudes in a world of changing roles. *Journal of Marriage and the Family, 59,* 281–293.

Mortimer, J. T. (2003). *Working and growing up in America.* Cambridge, MA: Harvard University Press.

Parsons, T., & Bales, R. F. (1955). *Family socialization and interaction process.* Glencoe, III: Free Press.

Pierce, K. (1989). Sex role stereotyping of children television: A content analysis of the roles and attributes of children characters. *Sociological Spectrum, 9,* 321–328.

Peirce, K. (1993). Socialization of teenage girls through teen-magazine fiction: The making of a new woman or an old lady? *Sex Roles, 29,* 59–68.

Ridgeway, C. L., & Smith-Lovin, L. (1999). The gender system and interaction. *Annual Review of Sociology, 25,* 191–216.

Sadker, M., & Sadker, D. (1994). *Failing at fairness: How America's schools cheat girls.* New York: Charles Scribner's Sons.

Scheff, T. J. (1988). Shame and conformity: The deference–emotion system. *American Sociology Review, 53,* 395–406.

Schlenker, J. A., Caron, S. L., & Halteman, W. A. (1998). A feminist analysis of seventeen magazine: Content analysis from 1945 to 1995. *Sex Roles, 38,* 135–149.

Schur, E. M. (1984). *Labeling women deviant: Gender, stigma and social control.* New York: McGraw-Hill.

Sigfusdottir, I. D., Farkas, G., & Silver, E. (2004). The role of depressed mood and anger in the relationship between family conflict and delinquent behavior. *Journal of Youth and Adolescence, 33,* 509–522.

Signorielli, N. (1991). *A source book on children and television.* New York: Greenwood Press.

Simpson, S. S., & Ellis, L. (1995). Doing gender: Sorting out the caste and crime conundrum. *Criminology, 33,* 47–79.

Smart, C. (1976). *Women, crime and criminology: A feminist critique.* London: Routledge & Kegan Paul.

Snow, M. E., Jacklin, C. N., & Maccoby, E. E. (1983). Sex differences in father–child interaction at one year of age. *Child Development, 52,* 227–232.

Starrels, M. E. (1992). Attitude similarity between mothers and children regarding maternal employment. *Journal of Marriage and the Family, 54,* 91 103.

Sutherland, E. H. (1947). *Principles of criminology* (4th ed.). Philadephia: Lippincott.

Svensson, R. (2004). Shame as a consequence of the parent–child relationship: A study of gender differences in juvenile delinquency. *European Journal of Criminology, 1,* 477–504.

Swaim, R. C., Oetting, E. R., Edwards, R. W., & Beauvais, F. (1989). Links from emotional distress to adolescent drug use: A path model. *Journal of Consulting and Clinical Psychology, 57,* 227–231.

Thompson, T. L., & Zerbinos, E. (1997). Television cartoons: Do children notice it's a boy's world? *Sex Roles, 37,* 415–431.

Thorne, B. (1993). *Gender play: Girls and boys in the school.* New Jersey: Rutgers University.

Thorne, B., & Luria, Z. (1986). Sexuality and gender in children's daily worlds. *Social Problems, 33,* 176–190.

Walby, S. (1990). *Theorizing patriarchy.* Cambridge, MA: Basil Blackwell.

West, C., & Zimmerman, D. H. (1987). Doing gender. *Gender and Society, 1,* 125–151.

White, L. K., & Brinkerhoff, D. B. (1981). Children's work in the family: Its significance and meaning. *Journal of Marriage and the Family, 43,* 789–798.

Willemsen, T. M. (1995). Widening the gender gap: Teenage magazines for girls and boys. *Sex Roles, 38,* 851–861.

# COMMENTARY ON PART I: THEORY AND RESEARCH IN THE SOCIOLOGY AND SOCIAL PSYCHOLOGY OF CRIME AND DEVIANCE

Ronald L. Akers

## ABSTRACT

*In this commentary on the chapters of Part I, Ronald L. Akers discusses the link between theory and research at micro and macro levels of analysis. He addresses the chapters' indebtedness to the classic scholars of sociology and the various ways in which theory informs research. Akers then reviews each of the chapters in Part I individually.*

## INTRODUCTORY AND GENERAL COMMENTS

The major theories in the sociology of crime, law, and deviance (criminology, criminal justice, and sociology of law) provide answers to sets of significant and enduring questions about behavior and society. Research in the field attempts to test the empirical validity of those answers, describe variations and distributions of the behavior in question, and evaluate efforts by society to define, affect, control, and change criminal and deviant behavior and patterns.

Sociological Theory and Criminological Research: Views from Europe and the United States
Sociology of Crime, Law and Deviance, Volume 7, 137–155
Copyright © 2006 by Elsevier Ltd.
All rights of reproduction in any form reserved
ISSN: 1521-6136/doi:10.1016/S1521-6136(06)07007-2

First, theories of law, social control, and justice attempt to answer questions about legal and social norms and definitions and reactions to conforming and deviant behavior such as: How and why do systems of law, formal and informal social control, and criminal justice develop, operate, and change? Why do the actors, agents, and personnel in these systems behave as they do? What impact do the social, political, economic, religious, and other institutions and factors in society have on these systems and what impact do these systems have on society?

Second, theories of criminal and deviant behavior attempt to answer etiological questions about the causes and consequences of crime and deviance in society such as: Why do people engage in behavior that conforms to social and legal norms and why do they engage in criminal and deviant acts that violate those norms? Why are there variations in the distribution of rates of crime and deviance across societies and across groups, categories, and locations within the same society? Why are there differences across individuals in the general tendency, frequency, probability, and seriousness of criminal and deviant behavior? Theories addressing the question about rates of crime and deviance are said to focus on the *macro or structural* level of analysis, while those offering answers to the question of differences across individuals are said to operate at the *micro-processual* level.

These important questions, in one form or another, have puzzled thinking people almost from the beginning of human society and have confronted us in more systematic form since the beginning of academic and scientific interest in crime, law, and deviance in sociology, psychology, and criminology. We have clarified and found more precise ways of asking these basic questions, but the questions remain essentially the same. There have been many different theoretical answers offered, and which theories seem to be preferred vary somewhat through time and across space. We are not likely ever to reach completely satisfactory, agreed upon, and validated answers. Nevertheless, as reflected in the chapters in this volume, as long as we continue to address the important questions, we will continue to make important strides in providing better and more empirically validated theories.

All of the chapters in Part I address primarily the second set of questions. They show clearly that the theories answering these questions today build upon classic or nearly classic sociological theories of social structure and social behavior of the late-19th century and the 20th century. Those classic theories did not suffice at the time as adequate answers and will not suffice today, but as shown in the chapters here, they become more sufficient in the modified, reformulated, and empirically grounded form found in contemporary theory.

Classic Weberian theory informs "Work and Crime: Can the Missing Link be understood through Max Weber's Protestant Ethic?" by Karl Schumann. Imke Dunkake relies upon Merton's anomie theory (which itself is a derivation of Durheimian theory) in "Truants and the Family: An Empirical Study of Deviant Behavior in Early Adolescence." She provides an empirical test of modified models of anomie theory. Anomie theory is also the subject of the paper by Sanjay Marwah and Mathieu Deflem, "Revisiting Merton: Continuities in the Theory of Anomie-and-Opportunity-Structures." They do a masterful job of analyzing, clarifying, and updating Merton's theory (and extensions of it), indeed relying on Merton's last statements on anomie theory just before the end of the 20th century. Ross Matsueda, "Criminological Implications of the Thought of George Herbert Mead," continues his work on the application of symbolic interactionism to crime and delinquency based on Meadian social psychology and its implications for differential association/social learning (Sutherland, Akers, Bandura, and others), labeling and shaming (Tannebaum and Becker), control (Hirschi, Kornhauser, Sampson, and Laub), and other contemporary perspectives. Some of his prior work along these lines has been done with Karen Heimer. Her paper with Stacy DeCoster and Halime Ünal, "Opening the Black Box: The Social Psychology of Gender and Delinquency," links gender to social psychological processes found in some of the same theories considered by Matsueda, differential association/social learning, labeling and shaming, and control as well as strain (Agnew) and power-control theory (Hagan).

Theory is central to all of the chapters in this Part, but the first two can be fairly characterized as concentrating more on reporting data analysis related to theory, while the other three are more devoted to theoretical analysis and argument, referring at times to published research but not presenting original data. Also, the theoretical perspectives move from the macro/meso (Schumann, Dunkake and Marwah and Deflem) to the meso/micro with symbolic interactionism (Matsudea) and the social psychological processes that may account for the gender differences in rates and individual differences in criminal and deviant behavior (Heimer et al.). I should note here that I consider both Matsueda's and Heimer's past and present work to be very compatible with social learning theory. Although we move with somewhat different gaits, we walk the same side of the theoretical street. Cognitive/behavior concepts drawn from or similar to those in differential association/social learning theory play an important role in their analyses.

Sociology is not defined exclusively by either purely macro/sociological or purely micro/social psychological theories and levels of analysis. These chapters taken together illustrate how any theory, while focusing on one level, actually assumes, refers to, or has implications for, factors and processes operating at the other level. The question of human agency and determinism is relevant to any theory whether macro, micro, or integrated theory. This is most directly addressed by Marwah and Deflem and by Matsueda, both preferring models that accommodate active human agency, but it is implicit in the other chapters as well. I agree with their preference for incorporating or at least accommodating human agency in theory. I also concur with their remarks on the proper approach to causation and determinism in sociology. No sociology has ever lived up to a strict model of determinism that meets the standard of specifying necessary and sufficient conditions fully causing behavior. In reality, sociologists have long since abandoned these older notions of strict determinism and have moved to what David Matza called "soft determinism." The more appropriate conception of cause is a probabilistic one that asserts that deviant behavior is more likely in the presence of a set of variables or processes, less likely in their absence, and different values of the variables produce different probabilities of behavior occurring. Humans are not passive, empty organisms who bounce in response to external forces like billiard balls. They act, react, and create, and therefore the path of actions, by individuals, groups, or societies is not completely determinable by causative factors and variables. Also, it should be noted that Schumann's research examining the differential effects of unemployment not only on delinquency but also on court sanctioning as well as the references to differential societal reactions (informal and formal) and to labeling/shaming theory in both Matsueda and Heimer et al. shows that some of the same theoretical perspectives addressed to issues of causes of crime and deviance, may also relate to issues of social control, law, and criminal justice.

There are places where I offer disagreement with or raise questions about the analysis or conclusions, but these are offered in the spirit of suggestions for future work and do not diminish my appreciation for the contributions of the papers in Part I. Each chapter is impressive on its own. Taken together they provide the reader with an excellent review of central issues in the sociology and social psychology of crime and deviance.

## COMMENTS ON SCHUMANN'S "WORK AND CRIME: CAN THE MISSING LINK BE UNDERSTOOD THROUGH MAX WEBER'S PROTESTANT ETHIC?"

One of the common assumptions in political discourse is that crime is concentrated in the lower classes because poverty, low income, or economic deprivation are among the most important "root" causes of crime in society. It is also a common belief that this relationship has been amply and fully documented by sociologists, psychologists, and other social/behavioral scientists. These views are shared by governmental decision makers and much of criminal justice policy and practice such as programs of training, re-education, and job skill development in prisons and in the community, and post-release vocational advising and placement for both juvenile and adults is based on this assumption. I believe that this appeals to the liberal/left because it can be seen as a way of denying individual responsibility for crime and showing the flaws of capitalistic society. When these "puritan" ideas as Schumann calls them are espoused by the right, it is seen as upholding the dictum that idle, unemployed hands are the devil's workshop and need to be counteracted by useful and gainful employment (along with sufficiently tough and sure criminal penalties). But probably the majority of those holding to these notions simply take for granted on commonsense grounds that the unemployed find economic incentive in crime and that being employed counters crime because it provides a legitimate alternative to criminal gain. Further, honest work is good and ennobling in its own right. From whatever source, there is the general expectation that unemployment or unskilled and low paying employment produces crime both at the individual and societal level while job skills and employment counters criminal motivation. As Schumann reminds us, however, the validity of this belief about work and crime is far from a settled sociological issue either theoretically or empirically.

To test the relationship between work and crime, Schumann has at his disposal an imposing set of longitudinal data collected over a 10-year period with both self-report and official delinquency data that "allow for the study of the impact of the German system of apprenticeships on the school-to-work-transition" for those youth who will not graduate high school and attend a university. The longitudinal data are true panel data from "four waves for the whole panel of respondents and five waves of qualitative interviews in a smaller panel." The findings from these data, in agreement with other studies in the United States and the United Kingdom, do not support the expectation that failure to acquire job skills and employment is a cause of criminal behavior or that doing so is a strong protective factor against criminal influences. Specifically, the hypothesis that greater success in completing the German job-training apprenticeship the lower the probability of delinquent behavior is not supported by the findings. There were no significant differences between those who successfully completed apprenticeship and became "qualified" for better jobs and the "unskilled" youth who did not. In fact, the unskilled and unemployed respondents were actually less involved in delinquency than the successful apprentices, although they tended to be sanctioned more severely by the justice system, which in turn adversely affected the youths' work careers.

Schumann is quite aware that work status and its changes with age are among those elements of social bonds (along with marital status) to which life course criminology has paid attention. He also recognizes that the life-course perspective is not itself a theory that can shed much light on the work–crime relationship, but primarily a framework for conducting longitudinal research and raising questions about what accounts for persistence or change in criminal behavior over time. I agree and would add that life-course criminology has yet to provide a single new causative variable or explanation of crime and delinquency. Rather life course criminology concentrates on age variations in deviance (just as Marxists focus on class, feminists focus on gender, and conflict theorists focus on class, gender, and race), and relies on existing etiological theories to explain age variations and make sense of the trajectories and patterns of crime in the life course. Therefore, Schumann turns to these theories and takes the reader through the basic issue of why, theoretically, we would expect a negative relationship between work and crime. Why would employment protect against criminal tendencies and why would failure at legitimate employment motivate crime? He considers anomie/strain theory (Merton's classic statement to Robert Agnew's more recent statement of general strain theory) as well as control/social bonding, rational choice, interactional, and other theories. He dismisses these theories as "too general" to explicate the work–crime relationship, and to the extent that any of these predict a strong negative relationship between work and crime, they are not supported by the research.

Finding little help from these theories, Schumann turns to Max Weber. His argument is that Weber's famous thesis linking the Protestant ethic with the spirit and growth of capitalism in Europe and America offers the best hope for understanding the link between work/employment and both the commission of criminal behavior and the justice system reactions to criminal behavior. I think this is an intriguing notion that deserves further exploration. While we have certainly taken from Weber in the sociology of law and justice, we lean much more heavily on Durkheimian perspectives in the study of crime and deviance, and have not examined as carefully the implications of Weberian theory for the etiology of crime. I would encourage Schumann to carry on that exploration. However, I have some reservations at this time about how far that enterprise will take us in etiological theory. The Weberian thesis with regard to the Protestant ethic and capitalism may help us to understand the popular assumption of the positive effects of gainful employment on conforming and lawful behavior, or as Schumann says, "One might even say: there seems to exist a 'prison for thoughts' (Quensel), created by the common shared values of the Protestant ethic in the industrial societies, which makes everybody believe that there must be a connection between not working and crime." And given the Weberian backdrop to sociological (non-partisan and non-Marxist) conflict theory, Weber's Protestant ethic thesis may help to understand the societal attitude, shared by judges and criminal justice workers who apply criminal sanctions, that offenders who are skillfully employed qualify for less severe punishment than unskilled or unemployed offenders. But it is difficult for me to see how Weberian theory sheds much light on the behavioral question or the findings in the study of no relationship between working and the commission of criminal behavior better than the other theories that Schumann discusses and finds lacking. What is it about Weberian theory that would predict that there is a zero or a positive relationship between work and crime?

I believe development of the implications for criminal etiology is the most challenging aspect of further application of Weber's theory in the sociology of crime and deviance. But I think Schumann has shown that it is a challenge worth taking. If Marx, Durkheim, and Weber are the three foundational legs of the sociological stool, then sociological theory of criminal behavior may benefit greatly from better grounding in Weberian thought.

# COMMENTS ON DUNKAKE'S "TRUANTS AND THE FAMILY: AN EMPIRICAL STUDY OF DEVIANT BEHAVIOR IN EARLY ADOLESCENCE"

Truancy is a minor form of adolescent deviance, but we have known for a very long time that it is related to, and predictive of, involvement in more serious delinquency. At one time it was routinely included as a status offense in self-report checklists to measure overall adolescent delinquency. Therefore, we can examine the motivation and constraints on truant behavior from the perspective of general theories of crime and deviance. This is exactly what Imke Dunkake does. She offers a viable sociological alternative to the dominant (in Europe) psychiatric/medical perspective on truancy, which sees it as a symptom of a personality disorder. Her alternative begins with the original version of Merton's anomie theory and its modes of adaptation and "extends" it with concepts of value expectancy and social/cultural capital.

From these, she proposes a series of detailed hypotheses that she tests with data on school students and their parents from a first-rate, large-scale study. In these data, she finds good operational measures of the modes of adaptation and the other theoretical concepts. Her data analysis is quite complex, but produces findings that offer at least some support for the hypotheses. She does admirably in showing how the hypotheses are derived from her extensions of anomie theory and in delineating concepts and their empirical measures. Her research makes significant contributions to the sociology of truancy and to testing of modified models of anomie theory.

Merton defined material, monetary success as the culturally desirable goal to which all segments of industrialized society are socialized to aspire with the expectation that it will be pursued through legitimate educational, occupational, and other means. One form of anomie exists when disadvantaged segments (such as lower classes) experience limited access to those socially acceptable means. Among the modes of adaptation to this condition of anomie is the deviant mode in which one turns to effective but illegitimate means to achieve the end of economic success. In operationalizing anomie for Hypotheses I, Ia, and Ib, Dunkake follows this schema with regard to "economic prosperity" as a goal, but she begins by defining school achievement as the means and educational success (not economic prosperity) as the goal. Then she adds in "social recognition" as an alternative goal. Lower social class position is hypothesized to inhibit school achievement because it indicates blocked opportunity to achieve in school or "limited access to social and cultural capital." Truancy is the deviant act she wants to explain but is not itself the illegitimate means to desirable goals. Rather truancy is caused as a necessary byproduct of pursuing alternative goals "aside from school." This is an interesting way of conceptualizing deviance as an adaptation to a means–ends disjuncture. But it is a bit confusing because it refers not to using alternative means to the same goal but of pursuing alternative goals, and it is not clear what adaptation this represents because "innovation" involves utilization of alternative means to the same goal.

Schumann in the first chapter finds that, contrary to theoretical expectations, lack of work skills and unemployment (as indicators of disadvantaged socio-economic status) are not related to delinquency. Dunkake's findings are similar in that the social class of the student's family of origin does not predict differences in truancy. To the extent that anomie theory expects truancy to be strongly related to class, it is not supported by the findings, although it supported to some extent by the findings on the effects of school achievement. Other family (social and cultural capital) variables not included in the original anomie theory (supportive home environment, parental monitoring, and family cultural resources) are related to truancy. Also, "deviant peers" (which has the highest odds ratio) and "side job" are significant predictors of truancy. Dunkake sees seeking a part-time job and attachment to deviant peers as resulting from a perception that, first, there are few benefits to school and, second, that monetary gains will come from gainful employment outside of school and social gains will come from associating with deviant peers. These findings are interpreted primarily as supporting expectations based on concepts of social capital and value expectancy theory.

I would suggest that such findings also support expectations from social bonding theory (especially the family variables) and social learning theory (especially peer variables). The references to parental monitoring and other family variables are directly in line with the concept of attachment in Hirschi's social bonding theory and the way in which it has been measured in the literature. The references to deviant peers and to perceptions of costs/benefits are directly in line with concepts of differential peer association and differential reinforcement in social learning theory (Akers). I believe one would find that a variable such as differential peer association (Dunkake, as have others, calls it "attachment to deviant peers") would have an even stronger effect on truancy than found in this study, if it were measured directly in the typical way using reported proportion or number of friends engaging in truancy rather than more indirect way in this study. If further work is undertaken to determine the explanation and predictors of truancy, it would benefit both theoretically and in terms of concept operationalization from paying attention to these major social psychological theories of deviance. I would also suggest consideration of Robert Agnew's General Strain Theory as a modern extension of the social psychological strain dimension in anomie theory because it allows directly for hypotheses about a variety of types and sources of blocked goals, strain, and negative experiences as individual level motivation for deviance.

# COMMENTS ON MARWAH AND DEFLEM'S "REVISITING MERTON: CONTINUITIES IN THE THEORY OF ANOMIE-AND-OPPORTUNITY-STRUCTURES"

Sanjay Marwah and Mathieu Deflem make a strong case that the "sociological paradigm of anomie-and-opportunity-structures underlies" Merton's classic theory. They do so by examining and clarifying Merton's original 1938 statement and his statements about the theory in the 1950s and 1960s. And to some extent they draw upon formulations and re-formulations of others. But they lean more heavily upon emphases found in Merton's last statements on the theory, primarily the 1995 paper on op-portunity structure, but also his remarks regarding opportunity in the 1997 article on the emerging macro–micro, cross-level synthesis of anomie and differential association theory.

The authors persuasively argue that understanding the full value of Mertonian theory requires not only the proper theoretical conceptualization but also proper measurement of the key concepts. Through the years there have been many missteps in the attempts to do this. It is worthwhile point-ing out, however, that Merton himself did not accomplish this either and did not provide much guidance to others, even in his last statements. Tests of the theory's explanation of variations in rates of crime across societies and segments within the same society still rely on indirect and proxy measures. And we still have not come up with much more satisfactory measures of strain at the individual level than the measures of the discrepancy between aspirations and expectations that have been in use since the 1960s (although, I believe that there have been some advances in measures of other strains in Agnew's general strain theory).

The authors explicate a number of misunderstandings, misinterpretations, and mischaracterizations of anomie theory in the literature. We would all do well to pay heed to them. Prominent among the erroneous views they iden-tify is that anomie theory is a one-dimensional theory. In fact, Merton con-ceptualized anomie as the dissociation or malintegration between means and ends in two related ways. The first has to do with the "imbalance between cultural goals and socially accepted means will result in a de-institutional-ization of means." Societies differ in the extent to which there is such an imbalance or disjuncture created by relatively greater cultural emphasis on one or the other (in the case of American society too much emphasis on material success goals and too little emphasis on acceptable, legitimate means to that end). The higher the level of this type of anomie in the society, the higher its crime rate. The second is "strain theory (of deviant behavior) to suggest that social barrier can restrict people under certain socio-economic conditions (such as anomie) from having access to the legitimate means to achieve culturally valid goals, presenting a pressure toward the adoption of illegitimate means to pursue culturally accepted goals." That is, assuming relatively even distribution of emphasis on and socialization into success goals across all segments of a given society, socially structured dis-tribution of access to legitimate means may disproportionately limit, deny, or block opportunities for some segments of society (presumed by Merton to be the lower class, but by extension would include racial minorities and other disadvantaged groups) to make use of or acquire legitimate educational, occupational, and entrepreneurial means to success. Faced with this relative lack of legitimate opportunities some will turn to effective, but illegitimate (deviant or criminal) means. Almost from the beginning much of the literature perpetrated the false notion that the theory only refers to this second dimension – lack of access to legitimate means by disadvantaged members of society. Marwah and Deflem are quite accurate in identifying and rectifying this interpretation. They also show clearly that Merton eventually moved away from seeming to identify the social structure with the distribution of opportunities to an "anomie-and-opportunity-structures paradigm" that differentiates between the two. While in the original theory "the distribution of means was awkwardly mixed with the production of means," this paradigm clarifies "that the social structure is defined as the organization and distribution of status positions, not institutionalized means."

These are important contributions by Marwah and Deflem to our understanding of anomie theory. But I am not sure that "Merton presented not one, but at least two theories." We need to be careful not to overstate the case and imply that anomie is not a unified theory. I would prefer to view not two theories but two dimensions of the same theory, the same concept of anomie, and the same mechanism (strain) by which anomie increases the probability of crime or deviance. Also, we need to be careful not to overstate the extent to which Merton's clarification and expansion in the 1990s "introduced" rather than clarified and further elucidated the notion of opportunity structure as something related to but distinct from the class structure. If not fully explicated in the original formulation, it became clearer in later statements by Merton and others. The extension of anomie to delinquent gangs and subcultures by Cloward and Ohlin's "differential opportunity theory," for instance, incorporated both the legitimate and illegitimate opportunity structures as avenues to material success. The distribution of these means is not identified solely with the class structure but with the social makeup of different lower-class neighborhoods.

Another, and perhaps the major, mischaracterization of anomie theory countered by Marwah and Deflem is the one fostered by Ruth Kornhauser and other control theorists that the theory relies "only on a notion of the cultural structure to explain the presence of strain and deviance." She was among the principal control theorists who paint an inaccurate picture of anomie theory as only a "strain" theory primarily in order to "defend alternative frameworks and models for the sociological study of deviant behavior." I agree completely with Marwah and Deflem on this point. Kornhauser and other control theorists developed a "straw man" version of the theory that could be easily dismissed. They do the same with differential association/social learning theory, which as I have shown, and which Matsueda shows in his chapter, Kornhauser, Hirschi, and other critics have erroneously characterized as merely "cultural deviance" theory. The strategy is to support the superiority of control theory by discrediting all other theories. The main critique by control theorists is that, other than control theories, all criminological theories mistakenly assume that everyone will be in conformity to conventional norms unless they are pressured, forced, or motivated to become deviant by forces over which they have no control. Control theorists believe all of these other theories only posit "positive" causes of crime and that none has a place for contextual or individual constrains on, or "negative" causes of, deviant motivations. In contrast, control theories are said to assume that the motivation to crime is uniformly distributed across all groups, segments, and individuals in society, and that therefore, "any real explanation of crime and deviance must aim to explain conformity rather than deviance." These critics ignore what Marwah and Deflem point out clearly, namely that Merton contented that social structure both constrains and provides motivation for crime. Control theorists are wrong in their characterizations of anomie and other theories. But it goes beyond that error because, as I have argued strongly over many years, the assumption of the universal distribution of deviant/criminal motivation, in fact, is not found in all varieties of control theories, is not necessary for the explanation of either conformity or deviance, and is empirically invalid.

Another problem in the literature that the authors identify is to misspecify the theory at the micro or individual level and take lack of empirical support at that level as constituting grounds for criticizing or dismissing anomie theory as a whole.

> While Merton has given some credence to the related notion of 'anomia' as the individual expression of the social state of anomie (Merton, 1964), he is otherwise quite clear that he is interested in studying the rates of deviance, their distribution, and structural strain ... [S]ince even the analytical scope and research domain of general strain theorists are different from Merton's original contribution, a dismissal of Merton's theory is premature on the grounds of these criticisms alone.

This is a very important insight into Mertonian theory. But again I would caution not to overstate the case. There is no doubt that Merton's focus in anomie theory was always on the structural differences in crime rates. However, the theory has never lacked a social psychological or individual-level dimension. If human agency has any meaning, anomie can produce differences in crime rates only if it has an impact on individual behavior and if individuals differentially react to social context. Crime rates are, after all, the summation of individual acts (or reports of acts) divided by a population denominator. The assumption even in classic anomie theory is that the conforming and deviant adaptations to anomie are made because individuals are able to perceive lack of opportunity or the disjuncture between means and ends and then are able to seek some resolution of the strain created by that perception. Some later theorists have emphasized the structural dimension, while others such as Agnew have expanded on the social psychological dimension. I fully agree that empirical findings or theoretical critiques at this level cannot be used by themselves to dismiss or deny the structural dimension of anomie, but I am not persuaded that this is what Agnew does in his formulation of general strain theory. I think he quite self-consciously keeps his predictions and conclusions at the micro/individual level.

Marwah and Deflem provide us with a very well reasoned, thorough, and much-needed corrective to the "unjust criticisms and misinterpretations" of Merton's theory that one still finds not only in textbooks but also sometimes in the professional research literature. The sociology of crime and deviance would be very well served if this chapter is widely read and incorporated into future interpretations and applications of anomie theory.

## COMMENTS ON MATSUEDA'S "CRIMINOLOGICAL IMPLICATIONS OF THE THOUGHT OF GEORGE HERBERT MEAD"

In this chapter, Ross Matsueda builds upon the highly respected work he has done in the past on symbolic interactionism, reflected appraisals, differential social control, and differential association/social learning (often with Karen Heimer as co-author). He has established himself as the leading Meadian scholar in contemporary criminology. Matsueda leaves little room for doubting the continuing relevance of Mead's social psychology for sociology and criminology. He illustrates in detail the extent to which current social psychological theories of criminal and deviant behavior rest on or draw from significant elements in Mead's thought, whether or not this influence is always recognized. Even the "classical theories of crime," have been influenced by, and can be elucidated through, the social psychology of George Herbert Mead "including human agency and creativity, identity and the self, differential association and social learning, rational choice and deterrence, and temporality and the life course."

Matsueda notes that Mead's writings "may have had an indirect influence on the general approach of Sutherland's differential association theory" as well as direct and indirect effect on other theories. Sutherland did not cite Mead directly as a basis for differential association theory, but he did list Mead along with Dewey, Cooley, and Thomas as progenitors of the social psychology underlying the sociological approach to crime (contrasted mainly with the psychiatric school which was at the time the major alternative) that criminal behavior is learned as is any behavior. The direction and content of the learning differ but not the basic process. There is no denying the connection, even if indirect, of Meadian psychology and Sutherland's theory. And since the beginning of my work on social learning theory (a reformulation and integration of differential association and behavioral theory), I have acknowledged the symbolic interactionism in the theory, social learning also rests on behavioral psychology. As such, it is *social behaviorism,* which McPhail and Rexroat (1979), cited by Matsueda, show is how Mead referred to his own perspective. And as John Baldwin demonstrates, there are many similarities between Mead's theory and modern behaviorism.

"Taking the role of the other" is perhaps the best known and key concept in Mead's theory. In the process, individuals "learn to relate the rules, expectations, and obligations of their own roles to those of others." This process is reflected in a number of ways in theories of crime and delinquency, and I would argue, as did both Sutherland and Cressey, that in one form or another, symbolic interactionism underlies social psychology in virtually all of sociology (including as I have just noted social learning theory). But it is true, as Matsueda argues, "the perspective on deviance most closely associated with symbolic interaction is labeling theory." The conceptual and empirical shortcomings of traditional labeling theory of Tannebaum, Becker, and Schur in the way in which it utilized symbolic interactionism have become well known. Current theory rectifies some of those shortcomings, including John Braithwaite's "reintegrative shaming," and Matsueda's "reflected appraisals" which is incorporated as one of the major elements (along with differential peer association and anticipated reinforcement) in Matsueda and Heimer's own "differential social control" theory.

Just as Marwah and Deflem do, Matsuda endorses the necessity of allowing for human agency in criminological theory and argues that strict determinism is not an adequate model for human behavior. Human agency is found in Mead's writings both in the concept of taking the role of the other and in the theory of temporality. Application of this to theories such as labeling and Sutherland's differential association theory could "free the theory (differential association) of its statement of determinism ... and provide a stronger link between differential association and differential social organization (see Matsueda, 2005). Moreover, it can provide the theoretical mechanism by which labeling can amplify crime or lead to desistance." Although I would argue that Sutherland's theory implicitly does allow for human agency, it is true that Sutherland's own epistemology was deterministic. He adhered to the methodology of "analytic induction" which is predicated on identifying the necessary and sufficient causative conditions that fit each and all cases of the behavior in question (see my comments on Marwah and Deflem).

Matsueda refers the reader specifically to the "temporal orientation of agency" or the "sequential phases of agency" in Mead's "theory of temporality," particularly as it relates to the stability and change in behavior through the life course. This is a less well-known part of Meadian theory than is "taking the role of the other," but Matsueda believes it is a major unifying concept that could pull together Mead's "theories of the self, social control, and cognition to shed new light on questions of agency and creativity, identity and the self, structure and culture, process and life course, and rationality and decision making." I like this analysis and would encourage Matsueda to continue to explore the extent to which the theory of temporality can do all of this and also do a better job than alternative conceptualizations in life-course criminology. For instance, I agree very much with Matsueda when he recognizes the weaknesses of Sampson and Laub's concept of human agency and their application of control theory assumptions to trajectories of crime through the life course. This weakness results, according to Matsueda, because of control theory assumptions made by Sampson and Laub which lead to their dismissal of learning, peer group, and subcultures as important variables in behavioral stability and change at different ages. Marwah and Deflem point to control theorists' errors regarding anomie theory, and Matsueda identifies their wrong characterization of subcultural and learning theories.

Matsueda ends with four important issues for future research on the application of Meadian social psychology to criminal behavior – which groups are relevant, internal roles and processes of groups, more specific operationalization and quantitative measures of concepts such as self and role relationships, and the relationship between decision as rational choice and decision as role taking. This is a challenging agenda, but one that Matsueda and perhaps some readers of his chapter should pursue.

# COMMENTS ON HEIMER, DECOSTER, AND ÜNAL'S "OPENING THE BLACK BOX: THE SOCIAL PSYCHOLOGY OF GENDER AND DELINQUENCY"

Gender is both a structural factor (indicating location in the social system and hedged about by cultural and subcultural role expectations) and a so-cial/ personal characteristic (with biological, psychological, and social psy-chological elements). Sociologists have always included gender (sex, sex roles) as an important indicator of status differentiation, but for a long time, it was class and race differentiation at the center of sociological theory and research in general, in certain specialties (social class/stratification and race/ ethnicity) in particular, and in particular theories such as conflict/ Marxists/ radical theories. In the latter third of the 20th century, these were joined by gender (sex roles/status) and feminist theory to form a central sociological triad of race/class/gender. To a lesser extent, the same description could be applied to age and the specialty of gerontology (sociology of aging and the life course) and for a brief period, a sociology of adolescence. This same history applies to the sociology of crime and deviance and to criminology as an interdisciplinary field, with courses on gender and crime added to the curriculum or combined into courses on race, class, and gender in crime and criminal justice and more recently with age-related crime patterns and life-course criminology assuming an increasing central place in the field.

All of the these have nearly always been routinely included (along with other socio-demographic variables) as background or control variables in multivariate models in sociology and criminology without attaching much theoretical significant to them. Class and race have turned out to be incon-sistently and often weakly related to criminal and deviant behavior and not nearly as good predictors of differential treatment in the criminal justice system as expected. Gender is a stronger correlate than either race or class for a wide range of deviant and criminal behavior throughout history, across all societies, and within all societies. Going beyond this empirical description of the relationships among variables to greater theoretical focus involves more than determining what causative significance can be attached to the corre-lation. Because it does not make a lot of sense to call gender or race (and also probably social class) a direct "cause" of crime, the key question is how to explain whatever correlation with crime is found. It is to this question of what lurks in the black box connecting gender to delinquency that Heimer, DeCosta, and Ünal devote themselves in this chapter. Which social psycho-logical processes and variables best account for the gender ratio in crime and within-gender individual variations in criminal and delinquent behavior?

The erroneous assumption (informed more by ideological predilection than theoretical insight) in much of the feminist literature is that all "traditional" theories of crime and delinquency (such as control, anomie, conflict, labeling, and social learning) were developed only to explain male criminality and have been tested only with male populations. All existing criminological theories are so tainted by male bias that they should be rejected as explanations of female criminality and male–female differences in crime and replaced by new theory resting only on female-centered theory. Heimer and her co-authors do not make that mistake. Rather they criticize efforts to apply "unmodified constructs" from "traditional" theories to gender and crime and then suggest that we move to "reconceptualizing these constructs in light of feminist theory and research on gender, more generally." And that is what they do in this chapter. They make no claims to have developed a specific theory and do not introduce any social psychological processes not already found in the traditional theories. Their goal, instead, is to provide a theoretical "road map" or framework for reconceptualizing or modifying social psychological constructs. The key signpost in this well-drawn and well-lighted road map is "hegemonic gender definitions," the prevailing cultural stereotypes, sex role expectations, and "beliefs about the nature of genders" into which both boys and girls are socialized. Drawing upon extant theory and research they illuminate how these gendered definitions can be found in many social contexts in childhood and adolescence, identifying the social psychological processes that "shape the development of gender" and by which gender expectations and behavior are learned.

The reader will get a good lesson on the research literature revealing how family, peer groups, school experiences, and exposure to mass media help to shape gender-relevant attitudes and behavior. The dominant cultural expectations of aggressive, physical activity by boys and passive, nurturing activity by girls are found and reinforced even in unsupervised playgroups and peer settings. In school, the findings seem to be that girls and boys are guided toward different courses or different topics in the same courses and gender-differentiated extracurricular activities. But the analysis does not stop there. It moves next to showing how all of this might be related to both the gender-ratio and within-gender differences in delinquency. For instance, a certain level of deviant behavior by boys may be more tolerated, while some of the same acts by girls are seen as not conforming to the hegemonic definitions making them "doubly deviant" and subject to stronger sanctions. I think this could be true but generally girls and women tend to be treated more leniently, both informally and formally, for violations of law and social norms than are boys and men. I would want to see if research supports the hypothesis. Among girls, more complete internalization of the

hegemonic definitions decreases, while among boys it increases, the probability of engaging in delinquency. Control theory applies to this difference,
but direct sanctioning seems to have a greater effect on boys' conforming or
deviant behavior whereas girls seem to respond more to indirect control
through bonds of attachment. Social learning concepts such as "definitions
favorable" to deviance apply because across family, peer, and other contexts
boys are more likely than girls to be exposed to and reinforced for delinquent definitions and behavior. Among these are male-preferred "morality
of justice" which "may be viewed as special instances of definitions favoring
law violations," and female-preferred "morality of care" that provides definitions unfavorable to violation. At the individual level, however, learned
definitions favorable and unfavorable to delinquency affect boys and girls
the same, and "in cases where girls and boys hold identical beliefs and values
about aggression and violence, they are equally likely to engage in aggressive, antisocial ways." I like this analysis because it is essentially the same as
that found in my Social Structure Social Learning (SSSL) model. In the
SSSL model, gender is viewed as an indicator of differential location in the
social structure and social learning variables are hypothesized to substantially mediate gender effects on deviance. But we need to take a closer look
empirically at how substantial that mediation is. Main gender effects on
crime seem to be more robust in the face of mediating social psychological
variables (including social learning variables) than race, class, or age. For
some kinds of deviance, non-trivial direct effects of gender may remain even
after inserting learning or other social psychological variables into the
model. And there are probably moderating effects of gender on the social
psychological process not presently anticipated by the model. The analysis
shows that concepts taken from reintegrative shaming, strain theory, and
power control theory also are helpful in finding what goes on inside the
black box of gender and delinquency.

I find the arguments by Heimer, DeCoster, and Ünal commendable and
persuasive, although I am not always clear how they are modifying extant
social psychological concepts and theories. For instance, the standard sociological concept of socialization seems to be intact throughout the discussion, including notions that the family is the primary institution of
childhood socialization and that sex roles are learned in the family, among
peers, in the school, and from the media. Also, boys and girls learning and
being rewarded for conformity, and punished for not conforming, to hegemonic gender definitions seems a pretty straightforward application of the
differential reinforcement process. The authors identify gender differentials
in the application of informal and formal social control and possible gender

differences in responding to that social control. But this does not seem to me to go beyond unmodified sociological perspectives on why there are behavioral differences across gender and within gender. Nevertheless, this is a very fruitful and promising line of inquiry that should help us move beyond gender as simply a control variable to be inserted into models with other theoretical constructs. I look forward to the next steps that Heimer and her colleagues take in theory and research on the social psychology of gender and crime.

# PART II:
# CRIME AND CRIMINAL JUSTICE IN SOCIO-HISTORICAL CONTEXTS

# IDENTITY AND INTELLECTUAL WORK: BIOGRAPHY, THEORY AND RESEARCH ON LAW ENFORCEMENT

Nigel G. Fielding

## ABSTRACT

*Biography provides a compelling but often invisible thread informing intellectual labour. Both the empirical topics of our work and the conceptualisations we use to understand them can be traced to the researcher's background and sensibilities. The chapter develops this perspective in relation to a study of police training and the conceptualisation of formal and informal socialisation to police occupational culture and a study of community policing and the role of systems theory in operationalising 'structuration'. The chapter discusses the underlying conceptualisations and policy dimensions of the studies, and their intersection with the author's biography.*

## BIOGRAPHY AND INTELLECTUAL WORK

Biography provides a compelling but mostly invisible thread informing intellectual work. In recent years, its role has increasingly been acknowledged,

Sociological Theory and Criminological Research: Views from Europe and the United States
Sociology of Crime, Law and Deviance, Volume 7, 159–181
ISSN: 1521-6136/doi:10.1016/S1521-6136(06)07008-4

but in a literature often akin to the confessional, when accounting for the researcher's own intellectual career (Wolcott, 1990), or the expose, when accounting for that of another (Freeman, 1998). Just as many intellectuals deny an interest in gossip while quietly reading the 'celebrity news' columns now found even in the most highbrow newspapers, there is considerable fascination in the intellectual confessionals and exposes. The argument that makes this somewhat more than a mild form of intellectual deviance is the idea that we might better understand the research, given a glimpse of the researcher's offstage biography. This is an approach more often encountered in respect of fieldwork and qualitative research, although a researcher's orientation to quantitative methods may well reflect biography, and fieldwork is not the sole preserve of qualitative researchers.

Amongst elements of research that we might better understand when provided with some information about the researcher are the choice of given methods and research designs, the adoption of particular analytic perspectives and conceptualisations, and connections between a series of research studies that may otherwise seem to be discrete. These affordances of researcher biography suggest that the official face of research methodology presented in graduate training and the methodology literature does not tell the whole story: a researcher's competences, interests and commitments play a substantial, undeclared part.

This perspective is particularly pertinent to criminological research. It is widely remarked that research in the field follows policy initiatives in a close way (Young, 1997; Morgan, 2000). Criminological researchers in western Europe and North America are closely attentive to criminal justice policy, engaging in pilot studies of programs reflecting new policy initiatives and evaluating the delivery and output of programs when they are fully implemented. Against this stands a substantial analytic genre independent of such stimuli, but it has to be acknowledged that research inspired by a deviancy perspective rather than a criminological one is, proportionately, in the minority in studies of criminal aetiology and the control apparatus represented by the criminal justice system.

In the spirit that both the empirical topics of our work and the theoretical conceptualisations we use to understand them can be traced to the researcher's background, experiences and sensibilities, this chapter will develop this perspective in relation to two research studies: a study of UK police training and socialisation to police occupational culture, and a study of community policing and the role of systems theory in modelling its effects.

A few biographical tokens are necessary. My early experiences of criminal justice were in the United States. These experiences were at the receiving end and came as a result of my involvement in student politics and the counter-culture of the 1960s and 1970s. With the radicalisation of the middle-class youth of the time, the experience of public order policing and the interventions of the drug squad briefly extended to a new fraction of American society. When I returned to the UK, which I had left at age five, it was with intellectual interests that crystallised around the interaction of political and criminal deviance. As a student, my attempts to find a group that reflected my particular commitments led me into encounters with a political organisation whose test for membership was willingness to kill for the cause, and encounters with poly drug users whose lives focussed on explorations of inner consciousness. It was an encounter with the extremes, and that gave my engagement with sociology a set of intellectual concerns relating to how people make the personal the political, and vice versa. My transatlantic background, and the sharp cleavages and social changes of the times, led to an abiding concern with identity, and how its construction is forged in social interaction. Uncertain of my own identity, I wanted to understand how others became certain of theirs.

My interest in political sociology and the sociology of deviance, specifically the convergence of political and criminal deviance, suggested empirical work on political extremism. The early 1970s saw the emergence into prominence of new extreme Left and extreme Right organisations, some orientated to electoral politics and some to direct action. We often take inspiration from folk wisdom, and one homily is that those committed to either extreme have more in common than either does with the mainstream. It seemed clear that I should conduct research that compared the extreme Left and extreme Right.

There is a further thread to add. During graduate studies I had begun teaching, and while I waited to accumulate enough years in the UK to establish eligibility for doctoral funding, I confronted a labour market congested with people who could not find the work for which their credentials qualified them. I eventually decided that I had to ignore my adverse experiences with the police and take the only social science job I could find, a lectureship at Hendon Police College.

I soon learned that far from the cardboard cut-out image I had formed of the police, the organisation harboured individuals of every political stripe, some of whom quietly shared the perspective of those on the Left who they spent time controlling at public order events. When I left Hendon for a doctoral place at the LSE it was to conduct a study of the National Front, an extreme racialist party whose successor, the British National Party, has latterly gained disturbing success in electoral politics. I had realised that it would be hard to study the extreme Left and discount my own sympathies, and I had discovered that no one had yet done an empirical study of the National Front. Motivated by being the first on the scene, I conducted a participant observation study that allowed me to exercise my interest in political extremism, political violence and the construction of a social identity around the two (see Fielding, 1990, 1992).

## FORMAL AND INFORMAL SOCIALISATION TO THE POLICE OCCUPATION

The fundamentals of UK police training are remarkably persistent. There is a period of 'probationer constable' status, during which classroom instruction alternates with field training assignments. There is a belief that all police should begin with experience as an ordinary constable, and although there are accelerated promotion schemes for prospective high-flyers, there is no direct entry to the officer class. Following the reforms mooted by the Sheehy Inquiry (Home Office, 1993) there was, however, increased interest in circulation of personnel among the police service, other public sector organisations and the private sector; and programs based on nationally recognised professional education qualifications sought to make police experience 'portable', enabling officers to gain experience of how other organisations work and transfer new skills to the police.

In recent years, undergraduate programs in police studies have been amongst the fastest growing in the UK, and latterly colleges have taken this a step further by inaugurating degree-level programs explicitly designed to train for a police career. These are designed in consultation with established providers of police training and government agencies responsible for coordinating police training and defining its curriculum. The negotiations have indicated society's continuing uncertainty over policing as a profession, with debate over whether the students should wear uniform while participating in classroom sessions, whether the curriculum should include parade ground drill and whether a central plank of the new approach to professional education, transferability of expertise, should see police students participate in instructional sessions alongside the other main occupational target of the programs, trainee nurses and midwives.

These contemporary concerns index differences to UK police training in the early 1970s. Even in cosmopolitan London, where Hendon Police College had a self-conscious role as the best-known and leading UK police recruit training establishment, the police college was much more akin to a military installation than a university campus. There was no question of probationers wearing anything other than uniform, drill was a significant part of daily routine, and instilling the outward signs of formal discipline was a preoccupation. Police-related elements of the curriculum were taught by uniformed police instructors, and although the role had emerged as a specialism and a long-term career for some incumbents, most served only for a spell before returning to 'the sharp end'.

A small number of civilian lecturers taught the academic elements of the curriculum. The idea was based on benign liberal principles of producing 'fully rounded' individuals for the police service. Topically, this meant subjects consistent with the secondary school curriculum and taught at the level at which school pupils were examined at age 16 ('O – Ordinary Level') and at age 18 ('A – Advanced Level'). Notwithstanding the fact that many recruits had left school at the earliest possible age (then 15), it was thought appropriate that they should engage with English, mathematics, modern languages, politics and the social sciences. They were permitted to enter for O and A Level exams, and if the qualifications were gained and the candidate wished to move on, the police rather impressively wished them well and did not require repayment of the wages and allowances received while at Hendon.

The civilian lecturers were accommodated in a rather bare staff room within a classroom block. They included several individuals who later became significant figures in police research, but the larger proportion were long-established community college lecturers more akin to schoolteachers than academics. Formally, we were employed by the local polytechnic, not the police, but had no contact with polytechnic staff. A sense of our real status is conveyed by the fact that at the time of interview the most emphatic point made to me was that I needed a haircut. Astonished to be offered the job, when asked as to what I could teach I replied that I could handle anything in which I had passed an examination. My schedule duly included music appreciation, mathematics and statistics, politics and English, as well as the sociology that had been the subject of the position announcement.

As well as training for the Met., Hendon trained recruits to the then Royal Ulster Constabulary, and several forces in northern England. There were very few ethnic minority recruits, and co-ed training of female recruits was an innovation, but regional differences made for some diversity. Indeed, recruits and staff had substantial communication problems with regional accents. Being the member of staff closest in age to the recruits, the only lecturer who routinely swore, having a US background, and a keen interest in contemporary music, it was perhaps easier for me to establish links with the recruits. From these I learned that many were as uncertain of their choice of career as I was about working for the police, that most could see no point in academic studies and were desperate to get on the street, and that while stereotypes and prejudices were freely expressed about minorities, it was accompanied by a cheerfully candid admission that the apparent prejudices had no basis in experience, those expressing them having had little contact with minority people.

My appointment board had made clear that the role of liberal education in the curriculum was to tackle prejudices and make recruits better at 'community relations' than their predecessors. I set about configuring the standard syllabus to highlight matters that addressed diversity, difference and prejudice. After leaving Hendon, a scandal occurred over racist views expressed in coursework for other police training lecturers (discussed in Coleman & Gorman, 1982). I had marked many such essays and had reason for not taking them at face value. These slender experiences led me to an interest in how the social sciences have understood police socialisation. Sociology's natural foil in that field has been psychology. Psychological accounts identified a self-selecting 'police personality' that gained reinforcement for its tenets from quasi-military discipline and conflictual encounters in early field training. Sociology was finding its way to something more subtle and dynamic, where career values were built in dialogue with experience. After taking my doctorate and a more permanent academic post, I was drawn to consider the relative influence of formal and informal agency in socialisation to the police occupation.

Sociology has elaborated a rich set of tools for conceptualising socialisation. The twin themes of socialisation are process and change. Chronology underpins the conceptualisation, from anticipatory socialisation to formal (classroom) and informal (on-the-job) socialisation and through to 'la deformation professionelle' and social closure. In case the conceptualisation seems unilinear there is the notion of 'career contingencies' (Becker, 1970) that prompt reflection and possible withdrawal, and to accommodate the fact that career progression is not necessarily unidirectional, there is the idea of horizontal mobility to match that of vertical mobility. These concepts, largely worked out in industrial and organisational sociology in the 1950s and 1960s, and associated with Chicago sociologists such as Everett Hughes (1958), well-equip sociology to understand occupational socialisation as a series of identity moves across a timeline. But the conceptual apparatus less well answers a question that preoccupies practitioners, their managers and those engaged in professional education and training. In essence, their concern is 'does all this training stick?' Moreover, if some of it does not 'stick', which agencies of socialisation are ineffective and what alternatives might be more effective?

Practitioner and policy concerns are naturally informed by the costs of training, but also by the need to respond to the public interest in securing effective and accountable professional practice. In the police context these are highly sensitive concerns, because of their fundamental relevance to the legitimacy of the police institution and the institution's keystone role underpinning and securing all other state institutions. In the context of the British police in the early 1970s, the specific concerns that police training had to satisfy were to produce officers better able to negotiate three points of tension potentially dividing the community and the police: increased racial tensions initially manifest in the Notting Hill disturbances of the late 1950s and that had by the early 1970s promoted racist political parties and a racialisation of mainstream political parties; the radicalisation of student politics largely via opposition to apartheid, US involvement in south-east Asia, and the rise of a 'counter-culture' amongst class fractions that customarily represented the future Establishment; and industrial militancy engendered by high unemployment, waning productivity, extensive unionisation, and the anachronistic nature of the country's traditional industrial base. Against these concerns, a belief in the curative power of a 'liberal education', particularly one applied to recruits who had largely joined the police out of an interest in action rather than intellectual labour, seemed quaint and over-optimistic.

Home Office and police management wanted to see better police/public relations and more effective resolution of the points of tension, they wanted a curriculum that focussed on such concerns, and they wanted officers to emerge with a skill-set that addressed such requirements. Research on British police training was sparse, and none of it much helped with this agenda. An evaluation research, experimentalist approach to assessing policy programs was little developed at the time, and absent in respect of police education. Indeed, the major historical debates about recruitment had come much earlier in the police service and had concerned the explicit preference to recruit as constables men who would obey orders and could cope with outdoors work in the British climate (Steedman, 1984), and at higher levels, an experiment with direct recruitment of the officer class, experience with which reinforced the bedrock belief in the importance of all police, high-flyers or not, starting with experience as a constable (Reiner, 1992).

Aware of the official concern to see police training more effectively serve the police/community relations agenda, but also of how police training as a process meshed with my interest in how people change as they practice occupations, I secured funding to conduct a study of socialisation to the police occupation. It would address the issue of identifying effective and less-effective socialisation agencies by comparing informal and formal socialisation, it would be a longitudinal study involving quarterly research interventions over a period of several years, it would also track the same cohorts of recruits as they negotiated training, probationary status and early service, and finally it would have a multiple-method research design combining quantitative and qualitative methods so it could secure both analytic range and depth. To test psychology's notion of a police personality, psychometric research instruments were included, and since US sociology offered some substantial and insightful studies of police training, notably that of Van Maanen (1982), the research instruments included items derived from US studies (John Van Maanen and Peter Manning served as advisors to the research).

The repeat applications at quarterly intervals of a survey questionnaire with attitudinal, occupational knowledge and socio-political items, combined with 10 percent subsample semi-structured interviews, over a 3-year period, enabled us to capture change in occupational perspectives and attribute these to given agencies of socialisation (such as first field training assignment, first solo patrol, etc.). We were also able to relate different accommodations to the role to gender, age at joining and previous occupational history. The intensive and extensive research design, and the logistics in tracking cohort members' negotiation of the various key stages, argued for a single research site. When I left Hendon, I maintained contact with the academic department's head, who I hoped would support research access. After yearlong negotiations my gatekeeper regretfully refused access; I was fortunate that an ex-student of my Ph.D supervisor had taken up command of a police training establishment in the English Midlands.

The broadest conclusion of the research, and no doubt news to nobody who worked in the system, was that formal agencies of socialisation had measurable early effects but that some movement was in a dispreferred (less tolerant) direction, although modestly outweighed by desired change; that informal agencies had increasing effect over time; and that much of what was imparted by formal agencies at an early stage was forgotten or atrophied from disuse (Fielding, 1988a). It was hardly a welcome message but it did provide a quite fine-grained picture (the broad trends mentioned vary by issue, target group, area of practice, and recruit demographics), and it also provided a set of instruments and measures that could be applied to specific initiatives, policies and training packages (some of which have been applied to training for uniformed service in occupations other than policing and in countries other than Britain; for example, in a recent study of fire service training in Sweden).

Academic, official (Home Office) and professional (staff association) research on police training subsequently expanded considerably, and began to provide sharper measures of training effects, still majoring on community relations (later 'human awareness') training. It is no satisfaction to say that the broad informal/formal and attrition effects noted in the original study were little modified by the later research. Indeed, in the most sophisticated studies, change in a dispreferred direction exceeded desired change (Bull & Horncastle, 1989). Such findings led to large changes in police training, with more emphasis on integrating field training and classroom training, greater focus on detailed examples from the field rather than general principles in classroom material, and more use of minority people serving as 'diversity trainers' in classroom sessions.

At a personal level, the research suggested to me that, if police/community relations were at the heart of effective policing, and the community was changing, it was necessary to document the practice of community policing in a substantial comparative study that could expose any contrasts between community and reactive modes of policing.

## POLICING AND SYSTEMS THEORY

My interest in researching community policing was facilitated by the climate following the urban riots of the early 1980s. It was acknowledged at policy level and amongst operational officers that change was necessary if the problematic police/community relations that directly triggered the riots were to be addressed. In four days prior to the Brixton riots, 943 people in the area, mostly black, were stopped by police using targetted and intensive stop and search powers under the tactlessly named 'Operation Swamp 81' (Bowling & Phillips, 2003). Gross disproportion in street stops between different ethnic groups was not the sole point of tension but encapsulated a wide experience of negative, sometimes hostile, relations between the minority ethnic community and the police. In the context of Britain's major cities, in which reside a diverse range of minority groups reflecting the country's colonial past, conflictual relations with the Afro-Caribbean community were but the most apparent amongst the groups whose relations with the police were problematic.

The riots impacted both on police and on public perceptions of the police. That such circumstances were best addressed by some form of community policing was already an orthodoxy, and the report of the Scarman Inquiry following the Brixton riots confirmed it (Scarman, 1982). Among others, Bowling and Foster (2002, p. 990) maintain that the ensuing emphasis on community policing was a direct response to the riots; '(d)eveloping closer contacts and reducing the gulf between police and public in these areas became a priority'. Community policing is the dominant response to police/public divisions in both the political and research spheres. Bayley and Shearing (1996, p. 604) see it as an essential prerequisite for policing by consent, especially in high crime areas, and the Patten Report saw community policing as 'the core function' of the reconstructed Police Service of Northern Ireland (Patten, 1999).

But community policing confronts many obstacles, including problems of definition, interpretation, implementation and evaluation. Indeed, community policing has proven particularly hard to achieve in just the high deprivation, high crime and social problem areas where it is thought to have most to contribute (Bowling & Foster, 2002). Community policing is nevertheless always in vogue, not least for its public appeal. There are a number of constructions of community policing within the police, policy and research worlds, but in the public's mind it stands chiefly for 'more bobbies on the beat', an enhanced level of patrol of the sort found to be rather ineffective by evaluation research based on systematic control designs and measures of crime rates with and without community policing (Sherman, 1992). Systematic research also finds that the role of senior police managers, line level officers and community residents, are all important to successful community policing, but that the commitment of all is hard to achieve and to maintain. There are organisational, operational and individual difficulties in delivering community policing. Frontline officer commitment and motivation is essential, and is reliant on managerial support (Lurigio & Skogan, 1994; Rosenbaum, 1994; Fielding, 1995), so community policing requires not only substantial organisational resources but sustained personal investment by individual officers. It can be knocked off course by failure in any of these factors, from the most 'micro' level of individual officer burn-out or tokenism through to the most 'macro' level of change in the external political environment, as Chicago's Alternative Policing Strategy ('CAPS') demonstrated at times of change in the city administration.

Chicago's CAPS program put major emphasis on the integration of city services – police, housing, social services and so on. It also emphasised involving residents in all aspects of community efforts against disorder and crime. As it developed, the policing element of the police/city services/civilian trio actually delivered least well, while there was a transformation of municipal services and real improvement in civilian involvement. The percentage of the public who thought police were doing a good job working with residents to solve problems rose from 39% to 59% during the first 5 years of the initiative. Satisfaction with crime prevention efforts rose from 45% to 60% between 1993 and 1999. The overall rating of how well police did their job rose from 36% to 50%. All this is perhaps the more remarkable because, in late 1999, the force had to completely re-think CAPS due to the innovation running into the ground, with officers reverting to traditional reactive policing while displaying the kind of lip service which is familiar to many who have attempted to bring about change in the police organisation (Chicago Community Policing Evaluation Consortium, 2000). In fact, the force nearly abandoned CAPS altogether. There is a message here about how positive impression-management on the back of a program largely supported by extraordinary civilian and non-police-agency effort can reflect well on a police force which was not latterly doing very much to earn its high satisfaction ratings.

There are arguments within political philosophy that suggest that the problems in achieving a closer police/public relation are not only practical but constitutional in origin. The police mandate derives from their status as an institution of government (Potts, 1982). In democratic societies, political-legal equality is the basis for personal liberty and a free society. Democracy is based on the capacity of citizens to engage in effective self-government, and bears a significant corollary:

> to the extent that government in general has been established as guardian of collective social interest, an implicit denial of the validity of the democratic principle has been made. All government officials may be tainted as enemies of democratic society to some extent. (*ibid.*, pp. 13–14)

The problem of democratic governance is to balance government's function as servant of the public with its function as coercer of the public. This challenge is acute for the police, who must constantly negotiate the space between the obligation to serve civil society as a whole by enforcing general norms and the need to serve individuals demanding mobilisation of the law in relation to their particular interests.

Community policing tries to modify policing's coercive dimension, but this dimension is fundamental and intrinsic to the political institution. *In extremis*, the state, as institutional expression of the general social interest, relies on the ability to coerce sub-groups of the population in order to secure their compliance and thus achieve civil order for many. Where community policing tasks police to lead community renewal and bring the community together despite its divisions, however mainstream the police construction of 'shared' values may be they necessarily represent a particular value set. Community policing inescapably challenges police apoliticality, and with it police claims to deliver their mandate in a way that is neutral between different interest groups.

The depth of the challenge represented by the problem of reconciling competing interests so as to advance the general interest is apparent by considering the distinction between 'community' and 'association' first advanced in the work of Tonnies (1955). Hillery (1955, p. 111) examined 94 different definitions of 'community', concluding that 'most ... are in basic agreement that community consists of persons in social interaction within a geographic area and having one or more additional ties'. Its essence is locality and communal sentiment (Rex, 1981, p. 52). In contrast, an association is a narrower entity, being a 'group organised for the pursuit of an interest or a group of interests in common' (*ibid.*). Both communities and associations can generate norms and social institutions. But communities and associations differ in their group dynamics, the calls they can make on their members, and in their degree of inclusiveness. Ever since the mid-nineteenth century, when Britain became the first nation to have more than half of its population living in cities, change in urban 'communities' has seen a transition in forms of affiliation from the generic and inclusive community to the particularistic and exclusive association. Contemporary urbanites are better understood as recognising and acting on the interests that *divide* them from others living in the same space. Associations cross physical boundaries (e.g., members of sports clubs) while the decline of communities bound by local values has been extensively documented. In Trojanowicz and Moore's (1988, p. 5) analysis, mass transit, mass communications and mass media have 'widened the rift between a sense of community based on geography and one based on a community of interest'. Yet it is on the basis of geographical communities that community policing targets its efforts, and it is on the basis of communities of interest that it seeks to engender the support of residents.

One response to such an analysis is for community policing to seek to capitalise on the lowest common denominator in order to stimulate a defined and restricted community of interest around the control of crime. Crime and social problems give police their best 'in' to create a mutual community of interest. If this is so, it is both in line with the broad police mandate and provides the police with a clear priority – to orientate their efforts in the community to gathering good (crime-relevant) information. This is the core of community policing's appeal within the community and the police.

This does not mean that the police can avoid their role appearing intrusive and sectarian within some social groups. Police overtures are more likely to register with some (home owners, business interests, the elderly) than with others. Geo-local ties are of declining importance for the generality of the population, but vary in strength by socio-economic and demographic factors, being relatively strong for older people, the poor and disadvantaged, and those with mobility problems. The police cannot embody 'the face of the community' unless they wish to reflect values including those of the criminal and the marginalised. Rather than claiming to reflect the whole community, the police need to determine at what threshold higher than at present they will use their discretion to ignore infractions regarded as tolerable by the various local groups with which they wish to engage and to act on the matters that concern such groups. The claim to police communities equitably is a strong tenet of police ideology, but only when they concede that civil order will vary by locale can community policing be distinguished from any other kind of policing. Community policing does not have to pretend to a universal appeal to reach those it has neglected in the past. With their transient population, fragmentation and physical deterioration, apathy is a greater problem in marginal areas than committed criminal attitudes or political disaffiliation, and the apathetic are prime amongst the groups whose support community police must secure. Despite all the obstacles, there is substantial evidence that the public gains much reassurance from community policing, and tantalising if more debatable evidence that the public is more inclined to provide police with crime-relevant information under community policing conditions (Chicago Community Policing Evaluation Consortium, 1997).

To understand the circumstances of community policing, empirical investigations need to measure the effects of sustained community policing initiatives in detail, show enough variation among case studies to identify factors related to effectiveness, and attend to the place of community policing at the relevant strata of the police organisation. Before the Brixton riots there already existed research testifying to the limited, non-existent or even counter-productive impact of community policing. Nevertheless, in the post-Scarman climate, a number of urban police forces were keen to revitalise community policing, particularly the Met., and the Police Foundation, an independent charity positioned between the police and the research community, drew together a program of research. The project I led employed the sustained observational methodology I had used previously, in a longitudinal design also involving interviews repeated over time with community policing practitioners and their managers.

The project's research design generated quantifiable information as well as qualitative data to illustrate community policing practice. In particular, we measured the relative time investment of community police and regular officers in different kinds of interventions. We prepared both qualitative field notes and quantitative observation forms, which enabled us to compare the working style of community officers and regular officers, and to assess whether citizens of different ethnicity, status or gender were dealt with differently. The forms were partly based on the observational schedules devised by Black and Reiss (1967) in their classic study of police/citizen encounters (a study itself motivated by widespread US race riots), and the version that we developed has lately informed design of forms used by the Home Office in monitoring on-street stops following the Macpherson Inquiry into the racist murder of the black teenager Stephen Lawrence. In our community policing study, we decided that each fieldworker should be attached to one group of officers throughout the fieldwork. I spent a year on fieldwork, and got to know 'my' officers quite well, not just on patrol but also in the canteen and after-hours. The other members of the research team spent 2 years in the field, achieving a detailed knowledge of the policing issues affecting the locale, the nature of the community and the differing approaches to their work of community police and regular officers.

Although organisational commitment and a clear focus on crime control can improve the effectiveness of community police, the necessary conditions demand much of the organisation. In an initiative operating in one of our research sites, community constables had their own inspector, vehicles and station, and determined for themselves their response to demands for service, the priority given to these demands being balanced against those arising from beat patrol and from meeting longer-term demands such as motivating Neighbourhood Watch coordinators and managing relationships with local informants. The organisational environment facilitated identification with a locale and sustained relationships with its members based on reciprocity of interest. But when the organisational environment changed the initiative withered (Fielding, 1995).

When we came to publish our findings, highlighting this initiative, along with evidence that the community policing officers invested more time and other resources in dealing with incidents than did their counterparts working in regular reactive mode (Fielding, Kemp, & Norris, 1989), other researchers suggested the work was unrepresentative. Our critics felt that as we had only studied three sites we could not show for certain that community policing was any better than regular reactive-mode policing. However, our purpose was not to say whether community policing was a 'success' but to document how it was done. We were certainly able to judge at a micro-sociological level the techniques that community officers used and the effects of these, and the comparisons we were able to make between different officers' working practices provided examples of approaches to interventions that were more, and less, effective within the confines of the incident. These were not highly sophisticated techniques or ones based on personal qualities, so we judged them to be transferable and a basis for illustrative examples that would be useful input to training, and they were subsequently incorporated into new recruit training materials that tried to bring more of a flavour of on-street practice into formal classroom sessions. The policymakers, police trainers and police forces that drew on our findings were not themselves interested in whether our analysis was 'representative' but in our identification of techniques and factors that affected practice in the fieldwork sites. A lone study seldom provides the complete answer to a research issue, and it is important both for researchers to be clear on what analytic claims their research design can support and for others to assess research on its own terms.

The research highlighted what organisational factors supported or obstructed community policing, and suggested that troubles in the police/community relation are not the only problems to be negotiated. From an intellectual biography perspective, the experience of the research, and the research community's response to it, gave rise to a recognition that a program-specific study had confines that artificially bounded the inquiry. The initiatives we had studied did not exist in isolation but were part of a policing system. The innovation we documented at one site depended on organisational factors and collapsed when it could not negotiate internal problems. A prominent problem was the status of community policing amongst police, who reserve a variety of pejorative terms for community officers, an indicative one being 'hobby bobbies'. Another problem of community policing is that, even where regular officers subscribe to it, community policing is often added onto their existing duties, and community police sections are the first to be plundered when there is pressure on police establishments. In other words, there are acknowledged problems of community policing that relate both to process and to organisation. Social science understands the interaction of dynamic process variables and variables relating to organisational form and function by employing a distinction between 'action and structure', and a spatial metaphor based on micro or macro 'levels' or dimensions of large organisations (Fielding, 1988b).

While contemporary social theory employs a bipolar distinction between 'structure' and 'action', it sees these elements as intertwined, a formulation in which Giddens' structuration theory (1976, 1991) is prominent. A classic application to policing of such a conceptualisation was Grimshaw and Jefferson's (1987) account of frontline patrol, in which the structural analysis used to understand the organisational placing of *community* police was augmented by a typology of cultural adaptations to *routine* policing, so that the (problematic) way that community policing was delivered was made explicable by the mismatch between officers' accustomed working practices and the new emphasis on community responsiveness without accompanying change in shift systems. Grimshaw and Jefferson's combination of structural theory with critical cultural analysis (following Gramsci, Althusser & Foucault) has proven an enduring heuristic, represented more recently in police research such as the work of Choongh (1998).

What ages less well is the analysis of the 'meta level' that accounts for the outcome of the processes articulating action and structure. Latterly, theorisation of the relationship between 'micro' and 'macro' in wider social theory has rendered accounts of the 'meta level' drawing variously on neo-Parsonian functionalism, systems theory, post-modern cultural theory, and structuration theory. Moving beyond the dualities of action/structure and micro/macro calls on analysis at a level 'above' that of structural and cultural concerns, which would account for their articulation in a way that, in the context of community policing, might better capture the wider influences determining the relationship of police and communities. One rendering of such a synthetic account would be by having culture play a mediating role between the action level, which draws on microsociological accounts of interactions, and the structural level, which uses macrosociological data to capture the organisational and community context of interactions. Culture mediates understandings of community policing emergent from patterns in the interactions of community police with the public. Such understandings also provide cultural resources informing bargaining for material resources within the organisation. The distribution of organisational resources is a structural matter, necessarily involving higher echelons of the police and policy-making hierarchy.

Interaction, culture and structure provide the framework of a synthetic account that can model the course of given initiatives. For Giddens, every interaction is also 'a *moral* and a *power* relation' (Giddens, 1976, p. 118). Empirically, this is apparent in the different resources individuals bring to their interactions. Foucault also saw power as omnipresent in 'a never-ending network of microstructures' (Walton, 1998, p. 9). Importantly, neither structure (legitimate force) nor action (interactional skills) is inherently pre-eminent; which element prevails, and in which precise combination with the other element, is an empirical matter varying between initiatives, implementations and interactions.

The value of Giddens' conceptualisation is that it departs from descriptive analysis of interactional relations, drawing on this to address 'systems of generative rules and resources'. In structuration theory, whenever we consider an account based on individual actions we inevitably invoke the structural level, because the theory sees the individual as both an agent producing action, and as the subject of action by others. It 'attempt[s] to provide the conceptual means of analysing the often delicate and subtle interlacings of reflexively organized action and institutional constraint' (Giddens, 1991, p. 204). This is valuable, but 'structuration' is not the only approach to developing an 'agency–structure' relation that can address empirically documented organisational processes such as the implementation and evaluation of a community policing program. Archer (1982) has developed an alternative conceptualisation based on a process of 'morphogenesis'. Her account differs from structuration in having a tangible end product, structural elaboration, while Giddens' process manifests simply as a 'visible pattern'. Insisting on simultaneity in the *duality* of structure, so that 'social structures are both constituted by human agency, and yet at the same time are the very *medium* of their constitution', obstructs empirical operationalisation. In contrast to Giddens, Archer sees the progressively elaborated structure as acquiring properties irreducible to the recurrent social practices from which they are derived.

Systems theory assumes a discontinuity between initial interactions and their product. All subsequent interaction will differ from prior action because it is informed by the structural results of the prior action. This introduces chronology to the picture, whereas Giddens rests with 'instantiation', an idea that makes it impossible to disentangle the respective and changing effects of structure and action.

> (T)he morphogenetic perspective is not only dualistic but sequential, dealing in endless cycles of structural conditioning/social interaction/structural elaboration – thus unravelling the dialectical interplay between structure and action. "Structuration", by contrast, treats the ligatures binding structure, practice and system as indissoluble, hence the necessity of *duality*. (Archer, 1982, p. 458)

This move contributes another dimension particularly significant in understanding innovations like community policing. Morphogenesis moderates Giddens' Parsonian over-emphasis on the orderly reproduction of practices, instead placing in the foreground those points of friction and deviance which make more apparent the 'flow' of power (Sparks, Bottoms, & Hay,

1996). The morphogenetic conceptualisation is more susceptible to operationalisation and empirical testing. Seeing individual action, cultural beliefs and structural considerations, in recursive relation and temporally elaborated, as all contributing to the effects of innovative police programs, is more amenable to systematic modelling than the somewhat mysterious concept of instantiation.

A research effort to understand the obstacles affecting a community policing initiative has to track the cumulative character of a series of interventions done under the aegis of the initiative. A conventional approach is to divide the program into recurrent kinds of intervention and represent given types of intervention by case studies, while acknowledging any distinctive incidents that contradict the general cases. Large-scale policing initiatives are affected by institutional relations at the level of structure, raising such considerations as how obstructive or facilitative are the relations of the police institution with other social institutions; how trade-offs between investment in this and competing initiatives are resolved, and so on. To capture at macro-level these kinds of consideration, a model would require empirically operationalisable components such as (i) the formal constitutional mandate of police; (ii) the law regulating policing; (iii) administrative regulations; (iv) the organisational role and status of community policing; (v) working practices in local police culture relating to community policing; (vi) managerial and supervisory policies. The bridge to process factors, the mezzo level, would include: (vii) numbers of officers available; (viii) available equipment and facilities; (ix) type of shift system; (x) availability of overtime payments, allowances and bonuses in kind; (xi) the performance measurement and promotion system. Micro factors would draw on case studies of types of demand regularly met by community policing under the initiative and showing, in relation to each principal form; (xii) officer capacities and motivation; (xiii) officer specialist knowledge; (xiv) degree of back-up and teamwork; (xv) spatio-temporal dimension of incidents (where on beat, when on shift); (xvi) presenting problems of the principal forms of incident; (xvii) citizen groups dealt with; (xviii) character of interaction during incidents; (xix) citizen-perceived outcomes; (xx) officer-perceived outcomes; (xxi) paperwork account of incidents; and (xxii) the susceptibility of the principal types of incident to actions by regular officers.

The aim of a model such as that outlined here is to provide a source of factors that can help us explain the impact of the program, informed by research assessing the relative importance of each factor. It can be used to derive an initial theory of program functioning. The theory also has to accommodate interaction between factors, building a picture of factors of greater or lesser significance. The framework of factors pursues the 'generative mechanism of rules and resources' that Giddens and Archer both use to capture the articulation of action and structure. The interplay of rules and resources across the 'level'-based framework of factors is the mechanism that generates – and therefore explains – actions. An empirically grounded theory is progressively constructed using the factors and what is known about them and their interaction, with case study and other sources of empirical information enabling us to assess which factors should be emphasised and which can be discounted.

It was noted that Archer's conceptualisation better accommodates the chronological dimension that corrects against an overly static and once-and-for-all picture of program impact. Temporality is critical because the meaning of programs like community policing changes as a result of implementation. The morphogenetic theory conceives this temporal dimension as an 'endless cycle' of structural conditioning, followed by social interaction, followed by structural elaboration. Once we have identified selected factors as important, they are used to inform the initial structural conditioning of the community-policing program. Case study and other data, and knowledge from previous research, support an initial estimate that these are the critical factors in the working of the new program. But we need to consider how we can be certain that observed changes relate to these rather than other factors. In research, we must often reason from the parts we know to the whole, 'to create an image of the entire organisation or process, based on the parts we have been able to uncover' (Becker, 1992), employing the mode of reasoning Peirce (1958) styled 'abduction'. Becker suggests questions like: 'what kind of an organisation could accommodate a part like this? ... What would the whole story have to be for this step to occur as we have seen it occur?' (Becker, 1992, p. 213). Like the theoretical practice of critical realism (Harre, 1970; Pawson & Tilley, 1997), which engages in iterative cycles of testing to determine whether the empirically manifest signs of inferred social structures account for patterns of observed action, alternative factors are tested that may have caused observed events, drawing on accounts of causal mechanisms in other cases. This approach seeks to understand policing as a system, and recognises a central problematic of community policing, that change in one part of a system has effects on other parts to which it is only indirectly connected.

Set against the predominant style of service delivery based on reactive, emergency-response interventions, community policing poses the police with major dilemmas. The police must reconsider instinctive modes of operational response to local demands, must revalue the kinds of information and other returns they get from low-level public contact, and reassess how they relate to elements of the community with whom past contacts have been marked by friction. To implement community policing requires rethinking both the police and the community role in crime prevention, restructuring command and control procedures and reward and supervisory systems, and reevaluating currently unmeasured police outputs (Fielding & Innes, 2006). In its relatively brief history, police research has made a great virtue of empirically grounded, field-based understandings of policework. It has fared less well in drawing upon these to construct a theory of policing with explanatory and predictive power. The value of a more sophisticated theory of police innovations employed in tandem with systematic and comprehensive empirical information is that it identifies the system-level interactions between factors that make for or obstruct effective program functioning.

## BEING TOLD BY THE STORY

The case of theorizing community policing suggests that the bifurcation many see between an adequately conceptualised theoretical understanding of problems of deviance and social order, and the pragmatic, problem-solving approach of 'administrative criminology', overdraws the picture. Like the field of police research itself, the conceptualisation derived from systems theory advances some way from an initial concern with occupational culture, whose principal heuristic is the typology of adaptations to the police role, a relatively static and shallow conceptualisation that implies that role incumbents of a given type will perform policework consistently according to the values associated with that type. Instead, a more sophisticated conceptualisation acknowledges that officer types are the beginning, not the end of analysis.

Identity work is an important corollary to playing any organisational or occupational role, but whatever one's construction of a working role by reference to one's self-identity, roles are played in a complex system of rules and relations. Identity work is important but it is a concern intrinsically tied to the early stage of engagement with the organisational object of study. As we become more familiar with the empirical field we encounter factors affecting the course of decisions and organisationally embedded actions other than those associated with the capacities and interests of individual organisational actors or groups of actors sharing the same adaptation to organisational life.

In the UK, criticisms of the move to an increasingly 'administrative criminology' have engendered heated debate (Garland, 2002; Walters,

2003). Stimulated by social democratic New Labour's enthusiasm for 'evidence-based policy', there has been an increasing incorporation of academic researchers into government research (and a trail of government researchers taking senior academic appointments), and there is a current move by academics particularly closely involved with the criminal justice system to replace 'criminology' with a 'crime science' explicitly oriented to providing government with tools to 'solve' crime problems and even specific criminal cases. The offstage elements of the research story are particularly unlikely to emerge in the context of such work but are no less important. Indeed, informal contacts suggest that both government researchers leaving for academe, and those going the other way, are quite preoccupied with the choices they have made, and their impact on intellectual biographies. It is worth considering whether more candour amongst researchers about their purposes and interests might provide a bridge between 'administrative criminology' and the more conceptual approaches.

In a sceptical analysis of the treatment of crime stories by the mass media, Rock and McIntosh (1974) coined the term 'eternal recurrence' to characterise the cyclical nature of media panics about crime. The notion of eternal recurrence helps in understanding intellectual biographies as well as how the media treat crime and deviance. In topically related work, researchers may tell the same story again and again, but the telling changes us, and we come to realise how our analyses have been about understanding ourselves.

# REFERENCES

Archer, M. (1982). Morphogenesis versus structuration: On combining structure and action. *British Journal of Sociology, 33*(4), 455–483.

Bayley, D., & Shearing, C. (1996). The future of policing. *Law and Society Review, 30*(3), 586–606.

Becker, H. (1970). *Sociological work*. London: Allen Lane.

Becker, H. (1992). Cases, causes, conjunctures, stories, imagery. In: C. Ragin & H. Becker (Eds), *What is a case? Exploring the foundations of social inquiry* (pp. 205–216). Cambridge: Cambridge University Press.

Black, D., & Reiss, A. (1967). Patterns of behaviour in police and citizen transactions. In: US President's Commission on Law Enforcement and the Administration of Justice (Eds), *Studies in crime and law enforcement in major metropolitan areas* (pp. 4–240). Washington, DC: USGPO.

Bowling, B., & Foster, J. (2002). Policing and the police. In: M. Maguire, R. Morgan & R. Reiner (Eds), *The Oxford handbook of criminology, third edition* (pp. 980–1035). Oxford: Clarendon.

Bowling, B., & Phillips, C. (2003). Policing ethnic minority communities. In: T. Newburn (Ed.), *Handbook of policing* (pp. 287–324). Cullompton: Willan.

Bull, R., & Horncastle, P. (1989). An evaluation of HAT. In: R. Morgan & D. Smith (Eds), *Coming to terms with policing* (pp. 97–117). London: Routledge.

Chicago Community Policing Evaluation Consortium. (1997). *Measuring what matters: Crime, disorder and fear.* Chicago, IL: Northwestern University.

Chicago Community Policing Evaluation Consortium. (2000). *CAPS citywide resident survey documentation.* Chicago, IL: Northwestern University.

Choongh, S. (1998). *Policing as social discipline.* Oxford: Clarendon.

Coleman, A., & Gorman, P. (1982). Conservatism, dogmatism and authoritarianism in British police officers. *Sociology, 16,* 1–11.

Fielding, N. (1988a). *Joining forces.* London: Tavistock.

Fielding, N. (Ed.) (1988b). *Actions and structure.* London: Sage.

Fielding, N. (1990). Mediating the message: The co-production of field research. *American Behavioral Scientist, 33*(5), 608–620.

Fielding, N. (1992). Affinity and hostility in research on sensitive topics. In: C. Renzetti & R. M. Lee (Eds), *Researching sensitive topics* (pp. 146–159). London: Sage.

Fielding, N. (1995). *Community policing.* Oxford: Clarendon.

Fielding, N., & Innes, M. (2006) Reassurance policing, community policing, and measuring police performance. *Policing and Society.* Forthcoming.

Fielding, N., Kemp, C., & Norris, C. (1989). Constraints on the practice of community policing. In: R. Morgan & D. Smith (Eds), *Coming to terms with policing* (pp. 49–63). London: Routledge.

Freeman, D. (1998). *The fateful hoaxing of Margaret Mead.* Boulder, CO: Westview.

Garland, D. (2002). Of crimes and criminals: The development of criminology in Britain. In: M. Maguire, R. Morgan & R. Reiner (Eds), *The Oxford handbook of criminology, third edition* (pp. 7–50). Oxford: Oxford University Press.

Giddens, A. (1976). *New rules of sociological method.* London: Hutchinson.

Giddens, A. (1991). *Modernity and self-identity.* Cambridge: Polity Press.

Grimshaw, R., & Jefferson, T. (1987). *Interpreting policework.* London: Allen and Unwin.

Harre, R. (1970). *The principles of scientific thinking.* London: Macmillan.

Hillery, G. (1955). Definitions of community: Areas of agreement. *Rural Sociology, 20*(4), 95–115.

Home Office. (1993). *Inquiry into police responsibilities and rewards: Report, Cm. 2280.* London: HMSO.

Hughes, E. C. (1958). *Men and their work.* Glencoe, IL: Free Press.

Lurigio, A., & Skogan, W. (1994). Winning the hearts and minds of police officers: An assessment of staff perceptions of community policing in Chicago. *Crime and Delinquency, 40,* 315–330.

Morgan, R. (2000). The politics of criminological research. In: R. King & E. Wincup (Eds), *Doing research on crime and justice* (pp. 25–48). Oxford: Oxford University Press.

Patten, C. (1999). *A new beginning: Policing in Northern Ireland.* London: HMSO.

Pawson, R., & Tilley, N. (1997). *Realistic evaluation.* London: Sage.

Peirce, C. S. (1958). *Collected papers.* Cambridge, MA: Harvard University Press.

Potts, L. (1982). The limits of police community relations programs. *Police Studies, 5*(2), 10–20.

Reiner, R. (1992). *Chief constables: Bobbies, bosses or bureaucrats?* Oxford: Oxford University Press.

Rex, J. (1981). *Social conflict.* London: Longman.

Rock, P., & McIntosh, M. (1974). *Deviance and control.* London: Tavistock.

Rosenbaum, D. (1994). Impact of community policing on police personnel. *Crime and Delinquency, 40*(3), 331–358.

Scarman, L. (1982). *The Brixton disorders, 1981.* Harmondsworth: Penguin.

Sherman, L. (1992). Attacking crime: Police and crime control. In: M. Tonry & N. Morris (Eds), *Modern policing* (pp. 159–230). Chicago, IL: University of Chicago Press.

Sparks, R., Bottoms, A., & Hay, W. (1996). *Prisons and the problem of order.* Oxford: Oxford University Press.

Steedman, C. (1984). *Policing the Victorian community.* London: Routledge & Kegan Paul.

Tonnies, F. (1955). *Community and association.* London: Routledge.

Trojanowicz, R., & Moore, M. (1988). *The meaning of community in community policing.* East Lansing: Michigan State University.

Van Maanen, J. (1982). Fieldwork on the beat. In: J. Van Maanen, J. Dabbs & R. Faulkner (Eds), *Varieties of qualitative research* (pp. 103–151). London: Sage.

Walters, R. (2003). *Deviant knowledge: Criminology, politics and policy.* Devon: Willan Publishing.

Walton, P. (1998). Big science: Dystopia and utopia – establishment and new criminology revisited. In: P. Walton & J. Young (Eds), *The new criminology revisited* (pp. 1–13). Basingstoke: Macmillan.

Wolcott, H. (1990). *Writing up qualitative research.* Beverly Hills, CA: Sage.

Young, J. (1997). Left realist criminology. In: M. Maguire, R. Morgan & R. Reiner (Eds), *The Oxford handbook of criminology, first edition* (pp. 473–498). Oxford: Oxford University Press.

# SOCIOLOGICAL THEORY IN THE STUDY OF SENTENCING: LIGHTHOUSE FOR A TRAVELER BETWEEN CONTINENTS

Joachim J. Savelsberg

## ABSTRACT

*Basic sociological concepts, specifically Max Weber's ideal types of law, prove most beneficial in the empirical research on sentencing and sentencing guidelines. The history of this research, particularly the work by Dixon, Ulmer, & Kramer, and Engen & Steen, demonstrates that such use has greatly contributed to our understanding of sentencing guidelines and helped us predict their effects. It has also shown how research can feed back into Weberian thought and help refine basic sociological categories, especially by considering the organizational and ecological contexts of legal decision making. Autobiographical notes suggest the benefits of general sociological concepts for an outsider and, possibly, the outsider's benefit for insiders. This chapter is thus about the mutual benefits of sociological theory and criminological and criminal justice research.*

Sociological Theory and Criminological Research: Views from Europe and the United States
Sociology of Crime, Law and Deviance, Volume 7, 183–202
Copyright © 2006 by Elsevier Ltd.
All rights of reproduction in any form reserved
ISSN: 1521-6136/doi:10.1016/S1521-6136(06)07009-6

# INTRODUCTION: ON AIRPLANES AND
# THEORETICAL CONCEPTS

Consider the experience of an outsider – a common position in an era of airplanes and international exchange programs. While outsiders face challenges when seeking to advance knowledge, these challenges turn into benefits when we use theoretical concepts to approach unknown worlds. What appears strange initially turns out to be part of the same species of social phenomena we observed in the world we left behind. Or, when it differs, it often does so along theoretical dimensions we used to describe things back home. In addition, what we learned on distant continents may help us, and possibly those we visit, understand their world. Such are the advantages of strangers (Simmel, 1971 [1908]), especially if they are equipped with theoretical tools.

Specifically, this is a story about how sociological concepts helped me understand the American world of sentencing policies of the 1980s and beyond. Just having completed studies on white-collar crime legislation (Savelsberg & Brühl, 1988; Savelsberg with Brühl, 1994) and on regional sentencing disparities in my native Germany (Pfeiffer & Savelsberg, 1989), I began a 1987–1988 John F. Kennedy Memorial Fellowship at Harvard University to conduct research on the U.S. sentencing guidelines.

The use of Max Weber's ideal types of law had proven to be most useful in the earlier studies. Clearly, it seemed to me, sentencing guidelines too could be understood through the application of Max Weber's ideal types of law and the tensions inherent in each of the forms of law they characterize. I used the academic year to read up on the subject and to understand the promulgation process in Washington, interviewing many of the central players and immersing myself in the reading of documents. The result was a theoretical argument, embedded in an in-depth case study, on the chances of sentencing guidelines to achieve their declared goals and on the risks of unintended and even counterproductive consequences. First presented at conferences between 1988 and 1990 (e.g., Savelsberg, 1990), the main argument was published in 1992 in the *American Journal of Sociology*, entitled "Law that Does Not Fit Society: Sentencing Guidelines as a Neoclassical Reaction to Dilemmas of Substantivized Law" (Savelsberg, 1992).

The argument developed in that article served a number of subsequent empirical hypotheses-testing studies as a reference point. Here, I first summarize the general idea. I then review empirical findings of three studies that made most explicit use of the Weberian concepts to examine consequences of sentencing guidelines (Dixon, 1995; Ulmer & Kramer, 1996; Ulmer, 1997;

Engen & Steen, 2000). I finally draw conclusions on the insights these studies yield with regard to the hypotheses developed in my original article, and on the usefulness of Weberian ideal types in criminological and criminal justice research generally.[1]

## SENTENCING GUIDELINES: WHAT HAS MAX WEBER GOT TO DO WITH THEM?

The idea of applying Weber's ideal types to the world of law making and sentencing may seem strange to those who misunderstand Weber to argue that formal rationality of law, a focus on procedure and legal criteria at the expense of extra-legal substantive concerns (e.g., ethical, political, economic), is a precise depiction of the modern world. Shortly before diving into the sentencing guideline project, our study of German white-collar crime legislation had shown that deliberations are not at all limited to internal legal criteria (Savelsberg & Brühl, 1988; Savelsberg with Brühl, 1994). Consequences of a criminalization of bid rigging for the well-being of the economy and the unemployment rate in the construction industry, for example, were among the chief concerns raised by legislators on the judicial committee of the *Bundestag*, the lower house of the German legislature. Such findings are neither limited to the legislative branch of government nor to Germany. Mann, Wheeler, and Sarat (1980) find that federal judges in the United States are prone to using extra legal considerations, such as the well-being of dependents, when they ponder the sentencing of high-status offenders. Hagan and Parker (1985) show for Canada that capital-owning offenders are more likely to be channeled through institutions of administrative law, whereas similar non-capital owners (managers and lower level workers alike) are processed through criminal courts. The secure influx of capital to Canada is of crucial concern in this case. Also in other areas of law, such as abortion law, extra legal concerns frequently take center stage (Deflem, 1998).

An appropriate reading of Weber's (1978) arguments and a consideration of the history of sentencing law in the United States suggest the usefulness of his ideas about the central role of formal rational law in modern societies while acknowledging the challenges such law faces. I can be brief on summarizing Weber's well-known ideal types of law, fine presentations of which are now available to students at different levels (e.g., Marsh, 2000; Sutton, 2001, pp. 114–128). Weber uses two dimensions to construct his typology. The first is the rational–irrational dimension. Law is rational, following

Kronman's (1983) interpretation of Weber's writings, the more four conditions apply: the means of settling disputes are defined by rules; rules must form a logically clear, internally consistent, and gapless system; legal analysis depends on the abstract interpretation of meaning; and finally, means used for making legal decisions must be controlled by the intellect. Regarding the second dimension, law is formal when decisions are made with regard to legal principles alone; it is substantive when legal decision making is based on or affected by extra legal criteria such as political, religious, or ethical considerations.

These two dimensions form the famous set of four ideal types. First, formally irrational law is based on strict formal proscriptions, but does not involve intellect at all. Oracles are an example. Second, substantively irrational law invokes decision making that is oriented toward ethical or political criteria, drawn from the extra legal sphere, and applied in an ad hoc fashion. Third, substantive rational law is based on extra legal (often religious) standards that are organized in a coherent system of norms. Finally, formal rational law is oriented toward legal procedure. It refrains from any reference to extra legal, political, religious, or ethical standards, and it involves a logical and systematically integrated system of rules. Formal rationality is primarily institutionalized through the separation of judicial powers from those of the legislative and executive branches of government (Unger, 1976). Only so can the autonomy of law be secured and political, ethical, and religious motives kept at bay.

Ewing (1987) introduces an important, but difficult and often overlooked distinction that somewhat complicates Weber's typology. She shows that formal rationality involves two distinct but related phenomena. First, logically formal rationality refers to the generalization and systematization of legal subject matter so that it constitutes a deductive, logical, and gapless system of rules. This is a feature of civil law countries. Second, sociologically formal rationalization of formal justice signals the rational legal state emphasizing calculable enforcement of guaranteed rights. Here the state is seen as non-interventionist, simply providing a basis for social and economic exchanges among formally equal and free individuals. This may be a characteristic of common law and of civil law countries.

The temporal order in which these four types of law emerge has been an issue of considerable debate. Some argue that Weber had a quasi-evolutionary model in mind, where formally irrational law is followed by substantively irrational forms, then by substantively rational ones, finally leading up to formal rational law. This interpretation is in line with Weber's "iron cage" (really "steel-hard casing") prophecy (Weber, 2002 [1904–1905],

p. 123) and with the concluding sentences of his Sociology of Law (Weber, 1978, p. 895). Others object to this interpretation of a streamlined evolutionary process. They support their position with a number of strong arguments. First, Weber argued that the rationalization he described was limited to the occidental world. Also, like all major social changes, it was the outcome of the coincidence of a set of historic conditions. The latter include the rise of capitalism and, more importantly, modern state building, secularization, and the specialization of legal thought and training in universities. Second, in line with his historicist method, Weber always saw the potential for contradictions, instabilities, opposition, and reversals. Consider his note on opponents of formal rationality in law:

> In the modern world of law, legal clients often desire "to eliminate the formalities of normal legal procedure for the sake of a settlement that would be both expeditious and better adapted to the concrete case" (Weber, 1978, p. 882). Those concerned with social justice pose "new demands for a 'social law' to be based on such emotionally colored postulates as 'justice' and 'human dignity'" (Weber, 1978, p. 886). Finally, lawyers pursue professional interests and thus reject a kind of formal rationality under which they would be reduced to "a slot machine into which one just drops the facts (plus the fee) in order to have it spew out the decision (plus the opinion)" (Weber, 1978, p. 886).

Clearly, a formal rational order cannot be considered stable in light of opposition by legal clients, social justice proponents, and the practitioners of law alike. The story is further complicated as legal decisions, such as sentencing decisions, cannot be understood in isolation but only as part of a web of decision making.

The history of sentencing law reflects both the rise of formal rational elements in criminal law and the challenges it faced, beginning in the later part of the 19th century, when important substantive elements were introduced. It also entails the reaction to this process of substantivation, beginning in the late 1960s in the United States, a reaction that resulted in new legal forms taking the shape of sentencing guidelines among others. A very brief review must suffice.

While legal trends and forces are always ambiguous, the birth of the United States was clearly accompanied by ideas that are congenial with formal rational law, in line with the enlightenment spirit of the time that carried the American as well as the French revolutions, and revolutionary attempts all across Europe a good half century later. The Declaration of Independence and the Constitution stress, after all, the idea of inalienable rights of individuals. They perceive individuals as enlightened, rational actors, capable of engaging in free exchange, actors who ought to be unhampered by interventions of the state. The declared purpose was, in fact, the neutralization of the kind of state that had imposed, for centuries, its religious and political standards on increasingly reluctant legal subjects. This was a democratic revolution that sought to abolish an order where group membership trumped individual rights, to replace it by one in which individual rights would be sacred. In criminal law, only two principles of penal philosophy are congenial with this model of social organization: retribution and deterrence. Guilt matters and deterrence is possible where individuals are perceived as insightful, autonomous, intelligent, and rational. Also, enlightened individuals would obviously respond to the types of legal decision making that are clearly constrained by legal rules such as determinate sentencing principles.

Yet, the enlightenment spirit soon encountered limits, expressed by ills of the new democratic and capitalist times such as poverty, unemployment, labor exploitation, homelessness, and neglect of children. These limits were articulated, on the political front, by labor movements and their representatives in the political system. In intellectual life they were expressed by new intellectual currents, out of which new disciplines would be born. These disciplines included sociology with its focus on the social embeddedness of the individual and its challenge of the fictions of autonomy, rationality, and equality (Hamilton & Sutton, 1989). No wonder that the vision of rational and free actors was replaced, or at least supplemented, by a view of individuals immersed in and profoundly affected by the social and economic conditions under which they live. In the area of penal law and its philosophies, this insight would call for indeterminate types of decision making, flexible enough to allow for the adaptation of legal decisions to individual social circumstances. Such decision making would consider deviation from norms as the product of adverse circumstances and faulty socialization, factors that could be reversed through rehabilitation or prevented through social reform. It is no wonder then that, by 1922, 37 out of (then) 48 U.S. states had passed indeterminate sentence laws and 44 states had created parole boards. In addition, for those most malleable members of society, juvenile justice systems had been created where the state claimed to take the role of parents (*parens patriae*) to bring young delinquents back onto the path of righteousness, even at the expense of formal rules and legal safeguards. Clearly, substantive concerns with desired outcomes were winning the upper hand over formal rationality with its focus on procedural purity.

The celebrated resort to reason and substantive outcomes came with a price tag, of course. Flexibility tends to be accompanied by disparities in decision outcomes. In the 1960s, for example, a growing body of research began to identify sentencing disparities. Also, a flexible system could be used for repressive purposes. Decisions based on legal criteria alone allow for legal appeals. But decisions based on judgments of professional experts such as psychologists, psychiatrists, and social workers open the gates to a Foucauldian system of professional expert control from which there is little escape. The call for determinacy in judicial decision making could be heard again by the late 1960s. It intensified during the 1970s and 1980s. This call was, at times, brought forth by groups and activists with civil libertarian agendas (American Friends Service Committee, 1971; von Hirsch, 1976), at other times by those who paired the idea of determinacy with demands for more severe penalties (Wilson, 1975). The movement stretched all the way to the juvenile justice system, aiming at the "recriminalization of delinquency" (see Singer, 1996).

One of the prominent tools emerging from this movement were sentencing guidelines, first developed in reform-minded states such as Minnesota and Pennsylvania in the late 1970s and early 1980s. The federal government followed suit in the mid-1980s, and by the time I arrived in America in 1987, the promulgation of the federal guidelines was in full process. I read sentencing guidelines, in Weberian terms, as an attempt at (re-)establishing formal rationality of law. Let us remember Weber's criteria of formal rationality and apply them to guidelines to understand how this assessment is valid and where its limitations lie. First, formally rational law involves a logical and systematically integrated system of rules. This clearly applies to sentencing guidelines. Guidelines are typically based on a two-dimensional grid, one dimension representing the seriousness of the offense under consideration, thus the idea of retribution. The second dimension considers the number of prior convictions. The sense of culpability grows with every previous conviction, with it the likelihood of incarcerative sentences, and within the latter that of longer prison terms. In addition to the two dimensions, sentencing guidelines come with a limited and specific set of aggravating and mitigating circumstances. Second, formal rational law is oriented toward legal procedure. This is clearly in line with the application of guidelines. Deviations have recently been restricted when the U.S. Supreme Court argued that even penalty-enhancing aggravating circumstances must be determined by a jury rather than being left to the discretion of the judge. Third, formally rational law refrains from any reference to extra legal, political, religious, or ethical standards. Guidelines indeed do not allow judges to bring such criteria into the decision-making process. This argument is complicated by the fact, however, that guidelines might themselves entail substantive judgments. Finally, formal rationality is primarily institutionalized through the separation of judicial powers from those of the legislative

and executive branches. Judges simply apply the guidelines that were promulgated by sentencing commissions. Yet, debates have been raging if this
distribution does not mean that legislatures have usurped judicial powers.

In short, while some troubling issues remain unresolved, sentencing
guidelines do represent the idea of formal rational law. This reading then
allows us to apply to the case of sentencing guidelines, Weber's general
insights into the advantages of formal rational legal systems, and into the
contradictions, instabilities, and challenges they are likely to face.

Being equipped with Weberian concepts thus allowed me to shed new
light on a recent innovation in criminal justice. To examine the way in which
the federal guidelines were promulgated, I commuted between Cambridge
and Washington, and learned to appreciate the open doors a Harvard let-
terhead provides. I interviewed most current and former members of the
guideline commission and commission staff, Congressional staff who had
been involved in the legislation resulting in the guideline commission, and
Justice Department staff who worked with the commission. I spent many
weeks reading documents from legislative and commission records, especially transcripts of hearings, as well as the growing body of publications
on the early outcomes of state-level sentencing guidelines, especially in
Minnesota. Applying Weberian insights and drawing from my observations,
I proposed that several counterproductive consequences of the formal rational policy tool of sentencing guidelines were likely to occur in the promulgation and implementation processes. Here, I focus on implementation:

> [Sentencing guidelines] would have to be implemented through networks of decision
> makers in complex administrative environments and by actors with internalized sub-
> stantive rationales who often depend on constituencies with interests in substantive
> reason. [Further], implementers will oppose reformalization especially if attempted
> through central guidance, that is, if reformalization threatens to place restraints on their
> autonomy. Distortions of neoclassical instruments are thus likely to lead to unintended
> and counterproductive consequences (Savelsberg, 1992, p. 1361).

By now a substantial body of research has examined the consequences of
sentencing guidelines, providing us with empirical evidence regarding the
validity of this proposition. Many publications refer to Weber's terms while
some use the Weberian frame most explicitly, focusing on several of the
factors addressed in the quotation above: (1) networks of decision makers in
complex administrative environments, (2) lawyers with (a) internalized substantive rationales and (b) an interest in decision-making autonomy, and (3)
their dependency on constituencies with interests in the pursuit of substantive rationales. Let us consider then some central findings from empirical
research that most directly speak to these issues.

# USING WEBER'S CONCEPTS IN EMPIRICAL RESEARCH: LIMITS OF DETERMINATE SENTENCING SCHEMES

Three impressive empirical studies most directly address the concerns explored above. I briefly summarize their basic features and their findings as they pertain to predictions derived from Weber's insights into the inner tensions that engulf his ideal types of law.

## *Sentencing Guidelines in Varying Organizational Contexts: Dixon's Work*

Jo Dixon, in a 1995 article in the *American Journal of Sociology*, provides an impressive example of testing the Weberian models in a sophisticated empirical study, based on a rich data set collected in 1983 (Dixon, 1995). Her case is that of sentencing in the guideline state of Minnesota.

Dixon is concerned with explaining chances of a prison term and the length of a prison term separately. On the side of independent variables she first distinguishes between a formal rational model of legal decision making and a substantive political model as the two main contenders in the modern world of law. The former suggests that sentencing decisions will be based on criteria laid out in the law alone, especially the severity of the offense, the criminal history of the convict (operationalized by the number of prior convictions), the use of weapons in the offense, and the presence of multiple charges. Her data provide information on all of these variables. The substantive political model argues that legal decision making will reflect status variables and concern with substantive outcomes. Here Dixon's data are somewhat limited, and only the potential for discrimination along lines of race is taken into consideration. The application of welfare rationales or other extra legal criteria are not examined.

Yet, Dixon appears to deviate from the Weberian typology when she introduces a third model of sentencing, based on an "organizational maintenance theory." According to this theory, processing variables play a major role in sentencing decisions, specifically rewards for guilty pleas as a means to enhance organizational efficiency of courts. The argument is further complicated when Dixon introduces the possibility that organizational maintenance and substantive-political criteria may interact differentially depending on the more or less bureaucratized nature of courts and prosecutor's offices. She operationalizes the level of bureaucratization by measuring the complexity (specialized dockets with specific criminal docket) and centralization (decentralized judicial decision making/master calendar) of the organization. Dixon's is the first study to measure such organizational characteristics directly.

Dixon's findings justify her sophisticated and differentiated argument and analysis. It turns out that, on the one hand, formal legal theory is supported under conditions of low bureaucratization. In other words, sentences are largely explained by factors explicated in the guidelines where courts are less specialized and centralized. The organizational maintenance theory (in combination with formal legal theory) is supported, on the other hand, under conditions of high bureaucratization. This pattern is identified for both the imprisonment decision and (yet more strongly) the sentence length decision. Dixon finds this pattern to be in line with arguments and qualitative findings by Eisenstein, Flemming, and Nardulli (1988) according to which greater division of labor and decentralization in bureaucratized courts results in loosely coupled work groups that use high levels of discretion (thus allowing room for extra legal factors such as court efficiency), whereas less bureaucratized courts with little division of labor and higher levels of centralization result in tightly coupled work groups that produce consistent decision-making outcomes (and are more closely tied to formal legal criteria). Yet, Dixon does not directly examine tight coupling or the coherence of court room work groups. Finally and interestingly, substantive-political or combined organizational maintenance-substantive political models are not confirmed under either of the organizational contexts Dixon investigates.

Dixon concedes that her findings may be specific to the state she studied. First, Minnesota has a relatively small minority population; states with varying minority representation thus need to be studied. Second, Minnesota is a sentencing guidelines state, and, we may add, data were collected only three years after the introduction of guidelines when initial effects had not yet been circumvented. Both factors should increase the weight of formal legal variables. Third, Dixon does not examine potential "hydraulic displacement effects," meaning the likelihood that disparities will be shifted from sentencing to plea (especially charge) bargaining at the level of prosecutorial work. She pleads that this be examined in future research. Two further limitations may be added. First, the measurement of substantive-political factors is limited to the inclusion of the "race" variable. This is understandable in light of data availability. Yet, it does not do justice to all the potential substantive effects Max Weber had in mind when he predicted substantive challenges to formal rational law. Finally, substantive judgments that affect the construction of guidelines are, of course, outside the realm of studies that examine the implementation of sentencing law alone (see Savelsberg, 1992).

We shall link this analysis back to our ideal types of law to examine how Weber's arguments could be refined and how empirical studies can gain by taking Weber yet more seriously. But first we examine two further studies that partly address limitations of Dixon's work.

### Sentencing Guidelines Versus Court Communities: The Work of Ulmer and Colleagues

Another impressive project using Weberian categories to study sentencing was conducted by Jeffery T. Ulmer and collaborators. Results are reflected, among other sources, in a 1996 *Criminology* article, co-authored with Kramer (Ulmer & Kramer, 1996) and in a 1997 research monograph (Ulmer, 1997). While Ulmer does not measure court organization in as systematic a way as Dixon does, he clearly adds to Dixon's research in other respects. First, he studies Pennsylvania, a state with a larger minority population. Specifically, he compares three counties within that state, each of which differs substantially in terms of social structure, including racial composition. The largest and the most urban county has a very large minority population, differing substantially from a wealthy suburban and from a rural district. Second, while Minnesota guidelines might reduce substantive-political decision-making criteria, Pennsylvania adopted relatively open guidelines that leave judges more discretion than most other guideline systems do. While these features of Ulmer's work add information, his work shares other limits with Dixon's study. Information on initial charges is missing, thus not allowing for an examination of potential "hydraulic effects." Also, while age and gender are added as indicators for the consideration of substantive concerns, in addition to race, these three variables still constitute a somewhat limited measure of substantive considerations in sentencing decisions.

In short, Ulmer sets out to examine the empirical adequacy of the two Weberian models. The formal rational model is examined through the inclusion of measures for offense type and severity, the number of conviction charges, and a prior record scale (weighed for severity). The substantive model is represented by the consideration of race, gender, and age. Also, pleas are included to consider what Dixon refers to as the organizational maintenance model. Like Dixon, Ulmer examines the effects of these factors on incarceration decisions (differentiating between probation versus jail/prison and probation/jail versus prison) and on the length of prison terms separately.

Findings of the Pennsylvania study overlap in important ways with Dixon's results while also showing important variation. As in Minnesota, in Pennsylvania formal legal criteria have a decisive effect on sentencing outcomes, especially offense severity and prior record, much less so multiple conviction charges. Yet, also substantive and organizational efficiency variables show significant effects. African-Americans and men have higher chances of receiving a prison or jail sentence and a longer term than whites or women. The effect of age is minimal. With regard to organizational maintenance variables, sentences resulting from negotiated pleas are more lenient than others, while those resulting from bench trials are more likely to result in jail or prison terms. Sentences resulting from jury trials are by far the toughest. The price of a crime thus increases with the organizational efforts.

Ulmer and his colleagues also find important differences between the three counties under investigation, for example that jury trial convictions are most likely to result in incarceration in the wealthy suburban county; or that African-Americans are more likely to be imprisoned in the wealthy county, but less likely to suffer the same consequence in the rural country than in the other two; finally, that women are least likely to be incarcerated in the wealthy county.

Potential explanations for some of the findings are provided by in-depth interviews with judges, prosecutors, and defense attorneys in the three counties. The benefits from guilty pleas result, according to judges, from the efficiency they produce for an overburdened court, but also because pleas may be interpreted as signs of remorse. The extra risk for racial minority defendants may result from most whites' greater ability to afford costly alternatives to incarceration such as private treatment programs according to judges and defense attorneys. Yet, their higher risk in the wealthy suburban country is first attributed to the unfavorable appearance of their employment record when compared to that of typical defendants in this rather well-to-do context, but also to the reluctance of some judges to commit whites to prisons with a 60 percent Black inmate population. Judges attribute their greater reluctance to sentence women to prison with the fact that women are more often responsible for their children. Clearly, many of these rationales expressed in in-depth interviews and consistent with the statistical findings reflect diverse substantive rationales.

Elsewhere Ulmer (1997) adds an important theoretical argument, linking the Weberian concepts with a social worlds perspective that is rooted in ideas of pragmatist philosophy and sociological thought by the early Chicago School (Strauss, 1978; Fine, 1984). According to this approach, patterns of interaction generate social worlds that provide opportunities for action and simultaneously constitute constraints. Interaction in court communities, for example, results in "sedimentations" (Berger & Luckman, 1967), including "going rates," that is informal norms that determine decisions in most cases. Based on these theoretical ideas, the understanding of substantive criteria of sentencing can only succeed if we understand the processual order of court communities. Ulmer (1997, p. 33) proposes that

> court communities with greater familiarity and stability ... will exhibit stronger local going rates and thus less reliance on guidelines as a source of sentencing norms.

Dixon's findings presented above appear to indicate that one part of this hypothesis is right: court communities with greater familiarity and stability do exhibit stronger local going rates. Yet, the hypothesis is challenged in another respect as the going rates in those Minnesota counties that appear to have higher levels of familiarity and stability are strongly in line with the guidelines, thus directed by external formal rational legal instruments.

In short, Ulmer's findings partly support those of Dixon. Formal legal criteria are crucial in sentencing decisions. In addition, however, and in partial challenge to Dixon's Minnesota findings, substantive criteria clearly play an important role, including criteria that are tied to defendants' status characteristics. This may be due to the larger percentage of African-Americans in Pennsylvania, or it may result from the relatively great leeway the Pennsylvania guidelines grant judges. Finally, and again in line with Dixon, those substantive decision-making criteria are found to have substantial weight that Dixon discusses under the label of organizational maintenance theory, specifically bargaining mechanisms that result in greater efficiency of criminal courts.

### *Determinate Sentencing in Complex Organizational Environments: Judges, Prosecutors, and the Displacement of Discretion: Engen and Steen's Contribution*

A third study adds yet new answers to the puzzle of sentencing under guidelines. Rodney Engen and Sara Steen, in their 2000 article in the *American Journal of Sociology*, examine if the displacement of discretion under sentencing guidelines undermines the goals of sentencing reforms (Engen & Steen, 2000). They do so in the context of the relatively "tight" sentencing guideline system of Washington State, a system that is also primarily based on seriousness of the current offense and the number of prior convictions. Specifically, the authors examine changes in the conviction and sentencing of drug offenders in the time period between 1986 and 1995. During this period, the state legislature enacted changes to drug offender laws, different consequences of which would provide support for one or the other theoretical model. Partly following Dixon's modification of Weberian terms, Engen and Steen distinguish between formal legal and substantive models, supplementing these by an organizational maintenance approach to legal decision making. Yet, their conceptualization of "substantive rationality" is broader than Dixon's, as it is not limited to welfare rationales. The authors finally manage to overcome shortcomings of previous work as they analyze a longitudinal data set, allowing them to examine if prosecutorial behavior changes in response to reforms of sentencing laws.

What then are the changes in law and how did prosecutors react when legal changes constrained judicial discretion? First, in 1988 the legislature abolished the First-Time Offender Waiver (FTOW) for offenders convicted of delivery of heroine or cocaine. Then, in 1990, the legislature substantially increased the presumptive sentencing ranges for these offenses, almost resulting in double the number of months in prison. Finally, in 1992, the state Court of Appeals ruled that anticipatory offenses, that is the planning but not execution of a drug offense, is an "unranked" offense (i.e., has no seriousness level attached). The court thereby opened the possibility of a non-incarcerative sentence for defendants convicted of this offense.

Engen and Steen use these changes in the law to examine shifts in primary charges that should change in particular ways if prosecutors (or the court room work group) sought to hold on to their old practices against the new legal standards, an indicator of substantive justice. If prosecutors had a sense of substantive justice and were willing to hold on to that standard, even against formal law, then charges should decrease from delivery to simple possession, or – after the 1992 decision – from delivery to conspiracy to deliver. In the alternative, prosecutors would change their charging practices to increase organizational efficiency, for example by downgrading their charges only for those defendants who plead guilty.

What did Engen and Steen's analysis show? In line with the legislative demand, FTOW did vanish and the likelihood of prison terms for delivery offenses increased simultaneously. The length of prison terms did not increase initially. This is probably due to prosecutors reducing many delivery cases to simple possession, in line with the substantive rationality model. Yet, the length of prison terms did increase after the second legislative change of 1990. While this finding most strongly supports the formal rational model of legal decision making, other patterns show the strength of the organizational maintenance model: not only are those who plead guilty consistently punished less severely than those convicted at trial, the disparity between these groups increases substantially during the study period. This means that those pleading guilty are increasingly less likely to be threatened with more serious charges, multiple counts, and sentence enhancements than those convicted in a trial. As the legislature increases pressure on the court system, cooperative defendants reap yet greater benefits from their cooperation. Organizational efficiency becomes even more important.

Like the studies discussed above, Engen and Steen's investigation also has limits recognized by the authors. It covers only one state, characterized by a particular social structure and type of sentencing guidelines (in this case a tight guideline model that makes charge manipulations more likely). The study is also limited to conviction data, like the others presented above. Yet, it overcomes this limit to some degree by taking a longitudinal approach to examine changes in charging behavior over time. A third limitation is its focus on a particularly politicized crime, drug offenses. It is likely that prosecutors, themselves dependent on their constituency, will not counteract the punitive will of the legislature. Still, the authors conclude that

> the *hydraulic displacement* of discretion appears to be a very real phenomenon. Organizational adaptations subsequent to each of the sentencing reforms examined here appear to have produced very different sentences for similar offenders ... [T]he conclusion that sentencing guidelines have reduced inequality in criminal justice may be plainly wrong (Engen & Steen, 2000, p. 1336f).

# CONCLUSIONS: ON THE CONTROL OF DISCRETION AND THE USE OF SOCIOLOGICAL THEORY IN SENTENCING RESEARCH

In short, we have seen how Weber's ideal types of law have inspired empirical sentencing research. The initial application of these concepts to the study of sentencing guidelines (Savelsberg, 1990, 1992) inspired the adaptation of Weberian concepts in several empirical studies (most recently, see Johnson, 2005), three outstanding examples of which are reviewed and compared in this chapter (Dixon, 1995; Ulmer, 1997; Engen & Steen, 2000). This encounter between Weber's ideal types and his discussion of inherent tensions within each of them on the one hand, and the empirical sentencing research on the other yields several suggestions regarding future empirical research and the future development and use of the Weberian theory.

The use of Weber's ideal types has already much enriched recent research on sentencing guidelines as a contemporary policy tool, even if more comparative analyses across varying organizational, legal, and ecological contexts and more fine-grained measurement of substantive rationales are needed. It has helped organize features of sentencing law into meaningful theoretical concepts. These broader concepts facilitated the incorporation of previous insights of Weberian sociology into the analysis of sentencing guidelines, and it allows us today to draw broader conclusions from the specific findings of the empirical studies we reviewed.

In addition to providing conceptual tools, Weber also suggests substantive predictions. He clearly sees formal rationalization at work in modern law. Our empirical studies confirmed this prediction. Not only are guidelines a formal rational legal tool; they also contribute to a legal context in which legal decisions, here sentencing decisions, are strongly affected by the criteria specified in the law. Simultaneously, Weber also recognizes the impediments toward formal rationalization and the social forces that would spearhead the opposition and promote substantivation. Yet, whereas business actors are simply interested in flexibility and lawyers in status enhancing discretion, the carrier group of substantive rationales Weber considers most explicitly are those promoting the pursuit of welfare rationales in legal decision making. Weber was not naïve of course, and he recognized that open discretion might have substantive consequences different from the pursuit of welfare goals, such as repression and the defense of status and domination. Weber provides an example when he argues for his time that a male jury could never be convinced to find a fellow male guilty of rape (Weber, 1978, p. 893). Clearly, this argument can be extended to racial and class repression in court decision making. And indeed, the analyses at hand suggest substantial indications for discriminatory sentencing, even under sentencing guidelines.

While Weber's general sociological concepts and theoretical propositions thus provided a conceptual and theoretical basis for current studies, the Weberian approach can itself be further developed and enriched in light of these studies' findings. Consider the following exemplary insights:

1. It is astonishing that Weber, with his profound interest in organizations and influence on organization studies, did not alert us to the organizational efficiency concerns, a particular type of substantive rationality, that play such a strong role in legal decision making as all of our studies have consistently shown.[2] Such concerns will have to play a central role in future research on legal processes, as Dixon's work particularly indicates, and in the future development of Weber's 'substantive rationality' concept.

2. Weber also failed to recognize that legal decision making occurs in complex organizational contexts so that decisions made in one place will affect other decisions in ways that may neutralize the former. This is the 'hydraulic displacement' effect demonstrated in Engen and Steen's work. Such displacement may promote substantive concerns of different sorts, behind the pretense of strict adherence to formal rules. Future research on court decision making will have to take this factor into consideration, and Weberian sociology of law will need to become more intimate with organizational sociology.

3. Finally, Weber did not acknowledge that formal law is practiced in organizations of different degrees of bureaucratization. Dixon's work has shown that bureaucratization has significant effects on the degree to which formal rationality of law is maintained.

The future use of a Weberian frame for the study of court processes was recently suggested by a new collection of articles on the social organization of criminal courts. This collection makes also clear though that the value of a Weberian approach can be further enhanced if future work merges microsociological perspectives that explain the production of standards out of social interaction, and the consideration of macro environments with an analysis of the organizational structure of courts themselves (see Dixon, Savelsberg, & Kupchik, 2006).

Finally, this chapter suggests that general sociological concepts are crucial for criminological and criminal justice research, here illustrated for the case of sentencing research. Such concepts allow us to analytically organize the empirical world and to provide for explanations and predictions that are typically outside the reach of policy makers. They allow those whom airplanes take from distant countries to find their way, like lighthouses aid ships in the sea, but also alert those on the inside to potentially problematic consequences of well-intended programs. By doing so, they warn against criminal justice scholarship that loses sight of general sociological concepts and that navigates too closely along the shores of the criminal justice system (Savelsberg & Sampson, 2002; Savelsberg et al., 2002; Savelsberg et al., 2004; Savelsberg & Flood, 2004).

# NOTES

1. The benefit of drawing on Weber's concepts is not limited to the study of sentencing guidelines, of course. I later learned to appreciate their potential further when I applied Weberian ideal types of domination and authority to help explain

very different patterns in trends of criminal punishment in the United States compared to the Federal Republic of Germany (Savelsberg, 1994; Savelsberg with Brühl, 1994), and subsequently penal trends in these two countries compared to yet different patterns in the communist part of Germany and in Poland under state socialism (Savelsberg, 1999). These comparisons of changing rates of punishment in the context of country-specific societal and state institutions helped me understand the dynamics of penal policies in the United States. They later guided me to conduct research on the consequences of basic American institutions on second-order institutional change for knowledge production, especially criminology itself, its social organization and the knowledge its practitioners produce (e.g., Savelsberg, King, & Cleveland, 2002; Savelsberg, Cleveland, & King, 2004; Savelsberg & Flood, 2004).

2. It is open to future discussion if organizational maintenance rationales should be conceptualized separately from other substantive rationalities (as they deal with concerns internal to the criminal justice system). We could think of other internal rationales, of course, such as sensitivities of lawyers and judges, and their concerns with career opportunities. One option would be a distinction between internal and external substantive rationalities, with organizational maintenance concerns in the former category.

# ACKNOWLEDGMENT

The author thanks Jo Dixon, Rod Engen, and Jeff Ulmer for comments on an earlier draft.

# REFERENCES

American Friends Service Committee. (1971). *Struggle for justice: A report on crime and punishment in America*. New York: Hill and Wang.

Berger, P., & Luckmann, T. (1967). *The social construction of reality: A treatise in the sociology of knowledge*. New York: Anchor Books.

Deflem, M. (1998). The boundaries of abortion law: Systems theory from Parsons to Luhmann and Habermas. *Social Forces, 76*, 775–818.

Dixon, J. (1995). The organizational context of sentencing. *American Journal of Sociology, 100*, 1157–1198.

Dixon, J., Savelsberg, J. J., & Kupchik, A. (Eds) (2006). *The social organization of criminal courts (The international library of criminology, criminal justice, and penology)*. Aldershot, UK: Dartmouth Publishing Company.

Eisenstein, J., Fleming, R., & Nardulli, P. (1988). *The contours of justice: Communities and theirs courts*. Boston: Little, Brown and Company.

Engen, R. L., & Steen, S. (2000). The power to punish: Discretion and sentencing reform in the war on drugs. *American Journal of Sociology, 105*, 1357–1395.

Ewing, S. (1987). Formal justice and the spirit of capitalism: Max Weber's sociology of law. *Law and Society Review, 21*, 487–512.

Fine, G. A. (1984). Negotiated orders and organizational cultures. *Annual Review of Sociology, 10*, 239–262.

Hagan, J., & Parker, P. (1985). White collar crime and punishment. *American Sociological Review, 77*, 302–316.

Hamilton, G., & Sutton, J. (1989). The problem of control in the weak state: Domination in the United States, 1880–1920. *Theory and Society, 18*, 1–46.

Johnson, B. D. (2005). Contextual disparities in guidelines departures: Courtroom social contexts, guidelines compliance, and extralegal disparities in criminal sentencing. *Criminology, 43*, 761–796.

Kronman, A. (1983). *Max Weber*. Stanford: Stanford University Press.

Mann, K., Wheeler, S., & Sarat, A. (1980). Sentencing the white-collar offender. *American Criminal Law Review, 17*, 479–500.

Marsh, R. M. (2000). Weber's misunderstanding of traditional Chinese law. *American Journal of Sociology, 106*, 281–302.

Pfeiffer, C., & Savelsberg, J. J. (1989). Regionale und altergruppenbezogene Unterschiede in der Strafzumessung. In: C. Pfeiffer & M. Oswald (Eds), *Strafzumessng: Empirische Forschung und Strafrechtsdogmatik im Dialog* (pp. 17–42). Stuttgart: Enke.

Savelsberg, J. J. (1990). Neo-classical legal concepts in the political process: The making of the federal sentencing guidelines. Paper presented at the 1990 Annual meetings of the American Sociological Association.

Savelsberg, J. J. (1992). Law that does not fit society: Sentencing guidelines as a neoclassical reaction to the dilemmas of substantivized law. *American Journal of Sociology, 97*, 1346–1381.

Savelsberg, J. J. (1994). Knowledge, domination, and criminal punishment. *American Journal of Sociology, 99*, 911–943.

Savelsberg, J. J. (1994). *Constructing white-collar crime: Rationalities, communications, and power*. Philadelphia: University of Pennsylvania Press (with contributions by P. Brühl).

Savelsberg, J. J. (1999). Knowledge, domination, and criminal punishment revisited: Incorporating state socialism. *Punishment and Society, 1*, 45–70.

Savelsberg, J. J., & Brühl, P. (1988). *Politik und Wirtschaftsstrafrecht: Eine soziologische Analyse*. Opladen: Leske und Budrich.

Savelsberg, J. J., Cleveland, L. L., & King, R. D. (2004). Institutional environments and scholarly work: American criminology, 1951–1993. *Social Forces, 82*, 1275–1302.

Savelsberg, J. J., & Flood, S. M. (2004). Period and cohort effects in the production of scholarly knowledge: The case of criminology, 1951–1993. *Criminology, 42*, 1009–1041.

Savelsberg, J. J., King, R., & Cleveland, L. (2002). Politicized scholarship? Science on crime and the state. *Social Problems, 49*, 327–348.

Savelsburg, J. J., & Sampson, R. J. (2002). Introduction: Mutual engagement: Criminology and sociology. *Crime, Law, and Social Change, 37*, 99–105.

Simmel, G. (1971 [1908]). The stranger. In: D. L. Levine (Ed.), *Georg Simmel on individuality and social forms* (pp. 143–149). Chicago: University of Chicago Press.

Singer, S. I. (1996). *Recriminalizing delinquency: Violent juvenile crime and juvenile justice reform*. Cambridge: Cambridge University Press.

Strauss, A. (1978). *Negotiations: Varieties, processes, contexts and social order*. San Francisco: Josey-Bass.

Sutton, J. (2001). *Law/Society: Origins, interactions and change*. Thousand Oaks: Pine Forge Press.

Ulmer, J. T. (1997). *Social world of sentencing: Court communities under sentencing guidelines*. Albany: State University of New York Press.

Ulmer, J. T., & Kramer, J. H. (1996). Court communities under sentencing guidelines: Dilemmas of formal rationality and sentencing guidelines. *Criminology, 34*, 383–407.

Unger, R. M. (1976). *Law in modern society: Toward a criticism of social theory.* New York: Free Press.

Von Hirsch, A. (1976). *Doing justice: The choice of punishments.* Boston: Northeastern University Press.

Weber, M. (1978). *Economy and society.* Berkeley: University of California Press.

Weber, M. (2002 [1904–1905]). *The Protestant ethic and the spirit of capitalism.* Los Angeles: Roxbury.

Wilson, J. Q. (1975). *Thinking about crime.* New York: Basic Books.

# "THEY BRING YOU UP TO DO LIKE YOUR DADDY DONE": STRATIFICATION THEORY, EMPLOYMENT, AND CRIME [*]

Robert D. Crutchfield

## ABSTRACT

*This chapter makes the argument that theories of social inequality that were developed to explain how societies maintain social stratification can enhance criminological explanations. Social reproduction theory, which focuses on the role of education in continuing patterns of social advantage and disadvantage, and dual labor market theory, which was developed to explain why some, especially marginalized minorities, are intergenerationally disadvantaged, are discussed along with criminology research to support this position. Similarities in racial and ethnic disadvantage and the relationship to crime for the United States and Western Europe are briefly discussed.*

[*] From Bruce Springsteen's "The River," on *Bruce Springsteen Greatest Hits*. Columbia Records, New York, 1995. Initially released in 1979.

Sociological Theory and Criminological Research: Views from Europe and the United States
Sociology of Crime, Law and Deviance, Volume 7, 203–222
Copyright © 2006 by Elsevier Ltd.
All rights of reproduction in any form reserved
ISSN: 1521-6136/doi:10.1016/S1521-6136(06)07010-2

# INTRODUCTION

Bruce Springsteen sings the lyric, "They bring you up to do like your daddy done," in the song "The River." One of his working class ballads, expressing the dashed dreams of a young man with limited options; this one suggests a way toward a linkage between sociology and criminology that was well understood by the founders of both, but which too often is forgotten or perhaps ignored by some contemporary scholars. Criminologists frequently seek explanations for criminal behavior in the here and now, but that is not how peoples' lives are actually constructed. What and how we are, of course, are influenced by our personal circumstances, but not just by our current social positioning. How we act is also influenced by our familial and social histories. Bruce Springsteen understood this when he positions the protagonist of his dark song as a product of a system of social stratification that limited his father and limits him as well. The limits on the son are both the barriers external to the family that determined the available options for the father and the son's alternatives that were internal to the family, which were conditioned by the father's life. Much of criminology explicitly recognizes the latter, family circumstance as an influence on criminality, but only rarely today do we take as seriously the former, the limited options that the father faced. This is different from the early days when Chicago School disorganization theorists connected limitations on the social opportunities and segregated living arrangements of migrant families, both foreign and domestic, to their delinquency or criminality. It also differs from their colleague Edwin Sutherland, who argued that differential association grew out of differential social organization which was itself a product of intergenerational social structural arrangements.

Today we are more likely to explain crime as a product of various forms of individual alienation, shattered or underdeveloped bonds, or of immersion into subcultures. Those who use these explanations frequently at least tip the hat to social structure as an exogenous influence on these processes, but some, when asked, likely smirk and think or say, "of course I know that social arrangements and history are also important, but ... " My position here is not to critique my colleagues, but to advance the case that we can learn much and offer more by explicitly linking to broader sociology and here I will focus on links to theories of social stratification; specifically to theories that describe how social inequality is maintained.

Two widely read books provide useful examples; Butterfield's *All Gods Children* (1995) and Sullivan's *Getting Paid* (1989). Butterfield traced the history of the Bosket family from their origin in South Carolina where manly cultures focused on honor gave rise to pro-violent subcultures that were reproduced in succeeding generations. As the carriers of these values and beliefs are geographically dispersed they, including Butch Bosket and later his son Willie, were socialized by their families and communities, into, and came to embrace these beliefs. Butterfield ascribes their intergenerational pattern of violence to, in part, those pro-violent values and related conceptions of masculinity and honor. Butterfield describes how these values, whose beginnings he actually traces to the Scottish highlands, the cultural homeland of many Scotch-Irish settlers of South Carolina, were inculcated in the generations before Butch and Willie. What is clear from Butterfield's rich descriptions of the family's history, is that Springsteen accurately too described the Bosket history; they brought Willie up to do like his daddy done. Ultimately it was murder, but before that, it was to be economically marginalized and segregated from American opportunity. That intergenerational marginalization has the capacity to offer a counter account, or certainly interact with the subculture that Butterfield describes. Looking to theories of social stratification can offer, not necessarily a competing explanation to Butterfield's, but one that is certainly complementary, and maybe offers a more complete picture. And, for those interested in social policy, a hope for reform that is most unlikely if historically based subcultures alone or primarily, explain how multiple generations of black men become murderers.

In *Getting Paid*, Sullivan (1989) ethnographically studied delinquency among three groups of lower class youth; working class whites, poor minorities, and a group whose neighborhood fits descriptions of underclass communities (Wilson, 1987). All three groups were involved in delinquency, but their orientations toward the future, which influenced their current criminal involvement, were heavily conditioned by the educational and economic realities of the neighborhoods in which they lived. In the underclass sections, adults were marginal to the labor force. Most who had jobs worked in unstable positions that paid little and offered no or few promises for the future. In contrast, the white delinquents were unexcited about their future options, but knew that they had networks among parents and neighbors that would likely lead to employment in local or nearby manufacturing plants. In Sullivan's work, we again see lives lived that are consistent with Springsteen's line, for both groups, as well as the intermediate third group, were being brought up to do like their daddies done. The social structural positioning of parents and adult neighbors provided opportunities to one group, but the disadvantage of adults in the other two groups were translated into disadvantage in the next generation of children from those neighborhoods.

In both examples, the current social structural circumstances of the subjects of the research interacts with their history. In the case of the Boskets, history reaches back to Colonial South Carolina. Sullivan's treatment only focuses back one generation, but each preceding generation's options were constrained by the limited possibilities faced by peoples' parents. In both examples, we lose understanding if we fail to take both these histories and current social structural positioning into account when we try to explain criminality. Their current social circumstance and their histories are linked. Too often criminological work and theories are written without historical perspectives and with inadequate treatment of social structure (e.g. it is culture or peer influence without elaborating how values or peer networks have been affected by forces like discrimination and residential segregation). If we take seriously relevant sociological theories, in this case those explaining the maintenance of social stratification and social inequality, we can enrich our descriptions and explanations of criminality.

## SOCIAL CLASS AND CRIME

We should begin by taking seriously the lack of a strong relationship between social class and delinquency (Tittle, Villemez, & Smith, 1978). In studies using self-reported crime data, researchers have found no, or modest associations between social standing and delinquent involvement, but these studies generally focus on minor forms of misbehavior. Most people, no matter their class, or where they live, have stolen something of modest value, consumed alcohol (under age) or soft drugs, and among males at least have likely been involved in fights. More serious violations though are more frequent among the more economically disadvantaged (Hindelang, Hirschi, & Weis, 1981).

It is with very little skepticism that explanations attributing crime to a poor economy are accepted by the general public. But, recurring anomalies suggest that this may not, or at least, not always, be true. For example, during the worldwide "Great Depression" of the 1930s, American crime rates declined even though unemployment rates were at 25 percent for extended periods. Thirty years later, during the 1960s, along with sustained economic expansion, the U.S. experienced large increases in both property and violent crime rates. If we consider the link between economy and crime more globally, it is no secret among criminologists that comparative poverty rates are not highly correlated with comparative crime rates. Some of the poorest nations of the world do have high crime rates, yet most poor countries have relatively low rates. At the same time, even among industrialized nations it is difficult to explain their relative rankings based on their economies. Even with the declining crime rates of recent years, the U.S. continues to have astoundingly high rates of violence, even though it has one of the world's most productive economies.

But, there really is little reason to expect a linear relationship between social class and crime. There is no theoretical reason to believe that the group typically thought of as the working class, those in modest income blue-collar jobs and living in similarly labeled communities, would be any more crime prone than the middle class. The *wants* of the working class may be less satisfied, but that is different from having unmet *needs*. Expectations of a linear relationship between social class and crime though would require that they commit more crime and also that those in the middle class would, in turn have higher rates than those above them on the social-class ladder. Again, there is not a theoretical reason for expecting such. The poor though are a different story. There are reasons to expect that those living in poverty, especially those living in neighborhoods that Wilson (1987) characterized as "hyper poverty" would be more crime prone.

Links between economic standing and crime are popularly explained by reliance on simple-minded versions of strain theory or culturally based notions that "they," the "bad guys," are fundamentally different because they are flawed people or have pathological values. During the rioting that rocked many American cities after the police officers who assaulted Rodney King were acquitted by an all white jury, a local news anchor, after having sociological explanations for the events described, asked, "Well aren't they just thugs looking for an excuse?"[1] Her response used a less pejorative word but carried the same underlying explanation as the French Interior Minister, Nicolas Sarkozy, when he referred to rioters in Parisian suburbs as "scum" (Sciolino, 2005).

One set of explanations which purport to explain the connection between poverty and elevated rates of crime is the "culture of poverty" thesis. Banfield (1968) explained delinquency among a subset of the poor as a consequence of their failure to internalize middle-class values and especially the inability of some in the lower class to defer gratification. Critics of his point of view argue that Banfield's arguments are tautological – those with short time horizons (unable to defer gratification) are more likely to be poor and criminal and we know who has short-time horizons because they more frequently live in poverty or commit crimes. More recently Murray (1984) has convinced many policy makers that growing poverty in America, with its accompanying social problems, including crime, was caused by expansion

of social welfare programs. Murray's arguments provided conceptual justifications for much of the "welfare reform" that was implemented between
1985 and the end of the twentieth century. Some of his analysis, however,
has been called into question (Wilson, 1987). Both Banfield and Murray
mention social structural arrangements as a factor in the emergence of subcultures of poverty, but nearly all of their analyses, as well as their policy
recommendations, focus on the values of poor people; in particular the
values of the poor that are thought to be inconsistent with dominant middle-
class values.

Among the public, those who would not dismiss rioters and even those
who break the law alone or in much smaller groups, generally feel that the
poor are driven to utilitarian violation because of unsatisfied needs. They
believe in, not the anomie theory of criminologists, but what I have
described as the "Jean Val Jean theory of criminology." The hero of Victor
Hugo's *Les Miserables*, Jean Val Jean, was sent to prison for stealing bread
to feed his sister's starving children; a noble act of larceny because of his
motive. This imagery probably lies at the root of popular expectations that
when economic times are tough, some will turn to crime to satisfy needs. Of
course some among us, who are less noble than Jean Val Jean, turn to
villainy simply for wants that will not be satisfied by work and saving. It is
intuitively appealing to attribute criminal actions to material motives, so
many of us expect that unemployment will lead to crime, and that the
economically less fortunate will do more of it.

What is it about poverty that might make those experiencing it more
likely to become involved in crime? Here again, unless one relies on simplistic conceptualizations of strain theory (e.g. the Jean Val Jean version), or
subcultural explanations that are largely divorced from social structural
causes, it is not immediately apparent why the poor would engage in more
crime; that is unless we take social space and social history into account.
Wilson (1987) and Massey and Denton (1993) describe how the emergence
of urban underclass neighborhoods because of job losses, and racial residential segregation, respectively, concentrates the negative consequences of
poverty, including crime. A hyper-macho code of the street that is conducive to crime has developed in some deeply impoverished neighborhoods
according to Anderson (1999). What is common to these three arguments is
that they are tied to place. Poverty becomes criminogenic here when the
poor are concentrated together and isolated from the non-poor, and cutoff
from opportunity and reason to expect improvements in their lot. Sociological theories of stratification can help to develop explanations of how
impoverished places continue as such, and as a consequence these theories

can, when combined with criminological theories, give better explanations for crime than the oversimplified alternatives. Theories of social inequality are potentially valuable to us because it is vitally important that criminologists incorporate an intergenerational understanding of how people come to occupy both the place where they live and the social structural position in which their lives play out.

In the two examples that I began with, our explanations would be incomplete without an appreciation of the importance of the combination of the Boskets' familial history and the resulting deprived social life that first Bruce and then Willie come of age in. Residents in the communities studied by Sullivan do not live there simply by choice, but as a result of preceding generations' experiences with residential segregation and denial of equal access to education and the economic opportunities. The perspectives of two particular theories of social stratification appear especially useful for criminology, social reproduction theory and dual labor market theory. While some scholars continue to challenge these points of view, they seem especially well suited to help to explain persistently high crime rates in some places and the link between crime and inequalities observed by some analysis (Wilson, 1987, 1996; Massey & Denton, 1993; Anderson, 1999).

## Social Reproduction Theory and Crime

Social reproduction theory seeks to explain how social inequality is perpetuated in a society. Focusing largely on education as an institution that perpetuates the established class structure, theorists from this tradition describe how children from both the lower and upper classes are hammered into, or prepared for their respective stations. The former being discouraged and beaten down, while the latter's human capital is enhanced. Bowels and Gintis (1976) argue that schools prepare children for their place in the workforce, to be bosses or the bossed. Lower class children receive inferior education and come away with a sense of their inferiority. MacLeod (1987) describes black teenagers who begin with hopes and aspirations (which were encouraged by their families) but overtime this optimism is worn down by their experience in school and in the labor market. Rubin in response to those who argue that people of the lower classes are afflicted by a pathological subculture of poverty wrote of families she ethnographically studied:

> These families reproduce themselves not because they are somehow deficient or their culture aberrant, but because there are not alternatives for most of their children" (Rubin, 1976, p. 211).

Social class arrangements and unequal education reproduce in each succeeding generation of the poor, the conditions that lead to weak academic
preparation and limited aspirations, which eventually lead to low end employment, if any, and an economic life much like their parents. Critics (e.g.
Giroux, 1983) have argued that these perspectives are too mechanistic;
leaving out individual agency, but one need not argue that these processes
will be 100 percent successful in reproducing inequality for this theory to
provide a compelling explanation of why so many children remain in the
social class into which they are born. Nor do these theories require that the
disadvantaged cannot react by advocating, protesting, rioting, revolting, or
otherwise trying to change their circumstance.

If we accept Butterfield's argument that the Bosket family's intergenerational homicidal behavior is a product of their immersion in a culture beginning with their ancestors' experience of slavery, in a region of the south
that was obsessed with a code of honor buttressed by violence, we have to
explain why most of those with this legacy, both black and white, did not
end up acting like Butch and Willie. It is important to note that Willie did
not grow up in a household with his father Butch, but he was raised by
extended family members in deprived neighborhoods. So while Butch was
not there to influence him, the same shabby housing, unstable home life,
depressed community and bad schools were there. An answer is provided by
social reproduction theory. It is not the history alone, but that the Boskets
were, generation after generation, constrained to the bottom rungs of
American social and economic life. As a result, they were also constrained
by Jim Crow laws, the racial residential segregation of the north, the bad
schools of inner cities, and economic hardship, to live in places where both
their structural position and the culture that they were socialized into were
recreated in each succeeding generation. To more fully explain the behavior
of these two individuals we also would need the tools to explain their psychological makeup, but their social structural positioning and history of
disadvantage provide the context in which they developed and came of age.

Turning to less dramatic examples, recent studies report that parental
education and employment circumstance do in fact affect how children do in
school, which in turn affects delinquent behavior. Wadsworth (2000) examined parents' employment and juvenile misbehavior. He theorized that
parents who are marginally employed, out of work or employed in unstable
jobs, would have weaker social bonds to their children. He found this to be
the case and that when parental bonds were weaker; the children were performing less well in school, and were more likely to have misbehaved in the
previous year. Wadsworth's interpretation of his finding is that the affective

strength of the parent–child relationship is weakened with the parents' lack of labor market success, which in turn negatively affects school performance, increasing delinquency. Although MacLeod (1987) did not focus on delinquency, Wadsworth's results are consistent with his findings that black poor children lose the optimism that they begin with, and that white poor children early on develop pessimistic expectations about their future. Bellair, Roscigno, & McNulty's (2003) findings are also similar. They report that parents' work circumstance seems either to encourage or discourage children in the pursuit of academic success. Children whose parents have done well occupationally, like those whose parents accomplished more academically, do better in school and are significantly less likely to engage in acts of delinquency. Conversely, when parents' labor market experience is more marginal, so too are their children's performance in school, and these children are more frequently participating in delinquent activity. The children of marginally employed adults were significantly more likely to do poorly in school and to become involved in delinquency. As control theorists have found (e.g. Cernkovich & Giordano, 1992), when the social bonds to parents are weakened, children are substantially less likely to develop strong positive bonds to their teachers and school, which is associated with higher levels of delinquency.

The social conditions of where people live, place, can magnify these forces. In a study of the juvenile respondents to the National Longitudinal Surveys of Youth (NLSY), Crutchfield, Rankin, and Pitchford (1993) found that when parents were unemployed, their children do less well in school which in turn increases their involvement in delinquency and that this is especially the case in poorer central cities. More recently Crutchfield, Wadsworth, Groninger, and Drakulich (2006) used newer data from NLSY data sets[2] and found those children with poor school performance, and who live in socially and economically disadvantaged neighborhoods were significantly more likely to engage in acts of delinquency than poor performing children in other communities. It is not just the poor academic achievement of individuals, but as social reproduction theory suggests, it is the low-quality education in poor communities' schools (see Kozol, 1991, for descriptions of school inequalities), which leads to greater delinquency when young people have limited economic opportunities as they move into adulthood. To the extent that this delinquency is a precursor to later criminal acts these conditions will lead to higher likelihood of incarceration, which of course further lowers their labor market outlooks (Pager, 2003).

When families live where there is concentrated poverty, low educational obtainment, and joblessness, the economically struggling image of the parents are less likely to be mitigated by other adults in the neighborhood. A problem in underclass neighborhoods is that children do not see the models of people getting up, going out to work, and seeing it pay off, because too few adults in those neighborhoods are doing well in the labor market (Wilson, 1987).

## Dual Labor Market Theory and Crime

Dual labor market theorists base their explanation of the maintenance of social inequality on the premises that all jobs are not created equal and that there is not open competition for jobs (Piore, 1975; Kalleberg & Sorensen, 1979). The theory was developed to explain why some groups, notably but not exclusively, stigmatized minorities, are persistently disadvantaged in societies and economies. Central to dual labor market arguments is an oversimplified distinction[3] between primary and secondary sector jobs. Primary sector jobs are characterized by relatively higher pay ("family wage" jobs in contemporary political vernacular), good-benefits, reasonable expectation of future employment and even promotion. Often workers in these jobs begin in low, entry-level positions, and with time and seniority their pay benefits, but perhaps most importantly their job security increases. Included in this sector are a wide range of occupations from the classic professions of law and medicine to the blue-collar industrial jobs that many twentieth century American families built middle class lifestyles on. In the professions, income, security, and benefits are a function of training and credentials. In the case of blue-collar workers these benefits of their jobs were a consequence of the labor movement and the combination of the strength of their employing industry and the negotiating power of their union. Between the poles of the classic professions and unskilled blue-collar work the other primary jobs are arrayed, based on the extent to which positive benefits accrue because of the characteristics of the job and those of individuals occupying them, and the characteristics of the industries and the social organization of workers and work.

By contrast, dual labor market theorists describe secondary sector jobs as low paying, with few or even no benefits. Secondary sector workers' jobs have less security, employment is frequently unstable, and so occupants of these jobs are more likely to be in and out of work. The work place is structured so that there are very limited opportunities for advancement. One does not easily build a promising career in a secondary sector occupation. Examples of these jobs are the unskilled and non-unionized construction workers, many of whom are "picked-up" for "days work," unbonded security guards, most gardeners, those hired to unload trucks, many piecemeal workers, low end restaurants, and most retail workers, especially those in some "big box" stores. The prototypical secondary sector job may well be employment in a fast food restaurant, thus the title "McJobs" that has been used popularly to denote secondary sector jobs.[4]

Families whose heads are employed in the secondary sector are constrained to live in low cost housing. This perspective is especially useful to describe how African-Americans were kept marginal to the labor market and thus hit hardest by job losses that have occurred as a result of deindustrialization. In the cities of the U.S. industrial East and Midwest many black families built middle class lifestyles based on unskilled primary sector jobs in big steel, big auto, and other major manufacturers. Frequently, the sons of steel workers followed their fathers into the mills. Deindustrialization ended the jobs and the middle class lifestyles. These sons, and now their sons and daughters, are now more often than not, constrained to secondary sectors jobs or no jobs at all. Inner cities, where many of these people live, are now filled with neighborhoods composed disproportionally of people, who are marginal to the labor market; these are communities where crime can flourish.

Primary sector jobs are the right stuff for building middle-class conforming lives around. They are the jobs that we value sufficiently to get to work regularly and on time. They are the positions that we value enough that they influence and structure our days and habits, and we build our lifestyles around them. As a consequence, they are less conducive to crime, because we do not want to jeopardize such jobs. People who have to be at work on a job that they value, are less likely to lead a life of carefree late nights in bars, on street corners, and in marginal company engaging in questionable behavior. In addition to the immediate consequences of these behaviors; exhaustion, hangovers, jail, injury, etc., the loss of a valued job, because one cannot regularly perform up to par or is too often tardy or a no show, adds additional potential cost to criminal involvement. People with primary sector jobs have fewer motivations for involvement in low end pecuniary and entrepreneurial crime, and are less likely to lead lifestyles conducive to the chance occurrences that typify much violent criminal behavior.

While primary sector jobs give one something additional to lose, a prospective career, there is little to lose should one be fired from a secondary sector position. In other words, McJob holders are liberated from having to worry so much about being able to perform well or even up to par, and when the boss gets tired of late arrivals or no shows, there is little to lose.

As a result these people have motivations, because of low wages, to dabble in larceny and to seize opportunities to moonlight as a street corner drug dealer. Also, without the constraints of a job worth loosing, they can more freely lead a "street" lifestyle[5] that increases their chances of becoming involved in violence.

Elliot Liebow's (1967), classic study, *Talley's Corner* tells the story of day workers in Washington, DC in the early 1960s. Talley and his buddies worked irregularly in this system. The system continues to function in many cities. In most cities today there are gathering places where men seek day work. In Seattle along Second Avenue African American, Latino, and some white men gather near the "Millionaires' Club"[6] in the hope of finding a days work. In upscale Santa Barbara, California, mostly Mexican men gather within a few blocks of the scenic beaches for the same purpose. These men in Santa Barbara, Seattle's "millionaires," and Talley and company, are secondary sector workers, but they do not appear in employment statistics. But, day after day they are out there struggling for work. With limited education and few job opportunities it is likely that it is also where their offspring will someday seek work. Liebow did not describe the men that he studied as criminals, but law violations were a part of their lives, in part because of the instability of employment.

Dual labor market theory helps to describe how social inequality is perpetuated through the allocation of jobs to adults. Crutchfield and Pitchford (1997) found that young adults with unstable employment are more likely to have committed both violent and property crimes. Unstable employment, measured as the amount of time respondents were out of the labor force, is an important byproduct of secondary sector employment.

Crutchfield and Pitchford took advantage of the NLSY's "geo-coded" data feature to study the social and economic context of the local labor markets (counties) in which young adults are working (or not working). Counties are certainly not communities, but they can be thought of as local labor markets; the environment in which people seek employment. They found that the criminogenic effect of spending more time out of the labor market did not occur everywhere. The effect was only observable in counties that had above average unemployment rate. Where county unemployment rates were comparatively lower, being out of work for more time does not appear to increase criminal involvement. This is an important finding. It indicates that it is in the context of others who are out of work that an individual's employment circumstance matters for their criminality. This supports the contention that it is not just an individual's social class position that matters, but also characteristics of the place where they live and work that makes crime more or less likely because of circumstances of others who live there.

What each of these studies indicates is that crime and delinquency are, in an important way, in part a function of the school experience of children and of the work experience of young adults. In addition to having the same motivations that propel delinquents from other social classes, the poorest are also motivated by need, anger, and despair, and they live where there are more opportunities for serious offense. Yes, drugs are sold in the suburbs, but the open-air markets that existed in profusion during the height of the crack epidemic tended to be in poorer communities. Also, the cultural patterns that emerge when multiple generations of the residents of a community are marginalized, give rise to more serious crime and delinquency (Anderson, 1990, 1999; Patillo-McCoy, 1999).

In saying that young adults and poor children are additionally motivated by need, anger, and despair; which of course were important parts of Albert Cohen's (1955) description in *Delinquent Boys*, we should be careful not to paint a picture of morose, Dickens like characters. Just as middle-class suburbanites and their lives are more complex than the images presented in television's situation comedies, so too are the people of underclass neighborhoods. Anger and distress motivate the emergence of oppositional culture and propel some to serious crime, but there is more to life in ghettos and barrios than that. People who live in these neighborhoods are surprised in those rare cases when at work or school they make friends with middle-class people, who all too frequently eventually get around to expressing their sympathy "for you having to grow up there." Life in some inner city neighborhoods is hard, it is too frequently violent and dangerous, but that is not the sum total of the lived experience of residents. They have joys, fun, and enjoyment as well and sometimes, some juveniles there engage in delinquency for the same reason that their middle-class counterparts do; it is at times fun. Other children and young adults though may be drawn into serious crime by the despair and hopelessness that comes with being disadvantaged by systems that perpetuate social inequality.

One can see that Sullivan's observations are consistent with dual labor market theory descriptions of how social inequality is maintained. The residents of the underclass neighborhood have very constricted hopes for their future. Parents and other adults living about them frequently do not have good jobs, and the juveniles themselves have few reasons to believe that their prospects might be different. On the other hand, the working class kids, those who live where fathers and neighbors held unglamorous jobs in local factories and warehouses, did not especially want such jobs but they recognize that when the time comes, their social networks will make access to job opportunities available to them. Here again, just as with the Boskets, the class structure is maintained through a combination of access to education and access to the labor market; specifically the job sector that particular segments of the population are constrained to.

Of course strictly speaking, people are not "constrained" to these limited opportunities. Clearly through individual agency or luck, some are able to break away from the dim legacy and poor prospects handed down, not just by their parents, but very occasionally by the social institutions that reproduce intergenerational inequality. The chances of such luck, or the capacity of individual perseverance and ingenuity to overcome the odds, are limited by where people live. Here again we are back to that other legacy that succeeding generations must confront, place. Where people live is a consequence of systems of stratification that limit parents' options, limit their educational and occupational opportunities, and as a consequence will, in large measure, limit the choices available to their children.

## INTERGENERATIONAL SOCIAL INEQUALITY, PLACE, AND CRIME

Social space is a primary mechanism through which social inequality is maintained. Where one attends school and the job opportunities that are available are a function of where people live and that is determined by their status. Also, patterns of social life are determined by who lives in the neighborhood. When Anderson (1999) described the Philadelphia neighborhoods where he witnessed social life based on "the code of the street" it was not just a group of kids and young adults that elected to live according to these rules. What Anderson saw was sections of the city where hope and opportunity ceased to exist. These were not simply a group of people who, because they were poor, elected to develop an oppositional culture, but rather values and lifestyles emerged when similarly situated individuals were concentrated together in the face of intergenerational despair and isolation from jobs, good neighborhoods, and decent schools.

In a study of 1980 neighborhood violent crime rates in Seattle, Washington, Crutchfield (1989) found that rates of unemployment and work in the secondary sector were strong predictors of neighborhood crime rates. Seattle census tracts that had relatively large proportions of adults who were in "unstable work" had higher rates of violent crime, defined as murders, aggravated assaults, forcible rapes, and robberies. This study was replicated using 1990 data, with parallel analyses of neighborhoods and labor market participation in Seattle, Cleveland, Ohio, and Washington, DC (Crutchfield, Glusker, & Bridges, 1999). These three cities provide useful contrast on several dimensions; they represent different types of local labor markets, they are in different regions of the U.S., and they have very different crime patterns. Seattle, with Boeing Aircraft, Microsoft and other software producers, biotechnology, and shipping has what might be considered a twenty-first century economy. It has high property crime rates but very low levels of violence. Cleveland is a Lake Erie port city that took advantage of its location to build a shipping capacity that helped it to become a major steel producer. Like cities similar to it, a host of other industries developed in Cleveland because big steel was there. Cleveland in 1990 had high crime rates. Washington's industry is government. There are, of course, many other businesses there, but the city was founded as the seat of the Federal government and the defining characteristic of the local labor market is the government jobs that employ locals and attract others. DC's crime rates, especially violence rates are extremely high.

The earlier study, of 1980 violent crime in Seattle, was comparatively early in the manufacturing decline in the U.S., so by comparison the 1990 data gave us a picture after the decline was well along. The replication also added an indicator of neighborhood educational levels because research that took place in the interim (e.g. Crutchfield et al., 1993) emphasized the importance of education as a mediating force in the relationship of labor markets and juvenile delinquency.

The same pattern of results was found present in 1990 Seattle as existed in 1980; the distribution of labor helped to explain where homicide occurred in the city. In Cleveland, neighborhoods with more marginally employed people had higher homicide rates, but the relationship was not quite as strong as in Seattle. The authors' post-hoc speculation was that the results may have been weakened by the existence of large areas of the inner city that were virtually uninhabited, presumably in part because of deindustrialization and the accompanying loss of jobs, and consequent population decline. Our analysis found that in Cleveland, as in Seattle, neighborhoods, or census tracts, where relatively more marginal workers – secondary sector employees and the unemployed – lived had higher homicide rates than other places.

Employment patterns did not explain the distribution of homicide in Washington. There are several possible reasons why. The colinearity between the percent black in Washington neighborhoods and homicide rates is so high that it washes out all other associations. Although there are no results to support them, the authors speculated about how Washington might be substantively different from the other two cities. One possibility is educational differences. In Seattle and Cleveland the high school dropout rates are normally distributed; with the average number of dropouts in the latter's tracts significantly higher than in the former's. But in Washington, the distribution is bimodal. Most Washington neighborhoods have very high dropout rates but there are a small number of tracts with extremely low rates. This distribution captures the substantial inequality that characterizes the social life of the U.S. capital city. In terms of racial inequality, Washington, DC may be more like the apartheid cities of South Africa than like most other cities. It is a place where both the structure of labor and educational institutions appear to be maintaining very high levels of social inequality.

Returning one last time to the Sullivan and Butterfield examples, we see that where those families lived, and the social conditions of their neighborhoods are consequences of structural inequality and not just the particular circumstances of these individuals, but also of those who live in the same communities. Their labor market experiences are in part a consequence of educational institutions that reproduce social inequality. Even though Butch Bosket received an education late in life (as a result of contact with the criminal justice system), his primary and secondary school formative years were not likely to have been like those typically experienced by those coming of age in middle and upper class suburbs. The young men that Sullivan described can choose to try to break away, but the odds of overcoming inferior inner city schools and the lack of networks that are connected to the working world[7] are against them because of the limitations that come with where they live.

## BEYOND THE AMERICAN CASE

A virtue of generalizable theories is that that they help us to move beyond our observations. The research studies that are cited above have been completed in the U.S. They are studies of Americans, their schools, neighborhoods and cities. Social reproduction and dual labor market theories were developed to explain how inequalities are maintained across generations. They offer compelling alternatives to the bad people explanations of subcultural arguments and they provide a conceptual context that criminologists can use to add richness to our explanations. How might these theories aid us in understanding crime and social inequality elsewhere?

A number of European countries are experiencing two different migration patterns that include some racial or ethnic dynamics that are similar to those in the U.S., although of course they have very different racial histories than do nations of the Americas. As is the case in the U.S., these changes are associated with crime and law enforcement practices in those countries (for examples see the collection of papers in Tonry, 1997). Western European nations that had colonies as a result of the "age of conquest" increasingly have black and brown citizens electing to seek opportunity in the homes of their former colonizers. Britain, France, the Netherlands, and others extend citizenship, or at least eased entrance requirements, to those born in their former colonies. As a result, people can migrate relatively freely. In the United Kingdom the need for workers brought on by the world wars fueled immigration from the West Indies, just as the hunger for workers in the States drew blacks to Detroit and Cleveland during the "Great Migration." In Cardiff Wales, Tiger Bay became the largest black settlement in Europe, and continues as the continents longest existing black community, when Jamaicans moved there to work in ship building. Today Tiger Bay is subsumed in the Butte Town section of Cardiff and while it is not as segregated as the South Side of Chicago, it is set apart from the remainder of the city. London, Paris, Amsterdam, and Rome all have blacker and browner populations as a result of their nations' colonial histories.

The other force darkening Europe is the movement of cheap labor in the form of guest workers. In Germany, large numbers of guest workers have come from Turkey; in Italy from Africa. Economic strains resulting from German reunification have been exacerbated by anti-guest worker sentiments that have boiled up in some regions (Albrecht, 1997). Guest workers and dark skinned "foreigners" (called as such in some nations even if their families immigrated generations ago) typically occupy the low rungs of the labor market hierarchy – secondary sector jobs.

One can reasonably expect, to the extent that these countries are losing manufacturing as a result of globalization, that they may experience problems similar to those in the U.S. To the extent that racial and ethnic stratification focuses these negative consequences on populations of color, they may reproduce the same troubling patterns of inequality and crime as those in the U.S. as well. It is likely that the rioting that rocked Parisian suburbs in the autumn of 2005 are a consequence of processes described above. Rather than dismissing rioters as scum, French officials might do well to examine how their educational institutions and labor market segmentation has perpetuated a disadvantaged class. Rioting is but one of three possible outcomes of maintaining an underclass for generations, other options are crime, our topic here, and organized civil uprising.

Immigrants to France, like African Americans that moved to the industrial cities of the American north and west during the Great Migration, were seeking their promised land. These immigrants came with the belief that their hard work at the low end of the economy was an investment on behalf of their progeny. What many have found, because institutions of both nations have kept them and their children marginalized and their opportunities limited, is that their new nations have not fully admitted them, and have not kept their side of the bargain.

Little wonder then that the reality, so far short of the promised land, for minority people in America's urban slums and Barrios, and for Muslims and North Africans in France's suburbs, have sent some into the streets. In the U.S. some have, instead of becoming criminals or rioters, turned to nationalist movements. It was from the dispossessed and angry sons and daughters of America's Great Migration movers that The Nation of Islam, The Student Non-Violent Coordinating Committee (SNCC), and the Black Panther Party drew members.

When informants told Elijah Anderson that "they didn't want no damn slave job" (1999), it was not, as many in the wider society assert, because they do not want to work hard,[8] but instead they do not want to work hard at jobs with little future, low wages, and where they perceive (frequently very correctly) that they will receive little respect, in short, in secondary sector jobs. Children coming of age where quality education is not available and adults have no jobs, or only low end secondary sector jobs, are what Marxist scholars have referred to as "social dynamite." They are available to be mobilized by political leaders who offer them a rejection of the status quo, an ideology that offers them dignity, and hope. Today in most American inner cities young people are offered few such political visions, or organizations. Americans, the French, and citizens of other industrial nations with racially and ethnically heterogeneous populations, should take note that perpetuation of social inequality is likely to continue to lead to crime and rioting, if they are lucky. If their luck turns, the product of the dispossesseds' anger may be worst.

## NOTES

1. The question was to this author. The question was asked during an interview in a live news broadcast on KIRO TV in Seattle, Washington.
2. This study used the Children of the NLSY, which is following women from the original NLSY sample in 1979 who have given birth; and includes data on the women, their children, and some minimal information on their partners.

3. Critics of dual labor market theory (e.g. Baron & Bielby, 1984) have correctly argued that this dichotomy is oversimplified, but in published research criminologists have found even this crude categorization of occupations to have utility in explaining crime rates.

4. In the late 1980s when I presented early research on this topic to a group of county officials I titled the talk "McJobs ... ". One official issued the challenge that I was using an ethnic slur, but my defence was that the title was intended to cast aspersions on the characteristics of the fast food jobs, not an ethnic group. Then in early 2004, the McDonalds Corporation lost a lawsuit against the publishers of a popular dictionary for including "McJobs" as an entry. I, along with the publisher, I suppose, felt vindicated.

5. See Elijah Anderson's *Street Wise* (1990).

6. The Millionaires' Club is an assistance program for homeless men and those with alcohol or drug problems.

7. Most jobs are obtained not through broadly available information sources such as want adds or employment services, but rather through interpersonal networks where the employed convey information about future openings to those they interact with day to day.

8. Of course, some ghetto residents do not want to work hard, or even work at all, but any casual, or even cynical, but honest observers must admit that the "lazy gene" is unique to no class.

# REFERENCES:

Albrecht, H. (1997). Ethnic minorities, crime, and criminal justice in Germany. In: M. Tonry (Ed.), *Ethnicity, crime, and immigration: Comparative and cross-national perspectives.* Chicago: University of Chicago Press.

Anderson, E. (1990). *Street wise: Race, class and change in an urban community.* Chicago: University of Chicago Press.

Anderson, E. (1999). *Code of the street: Decency, violence, and the moral life of the inner city.* New York: W.W. Norton.

Banfield, E. C. (1968). *The unheavenly city.* Boston: Little, Brown and Company.

Baron, J. N., & Bielby, W. T. (1984). The organization of work in a segmented economy. *American Sociological Review, 49,* 454–473.

Bellair, P. E., Roscigno, V. J., & McNulty, T. L. (2003). Linking local labor market opportunity to violent adolescent delinquency. *Journal of Research in Crime and Delinquency, 40*(1), 6–33.

Bowles, S., & Gintis, H. (1976). *Schooling in capitalist America.* New York: Basic Books.

Butterfield, F. (1995). *All God's children: The Bosket Family and the American tradition of violence.* New York: Avon Books.

Cernkovich, S. A., & Giordano, P. C. (1992). School bonding, race, and delinquency. *Criminology, 30,* 261–291.

Cohen, A. K. (1955). *Delinquent boys.* New York: Free Press.

Crutchfield, R. D. (1989). Labor stratification and violent crime. *Social Forces, 68*(2), 489–512.

Crutchfield, R. D., & Pitchford, S. R. (1997). Work and crime: The effects of labor stratification. *Social Forces, 76,* 93–118.

Crutchfield, R. D., Glusker, A., & Bridges, G. S. (1999). A tale of three cities: Labor markets and homicide. *Sociological Focus, 32*(1), 65–83.
Crutchfield, R. D., Rankin, M. A., & Pitchford, S. R. (1993). Inheriting stakes in conformity: Effects of parents' labor market experience on juvenile violence. Annual Meeting of the American Society of Criminology, Phoenix, AR.
Crutchfield, R. D., Wadsworth, T., Groninger, H., & Drakulich, K. (2006). *Final report: "Labor force participation, labor markets, and crime."* Grant number 2000-IJ-CX-0026. National Institute of Justice, Washington, DC.
Giroux, H. A. (1983). *Theory and resistance in education: A pedagogy for the opposition.* South Hadley, MA: Bergin and Garvey.
Hindelang, M. J., Hirschi, T., & Weis, J. G. (1981). *Measuring delinquency.* Beverly Hills, CA: Sage.
Kalleberg, A. L., & Sorensen, A. B. (1979). The sociology of labor markets. *Annual Review of Sociology, 5*, 351–379.
Kozol, J. (1991). *Savage inequalities: Children in America's schools.* New York: Crown Publishing.
Liebow, E. (1967). *Tally's corner.* Boston: Little, Brown and Company.
MacLeod, J. (1987). *Ain't no makin' it: Leveled aspirations in a low-income neighborhood.* Boulder, CO: Westview.
Massey, D. S., & Denton, N. A. (1993). *American apartheid: Segregation and the making of the underclass.* Cambridge: Harvard University Press.
Murray, C. (1984). *Losing ground: American Social Policy 1950–1980.* USA: Basic Books.
Pager, D. (2003). The mark of a criminal record. *American Journal of Sociology, 108*(5), 937–975.
Pattillo-McCoy, M. (1999). *Black picket fences: Privilege and peril among the black middle class.* Chicago: University of Chicago Press.
Piore, M. J. (1975). Notes for a theory of labor market stratification. In: R. C. Edwards, M. Reich & D. M. Gordon (Eds), *Labor market segmentation.* New York: Heath.
Rubin, L. B. (1976). *Worlds of pain: Life in the working-class family.* New York: Basic Books.
Sciolino, E. (2005). Chirac, lover of spotlight, avoids glare of France's fires. *New York Times,* November 10.
Sullivan, M. L. (1989). *Getting paid: Youth crime and work in the inner city.* Ithaca, NY: Cornell University Press.
Tittle, C. R., Villemez, WJ., & Smith, D. A. (1978). The myth of social class and criminality: An empirical assessment of the empirical evidence. *American Sociological Review, 43*, 643–656.
Tonry, M. (1997). *Ethnicity, crime, and immigration: Comparative and cross-national perspectives.* Chicago: University of Chicago Press.
Wadsworth, T. (2000). Labor markets, delinquency and social control: An empirical assessment of the mediating process. *Social Forces, 78*, 1041–1066.
Wilson, W. J. (1987). *The truly disadvantaged: The inner city, the underclass, and public policy.* Chicago: University of Chicago Press.
Wilson, W. J. (1996). *When work disappears: The world of the new urban poor.* New York: Alfred A. Knopf.

# EMOTIONS, CRIME AND JUSTICE: EXPLORING DURKHEIMIAN THEMES

Susanne Karstedt

## ABSTRACT

*The process of 'emotionalization' of law and criminal justice has decisively changed criminological perspectives on the role of emotions in crime and justice during the last decade. 'Reintegrative Shaming' and Restorative Justice have been influential in re-shaping criminal justice around the globe, and the 'return of emotions' into criminological perspectives, theories and research is presently re-configuring notions of the 'rational offender' and criminal justice policies based on these. This paper seeks to carve out a distinctly sociological perspective on the link between emotions, crime and justice, and explores its potential through four 'Durkheimian themes'.*

## ENTER EMOTIONS

The first document of a systematic inquiry into the links between emotions, law and crime can be found in Plato's *Protagoras*. As he often did Plato cast his arguments in the narrative of a myth. At the dawn of humankind,

Sociological Theory and Criminological Research: Views from Europe and the United States
Sociology of Crime, Law and Deviance, Volume 7, 223–248
Copyright © 2006 by Elsevier Ltd.
All rights of reproduction in any form reserved
ISSN: 1521-6136/doi:10.1016/S1521-6136(06)07011-4

human beings were incapable of living together peacefully, their communities torn with strife and rife with violence. Thus, Zeus, the highest of all Greek gods feared that humankind was in danger of ultimately destroying themselves. He pitied these creatures and wanted to improve their lot. He sent his messenger Hermes, who notably, was the god of both merchants and thieves, down to earth with two gifts that should enable humankind successfully to establish communities and live together safely, amicably and in good order. These two gifts were *shame* and *law*. Zeus had given orders to distribute them equally amongst all human beings. Thus they were all endowed with a 'moral sense', which was based on a strong emotion, and a framework of common norms and principles, the law. The fact that the two gifts were enclosed in the divine package demonstrates that Plato thought that one could not work without the other (Plato, 1987).

This myth, which was well known to Hobbes and presumably Durkheim as well, already includes the basic and in the course of history most influential ideas and theoretical strands on the links between emotions, law and crime, which have shaped our conceptualizations of this link ever since. First, Plato contends that the social order has a strong and necessary foundation in emotions, which he identifies as shame. Second, emotions are countervailing forces, and one emotion can be overcome by a (suitable) other one. The anger and anxiety that is expressed through violence can be overcome by shame as a strong and countervailing emotion, and 'destructive' emotions can be overcome by 'constructive' ones. Finally and linked to the contrast of destructive and constructive emotions, his myth establishes the emotional forces that are present in both crime and justice. We find these ideas in the writings of the protagonists of the Scottish Enlightenment Adam Smith and David Hume, for whom social and moral order was based on 'moral sentiments' of sympathy and compassion, which acted as countervailing forces against unrestricted greed.[1]

The relationship between emotions and crime, penal law and criminal justice, as first outlined by Plato captured the imagination of sociologists, notably of Durkheim and Elias. Durkheim identified 'passions' as a driving force in (violent) crime as well as in punishment. Elias argued that the control of emotions was a powerful mechanism in the civilizing process, and he attributed a decisive role to shame. Elias and subsequently historians of crime have linked both, the long-term decline of violence since early modern times (see Eisner, 2003; Fletcher, 1997) and the changes in criminal justice, in particular the decline of more brutal punishments and sanctions that inflicted often visible signs of infamy on the offender (Whitman, 2003, Chapter 4) to changes in the emotional culture and practices of societies.

As compelling as Plato's narrative was, it simultaneously came with a legacy of dangerous routes in the conceptualization of the links between emotions, justice and crime. The most obvious one is that he posits *one basic emotion* as the foundation of law and justice, at the expense of a more nuanced view of a range of widely differing emotions. A number of contemporary authors have been tempted to take this route (e.g. see Kahan, 1998; Solomon, 1994; Karstedt, 2002; Nussbaum, 2004, for a discussion), in particular those who see retribution as the ultimate reason of penal justice. It comes as a striking fact that the 'moral sentiments' identified by these authors as foundations of law and justice, can be ultimately termed 'negative emotions', like disgust, hatred or revenge (Karstedt, 2002, p. 303). Further, Plato appears to imply that emotion is *constitutive* for law and justice, i.e. the edifice of law and justice is erected on moral sentiments, and would falter without them (see Taylor, 1987). However, the mythical narrative is less than clear here, and two other perspectives seem to be equally viable. These are the *functionalist* perspective according to which emotions produce compliance (e.g. Braithwaite, 1989) and the *indicative* perspective that emotions are expressions of moral engagement and attached to a moral principle or judgment, but do not motivate moral action (Nunner-Winkler, 1998; see for discussion Karstedt, 2002). However, in much of the current discussion, the constitutive perspective seems to prevail, and with it the dangerous notion that criminal justice and punishment ultimately need to give expression to those individual and collective sentiments on which they are imputedly based.

The 'return of emotions' to criminological theorizing and research during the last decade emerged as a most promising strand of fresh approaches and innovative thinking, with regard to conceptualization, research methodology, alternatives to criminal justice and crime prevention. It was exactly the link between crime and criminal justice established by a focus on emotions, which brought the paradox of three centuries of criminal justice to the fore, as Lawrence Sherman (2003) astutely pointed out in his Presidential Address 'Reason for Emotion' to the American Society of Criminology in 2002: *Criminals are rational, justice is emotional.* This paradox has presumably shaped criminal justice policies and criminological theorizing more than anything else during the last decades. A range of new developments in criminal justice policies demonstrated the intricate and volatile relationship between emotion and reason. Thus, the 're-emotionalization of law' or the 'reassertion of emotionality in law' (Laster & O'Malley, 1996; see Karstedt, 2002) was accompanied by new strategies of situational crime prevention, risk-based sanctions and deterrence, which built upon the imputed rationality of offenders (and victims). The move towards 'actuarial justice' as Feeley and Simon (1994; see O'Malley, 2004) had termed a range of new criminal justice policies that were based on rational and calculable risk assessments instead of moral sentiments, however, turned into criminal justice policies that were tuned to and driven by expressions of collective emotions of anger and fear in the public sphere. Freiberg (2001, p. 265) has argued that such a predominantly rationalist approach to criminal policy 'will fail to compete successfully with the more emotive law-and-order policies which tend to resonate with the public'. The simultaneity of such widely differing criminal justice policies demonstrated more than anything else how (rational) perceptions of risks are easily transformed into feelings of insecurity and ultimately fear, and consequently, how risk-based criminal justice policies are captured by to collective sentiments, and amplify emotions of fear and feelings of insecurity. Risk-based crime prevention and criminal justice, it seems, actually achieve the opposite of what they are supposed to do (Hope & Karstedt, 2003).

In a similar vein, Katz' (1988) path-breaking book *Seductions of Crime*, and Thomas Scheff's (1990a, 1994, 1997) work on the shame–anger–rage cycle and its relation to individual and collective violence had questioned the 'rationality' of offenders by demonstrating the powerful role of emotions in the commitment of crimes. Research on the decision-making process of street robbers (e.g. de Haan & Vos, 2003) showed that assumptions about the rationality of many types of offenders or offenses needed a thorough revision in favour of the emotional processes involved in the 'reasoning' of offenders before, during and after their offense. In drawing conclusions from the failures of 'expressive economics' in contemporary criminal justice, Sherman (2003, p. 2ff) called for a new paradigm of 'emotionally intelligent justice' that radically differed from 'expressive economics'. Whilst in the prevailing criminal justice paradigm of expressive economics 'the state reacts emotionally towards rational offenders' (*ibid*. p. 7), emotionally intelligent justice acknowledges the emotionality of offenders, and the state reacts rationally towards these emotions, as well as to those of the victims and the community. Emotionally intelligent justice seeks to restrict expressive emotionality as an institutional response and of those who work in its institutions, in particular where it becomes counterproductive to its objectives of repairing harm and promoting compliance with the law. However, it appears that politicians, criminal justice professionals and the public need a thorough '*éducation sentimentale*' in matters of crime and justice on the long road from expressive economics toward emotionally intelligent justice.

## SOCIOLOGICAL PERSPECTIVES AND DURKHEIMIAN THEMES

Whilst the return of emotions to criminology opens up new routes of inter-disciplinary research for criminologists in psychology, neurology and bio-logy (Sherman, 2003), there seems to be a need for sociology to assert its role in this endeavour. The contribution of sociological theorizing and research consists mainly in connecting micro-level emotional processes and interpersonal emotional dynamics with macro-level socio-cultural forces (Turner & Stets, 2005, p. 154). The sociological contribution therefore seems to be decisive in exploring in which ways emotions are linked to the institutional framework of criminal justice, how criminal justice policies are shaped by collective emotions and how emotional dynamics define individual encounters with the institutions of justice. Both micro- and macro-level research was involved in bringing emotions back to criminology. The work of Jack Katz, and Thomas Scheff invigorated a micro-sociological approach of emotion research, combined with a turn toward 'naturalistic' methodologies in the tradition of Goffman, Sykes and Matza. Elias' *Civilizing Process* currently functions as a framework for macro-level and historical research on violence and criminal justice. Durkheim provided the foundation and backdrop for the most successful contemporary criminal justice innovation, restorative justice and 'reintegrative shaming'. John Braithwaite's *Crime, Shame and Reintegration* (1989) actually inaugurated the return of emotions to criminal justice, and in many ways Scheff (1990b) was justified in referring to him as 'the new Durkheim'. In a very Durkheimian tradition, Braithwaite showed that shame was a decisive factor in both, the causation and control of crime. Sherman therefore identifies restorative justice as a seminal example of 'emotionally intelligent justice' (2003, 10ff), which takes emotions seriously enough to react rationally toward them.

Nonetheless, Durkheim has remained surprisingly invisible in the global success of restorative justice, and did not figure prominently in the return of emotions to criminology,[2] despite the fact that he had stated that 'passion is the soul of punishment' (Durkheim, 1893/1964, p. 86), and thus had provided a sociological lead for the criminology of emotions.[3] His theory has recently been named as a classic example of an account of modernity and criminal justice 'that is plainly wrong' (Whitman, 2005, p. 24).[4] At a first glance, the re-emotionalization of the public sphere and criminal justice in late modernity appears to prove Whitman's case. However, the rise of vigilantism and the support of capital punishment in closely knit and trusting communities (Messner, Baumer, & Rosenfeld, 2002, 2006), or the link between collectivistic orientations and punitive attitudes (King, 2005), point into a different direction albeit on a much lower level of aggregation than cross-national studies allow for. What emerges in these studies, and mainly in the way Braithwaite uses Durkheim, is a continuing influence of his ideas on emotions, crime and justice, which stem from his concern with the conditions promoting social solidarity, cohesion and social control in modern societies.

The sociology of emotions, as a field of systematic study, comprises a wide range of theoretical approaches from 'dramaturgical and cultural theorizing', symbolic interactionism to structural theories (Turner & Stets, 2005), thus mirroring the diversity in psychological research on emotions. In particular, it has not yet produced a body of systematic empirical research on which criminological research on emotions could draw. Criminology could therefore take a lead in contributing to a sociological body of research on emotions, based on a small but growing number of seminal studies. I will explore the role of sociological perspectives in the criminology of emotions through 'themes', which I have termed 'Durkheimian themes' as they are linked to or emerge from Durkheim's ideas and conceptualizations of the relationship between emotions, crime and justice. With these themes, I relate back to the classic, who Smith and Alexander (2005) call the 'cultural Durkheim', and to those parts of his work that analyses and theorizes the *affective-moral forces* in society. The 'cultural Durkheim' used both punishment and crime to elaborate how affective-moral forces functioned in society. Presently, the 'cultural Durkheim' emerges on the criminological scene with a number of studies that show how even today the sacred and the profane, rituals and moral boundaries underpin the social meanings of punishment and criminal justice. Seminal studies are Reiner's (1995) and Loader and Mulcahy's (2003) analyses of police organization, Smith's (1996) study of executions and Carlsson and Hoff's (2000) analysis of morality and the market.

Durkheim started from the basic assumption that crime and punishment are related to other social practices, and as such to social institutions (see Whitman, 2005, p. 20), which give expression to emotions on the one hand and which elicit emotions on the other.[5] Accordingly, specific types of crime and expressive practices of punishment illuminate or in a more technical way indicate the emotional culture and moral sentiments of society, and vice versa.[6] I identify four themes and show how contemporary criminology has developed new ways of engaging with them, and has incorporated other and more recent traditions in doing so. The first and perhaps most Durkheimian theme concerns the *transformation* of emotions in procedures (and rituals) of justice. Far from being based on a unique emotion, which finds its ultimate expression in punishment, the procedures of justice transform negative and more disruptive emotions into emotions of attachment and feelings of solidarity. A body of theorizing and research on restorative justice and procedural justice gives evidence of their capacity to facilitate and achieve such a transformation. The second theme takes up Durkheim's idea that the passions causing crime and its control are closely linked through the respective social practices in which they are both embedded: Anger, blame and revenge can as well cause crime as they are expressed through punishment. The third theme is based on Durkheim's juxtaposition of collectivistic and individualistic social practices and moral sentiments, and focuses on the *social embeddedness of expressive punitiveness.* The fourth and final theme explores how *the politics of status* impact on expressive punishment and moral indignation in the public sphere, and actually engages with a theme that Durkheim ignored.

## JUSTICE, RITUAL, AND THE TRANSFORMATION OF EMOTIONS: RESTORATIVE AND PROCEDURAL JUSTICE

Legal institutions and in particular the criminal justice system are the very institutions that are designed to deal with the most intense emotions and emotional conflicts, individual as well as collective ones. Criminal courts and procedures provide a prominent institutional space and mechanism for handling the emotions involved in and elicited by crime. Offenders, victims and witnesses bring their emotions to the courtroom; offenders feel shame and remorse, or humiliation; offences provoke feelings of moral disgust; victims as well as offenders elicit our compassion and sympathy (Karstedt, 2002, p. 300). Court procedures provide highly formalized rituals that restrict emotions on the one hand, and include strong expectations how emotions should be displayed on the other.[1] All criminal justice institutions, from the courts to the police follow a dramaturgy and make use of powerful iconography. This makes the topic of crime and justice so attractive to the media, which themselves appear to *reflect and amplify* the content of criminal justice drama and icons. *Feeling rules* and *display rules* are defining features of the proceedings in the highly formalized setting of courts, and they mirror the broader emotion culture and emotion ideology of society (Hochschild, 2003; see Karstedt, 2002).

Whilst the conventional story of modern penal law portrays a very restricted role for emotions in criminal justice so that emotions do not interfere with reason as the true preserve of law (Bandes, 1999, p. 2), the sociological narrative, starting with Durkheim and Mead, actually focuses on the role of emotions in criminal justice. Durkheim interpreted the emotional dynamics of the rituals of justice as a process of 'collective effervescence', and as a product of the 'moral density' that criminal justice procedures can achieve (Durkheim, 1912/1995; see Collins, 2001, 2004). Collective effervescence emerges in a physical assembly of people, who share a focus of attention, and it elicits feelings of group solidarity, 'emotional energy' in the participants and feelings of morality (Collins, 2001, p. 28). Collins, the contemporary proponent of theorizing rituals of emotions, calls this 'high ritual density' (*ibid.*). It is of highest importance that such social rituals as they take place in criminal justice *transform* one emotion into another. They initiate the sharing of emotions, like outrage, anger, fear or humiliation, which are brought to the courtroom or other procedures by the different parties involved in the first place. These are then transformed into feelings of solidarity, morality, sympathy and hope. Whilst Durkheim focused on the transformation of outrage into feelings of solidarity mostly at the expense of the offender and thus on the *exclusionary transformation* of emotions, restorative justice aims at the *inclusionary transformation* of emotions, as captured by Braithwaite's (1989) concept of 'reintegrative shaming'.

Contemporary programmes of restorative justice – from Truth and Reconciliation Commissions to 'sentencing circles' and restorative justice conferences – are all based on the emotional engagement of the participants. As such, they differ from 'court rituals' designed to determine guilt and sanctions, which only give miniscule and delineated space to emotions, and thus aim more at the suppression of emotions (Sherman, 2003, p. 11). The objective of restorative justice is to share 'inclusionary emotions' like remorse, guilt, shame and empathy among the participants, and thus to achieve the transformation of the initiating emotions of anger, fear and disgust. If restorative justice settings are to be successful in the process of emotional transformation they have to heighten the awareness of the initiating emotions, and not avoid them.[8]

Reports from restorative justice conferences often testify to high levels of emotional energy among participants and dynamics of collective effervescence (Rossner, forthcoming). One way to achieve this seems to be the decisively non-hierarchical setting of restorative justice procedures, which gives equal standing and voice to all parties involved, and provides network support for all participants. Such settings at least avoid the negative emotions aroused by inequality and highly differing power and status of participants (see Kemper, 1978; Barbalet, 1998; Turner & Stets, 2005, Chapter 7). Though the role of the situational setting of restorative justice procedures for the transformation of emotions has not yet been theorized, structural and exchange theories of emotion corroborate a distinct role for a non-hierarchical setting in the emotion dynamics of restorative justice. As far as restorative justice is successful in establishing reciprocal relationships, and/or generating a higher density of networks for offenders and victims in which such relationships can be embedded, it will elicit more positive emotions, and more emotions of cohesion (Lawler & Yoon, 1996, 1998; Markovsky & Lawler, 1994). In contrast, the distinct hierarchical setting of courts with strong power and status differentials will generate more negative feelings of resentment, anger and ultimately defiance (see below), and thus promote the exclusionary transformation of emotions.

Research so far seems to support claims by restorative justice to being 'emotionally intelligent', though there is some evidence that victims benefit more and consistently, from restorative justice than offenders (Sherman & Strang, 2004; Sherman, 2003). Strang (2002) shows that victims are in fact interested in apologies and explanations, and thus in an exchange that elicits inclusionary and positive emotions. Victims participating in restorative justice conferences show significantly less desire for revenge and harming offenders after violent crime (Strang, 2002, p. 139), and consequently less divisive affects. They are generally less fearful of the offender and crime in general (Sherman, 2003, p. 17). Both results support the claim of transforming emotions in the course of restorative justice procedures. Braithwaite and his colleagues (Ahmed, Harris, Braithwaite, & Braithwaite, 2001) provide evidence that for a range of offenses, offenders' attitudes about compliance with the law are not shaped by exclusionary emotions of stigmatic shame, but if at all, by inclusionary and exchange-related positive emotions. The fact that restorative justice works best for offenders of violent crime in reducing recidivism seems to confirm the transformative effect of a procedure that arouses strong and countervailing emotions against those that are related to violence like anger, fear or humiliation.

Even if restorative justice provides a particularly 'emotionally intelligent' procedure, formal criminal justice actually comprises settings and procedures that seem to be capable of accommodating emotions and initiating those transformative emotional dynamics that Durkheim saw as essential in sanctioning offenders. The growing body of theory and research on procedural justice by Tyler and his colleagues shows that specific procedural characteristics seem to have a vital role in future compliance with the law, and satisfaction with and acceptance of outcomes (see MacCoun, 2005, for an overview). Though research on how emotions are directly involved and affected by these procedures has been rare until now, evidence so far shows that the emotional overtones of criminal justice officials and in particular their disrespectful behaviour towards citizens has a significant impact on future law-abiding behaviour (Tyler & Huo, 2002; Tyler, 1998).

It is important in this context that procedural justice provides a setting that actually allows for the transformation of emotions, and that this is achieved by procedural characteristics that at least alleviate the impact of hierarchical criminal justice. These characteristics are (amongst others) 'standing' of the defendant, i.e. dignity and respect for individuals; hearing of all points of views, and ample opportunity for people to tell their story; and finally, unbiased consideration of all points of view. If these are provided, individuals are more likely to accept even outcomes adverse for themselves, and to comply with the law. In particular, the acceptance of adverse outcomes seems to point to the transformation of emotions of anger, feelings of injustice and revenge into feelings of trust and moral solidarity, thus attributing a much smaller role to the unrestricted pursuit of self-interest in court and justice proceedings than normally assumed for the 'rational' defendant. Further, proper procedures can alleviate insecurity and fear (van den Bos & Lind, 2002), and instill trust. The various effects of procedural justice that have been demonstrated by this body of research speak to its potential as an *affective moral force* that supersedes the pursuit of self-interest. This is classical Durkheim.

All three dimensions of procedural justice as detailed above are non-hierarchical, and their provision and observation clearly restrict justice officials from debasing, humiliating and otherwise disrespectful behaviours towards offenders that easily instigate feelings of anger and resentment. According to exchange and structural theories of emotion, the empowerment of defendants through procedural justice will contribute to eliciting more positive emotions, as far as these relationships are perceived as more reciprocal and cohesive (Turner & Stets, 2005, 194ff, Lawler & Yoon, 1996). If these instill generalized trust in the institutions of criminal justice they might prohibit victims from engaging in revenge; Pfeiffer and his colleagues found in their study of violence in German schools that juveniles who report a violent victimization to the police were less likely to engage in subsequent and presumably revengeful violent behaviour.[9]

The fact that victims are most dissatisfied if they do not receive a promised restorative justice conference (Sherman, 2003, p. 18) suggests that courts and alternative procedures as a space for the expression of their stories and feelings are hugely important in the transformative dynamics of emotions in criminal justice.[10] Restorative justice and procedural justice are closely linked in that they both offer routes towards procedures and settings that restrict the emotional impact of power differentials in criminal justice, and allow for the transformation of anger, revenge and disgust into feelings of social cohesion. Both embed moral suasion in (collective) emotional participation, though procedural justice obviously in more formalized ways and 'rituals'. Both restorative justice and procedural justice give equal weight to offenders and victims, thus restricting victims from (only) taking the high moral ground, which seems to be essential in repairing damaged social ties. As Sarat (2001) points out for capital punishment trials, the inclusion and empowerment of victims can have detrimental effects for the offender, and can actually increase punitive sentiments; here the transformation process amplifies the initiating emotions. This indicates conditions and procedures which are more conducive towards 'exclusionary emotions' (see also Laster & O'Malley, 1996; Karstedt, 2002; Zimring, 2003). However, the comparison between restorative and procedural justice suggests that the degree of formalization might be less important in achieving the emotional transformation – and formal procedures less inimical to emotions in criminal justice – then the implementation of non-hierarchical structures and procedures, which are emotionally sensitive and sensible.

## SOCIAL BONDS, EMOTION AND CRIME

As much as Durkheim saw punishment as an expression of passions, he assumed that crime, and in particular violent crime was related to the emotional foundations of social solidarity. Where social bonds are strong and elicit strong emotions, violent crime should be more prevalent than where these bonds are weaker. He found empirical support in the higher rates of violent crime in the rural communities of 19th century France in contrast to its urban regions (which has been corroborated, see Karstedt, 2001, 2005). In his sociological theory of emotions, Thomas Scheff explores central emotions of social bonds, and the ways in which these are linked to individual and collective violence. For Scheff, the central emotions of strong social bonds are pride and shame, with pride as the positive emotion through which social bonds are formed, and shame as a more ambivalent emotion. Shame is the emotion of damaged social ties, and if it is acknowledged and engaged with, it will contribute to re-attuning social relationships and restoring social bonds. In contrast, if shame is bypassed, suppressed and remains unacknowledged, it initiates shame–anger–rage cycles that can spiral out of control and ultimately result in individual and collective violence (and another shame–rage sequence). Shame–anger sequences that cause resentment direct anger and aggression against others. Scheff has explored such shame–anger–rage sequences and their relation to violence on the micro level as well as on the macro level of socio-cultural forces, with a seminal work on the Nazi regime in Germany and the origins of World War II (1994), and more recently on collective and genocidal violence in the former Yugoslavia (forthcoming).

Scheff's work has provided the framework for recent studies on hate crime, a crime that is seen as genuinely motivated by strong emotions.[11] Ray, Smith, and Wastell (2004) found that racist offenders in the UK directed their anger resulting from unacknowledged shame, against South Asians, who were seen as more successful, but illegitimately so. What emerges from their data is a mixture of lost pride, felt threat and shame. However, as Gadd and Jefferson (2006) astutely point out, it is questionable whether 'shame and pride are ... the 'master' emotions behind racist violence', which seems to be intertwined more with feelings of envy, fear and disgust. In their own study of a community in the North of England, particularly in their case studies, unacknowledged shame emerges as only one of the emotions in the motivational mix of young racist offenders (ibid., Chapter 4; Gadd, 2006). Interestingly, results from both studies show that shame is rooted in multiple disadvantages and perceived injustice, which define the cultural context, social background and networks of these offenders. Dixon, Gadd, and Jefferson (Dixon & Gadd, 2006; Gadd, Dixon, & Jefferson, 2005) found in discussions with focus groups from the area that deep-rooted feelings of loss and hurt pride prevailed, resulting from the 'fall of grace' in a once economically thriving area. Loss of former status and economic power, and ensuing feelings of alienation were pervasive, and strong feelings were directed against Asian – often erroneously perceived as immigrants – who were seen as 'not deserving', and a threat to scarce resources.

In fact Scheff (1994) himself had identified loss of power and alienation as conditions setting the emotional tone for the German people after World War I, and the scene for collective shame–anger sequences, which led them not only to adopt the Nazi regime but later also to engage in collective and genocidal violence. Two sociological theories of emotion focus on power and status relationships, the theories of Theodore Kemper (1978, 1990; Kemper & Collins, 1990) and Robert Thamm (2004; see Turner and Stets, 2005, Chapter 6). In particular changes in the relative power and status (or prestige) have large effects on the arousal of positive and negative emotions. Positive emotions such as satisfaction, security and confidence are attached to gains in power and status, and conversely, anxiety, fear and loss of confidence is experienced by individuals who have a low status or experience a loss of power. Thamm (2004) relates negative experiences of status–power relationships to a variety of emotions like resentment, hopelessness, powerlessness and shame, which all reflect deprivation and alienation. The findings of Gadd, Dixon and Jefferson on violent racist offenders indeed reflect the total spectrum of these emotions for the cultural context and social networks of these offenders, and highlight their relation with loss of power and status on the individual and group level (Gadd et al., 2005).

The large body of research on the relationship between inequality, deprivation, exclusion and violence lends itself to exploring emotional dynamics as the *mechanism* that connects the micro level of violent crime with macro-level socio-cultural forces. Inequality shifts the affective-moral forces of social cohesion and solidarity, and consequently affects the emotional experiences of social groups. Whilst the common experience of inequality, exclusion and injustice fuels anger and potentially violent reactions through processes of collective effervescence within the excluded group, it will evoke fear within the group of higher status (see e.g. Garland, 2001).[12] Bourgois' (1995) study of street culture and the 'search for respect', as well as other gang research provides evidence for such emotional processes that are linked to individual and collective violence. Inequality further pervades all institutions of society and reaches far into the system of criminal justice, thus determining how penal justice feeds into these affective-moral forces. Encounters with criminal justice officials that are perceived as unfair and unjust, namely on the street level of policing, have sparked collective violence and rioting, e.g. following the beating of Rodney King and the trial of the police involved. Lynching, as far as it is seen as an outburst of collective emotions and violence (see Messerschmidt, 1997; Garland, 2005), is a telling example of the intricate connections between inequality, perceived injustice, criminal justice, and violence. White Southerners felt that they had lost power and status in relation to black Southerners, which had been exacerbated by a difficult economic situation. Accordingly, the criminal justice system did not 'do justice' to what they felt was their legitimate status. Lynching had all ingredients of 'collective effervescence' and 'high ritual power' (Collins, 2001, p. 28; Collins, 2004, Chapter 3) in the way it was executed, and collective emotions were fuelled by the sense of injustice and anger that pervaded the small and tightly knit communities of white Southerners (Garland, 2005). It seems that it is through the lens of inequality and violence that criminology can realign the affective and symbolic perspectives with the structural and functional ones in Durkheim's work.

# COMMUNITIES, COLLECTIVE SENTIMENTS AND EXPRESSIVE PUNITIVENESS

The 'reassertion of emotionality in law' (Laster & O'Malley, 1996) and in public engagement with crime and punishment in contemporary Western democracies came as an unexpected development in these socially and culturally differentiated societies. In complex societies those who decide on punishment are separated from those who inflict it, and these agents are detached from victims, and the audience of criminal justice. Criminal justice procedures and policies are more or less 'insulated' against collective emotionality and direct pressure from politicians and the public. As Zimring and Johnson (2006) argue, harsh punishments are the result of a lack of such insulation, of which they cite the United States as a prominent example. The separation of institutions of justice in modern societies – and of democratic institutions as well – restricts and tempers the impatience and urgency of action that emotions elicit (see Elster, 2004, Chapter 8). Criminal justice and its procedures are organized in ways that avoid the impression of urgency and impatience, and we are suspicious of sentences that are too quickly meted out. The distance and impersonality of the punishment process, and the fragmentation of the audiences in contemporary societies all speak against the presently observed re-emotionalization of punishment in the public sphere.[13] Durkheim himself had argued that those forms of punishment that powerfully evoke the 'moral background structures of society' (Smith & Alexander, 2005) would give way to less emotive forms in modern societies.

It is obvious that the assumption of a uniform process of modernization in the realm of criminal justice and punishment – as Durkheim had assumed – is wrong. There is sufficient evidence that criminal justice systems developed differently (Whitman, 2003, 2005), and that societies of fairly equal levels of modernization differ considerably with regard to their criminal justice systems and policies (see O'Malley, 2004). If the re-emotionalization of punishment can be seen as an inversion of the modernizing (and civilizing) process, or if there is a universal and common undercurrent of revenge and emotive retribution, that different societies and their criminal justice institutions contain in various and changing ways in different historical periods (as Zimring and Johnson would argue), is presently hard to discern. However, a variety of factors have been made responsible for the return of emotions to the sphere of crime and punishment. First, this process is seen as responding to changes in the wider emotional culture, and of the moral imagination of late modern societies (Barbalet, 1998; Karstedt, 2002).

More specifically, general insecurity and fear in contemporary societies, as well as actual experiences of crime and victimization seem to fuel collective emotions around crime and justice (Garland, 2001; Girling, Loader, & Sparks, 2000; Young, 2003). Perceptions of risks of victimization are transformed into emotions of insecurity, anger and rage against (potential) offenders, and subsequently demands for harsher punishment (Ditton, Farrall, Gilchrist, & Bannister, 2004).

Even if we do not agree with Charles Taylor (1992) that 'victimization' is the defining feature of public discourse in late modernity, a certain imbalance in public interest, moral commitment and compassion towards victims and offenders is nonetheless obvious (Karstedt, 2002). In particular, Laster and O'Malley (1996) have attributed the reassertion of emotionality in law to the new role of victims in public discourse and criminal justice procedures. Franklin Zimring (2003) is the most prominent proponent of this perspective, and has developed the most advanced theoretical argument. According to Zimring, the death penalty was resurrected in the United States because it was reconstructed as a symbolic acknowledgement of the victim's rights, and as a form of compensation for the loss suffered by the victim's family. Capital trials and executions have been transformed into practices and rituals that should assist the victims. Sarat (2001) describes how victims have an impact in capital punishment trials, and (successfully) demand to witness executions. His study of capital punishment in the United States demonstrates that punishment procedures are becoming less distanced and impersonal, and the separation of spheres is replaced by integrative and symbolic action of high ritual effect. This generates moral density and symbolizes the emotive restoration of social cohesion (see Smith, 2003).

'Expressive punitiveness' can be defined as the demand for actions 'that seek immediate retribution' (Gault & Sabini, 2000, p. 499). In line with Elster's (2004) definition this conceptualization includes emotional content as well as the inherent impatience and urgency that characterizes emotion-driven action tendencies in the realm of criminal justice. As such, expressive punitiveness – as indicated by support for the prison build-up (Useem, Liedka, & Piehl, 2003), for the death penalty and harsh prison sentences even for less severe offences (Zimring, Hawkins, & Kamin, 2001; Zimring, 2003) – represents pressing demands by the public (and their fulfillment through crime policies) to replace the separation of spheres in criminal justice, drawn-out and cumbersome penal procedures and the fragmentation of audiences in favour of swift, visible and 'ostentatious punishment' (Pratt, 2000). Expressive punitiveness seeks to (re-)evoke the moral background structures of society that seem to be lost in contemporary criminal justice procedures, and to re-establish punishment as an affective-moral force. Two and paradoxically contrasting socio-emotional patterns should generate expressive punitiveness. Communities with comparably high social cohesion will produce collective sentiments, which coincide with high levels of expressive punitiveness. However, high levels of punitiveness might be equally found where feelings of loss of social solidarity and lack of collective sentiments prevail. In relation to the latter, Tyler and Boeckmann (1997, p. 256) observe in their study of support for three-strike policies in California that 'those citizens who feel that the moral and social consensus that holds society together is declining are more supportive of punitive public policies'. In a study on support for the death penalty, Messner et al. (2002) found that in fact individuals who trusted others less and found them less fair and helpful, showed higher support for the death penalty. Interestingly, and in line with the paradox outlined above, this relationship on the individual level was reversed on the collective level of communities. Levels of support for capital punishment were higher in communities with higher levels of social cohesion as expressed in feelings of generalized trust. Demands for expressive punishment seem to reflect the moral density within communities, and to indicate a communal opposition against criminal justice policies that are seen as not doing justice to the community, as sympathetic to offenders and treating them with 'inappropriate leniency' (Zimring et al., 2001, p. 231).

Support for capital punishment emerges as a type of community opposition against distanced and 'rationalized' criminal justice and government. Distrust of government increases support for several types of expressive punishment. Zimring et al. (2001, p. 232) found that citizens who were most distrustful of government were most supportive of sweeping, 'broad and extreme penal measures'. However, if this mirrors the affective-moral climate of communities and their moral consensus, this relation should differ between communities. Messner, Baumer, and Rosenfeld's (2006) findings corroborate this conclusion. Whilst whites who distrust the government and criminal justice are strong proponents of capital punishment, blacks who are distrustful are less likely to demand this extreme penal measure. It can be assumed that the disproportionate representation of black offenders amongst those executed, on death row, and in prison, as well as miscarriages of justice against poor, black offenders are fuelling anger and resentments against the government, and simultaneously render the death penalty a threat against the black community.[14]

Zimring (2003) evokes Durkheimian ideas and even nomenclature to explain the mechanisms underlying the resurrection of the death penalty in the

U.S. He argues that within the 'vigilante tradition' in the Southern states of the United States, punishment is viewed as a community responsibility rather than government power. Lynchings were in fact – as Garland (2005) has shown – fuelled by mistrust in criminal justice, and by the wish to overcome the imputed failure of remote and detached criminal justice procedures. As Zimring (2003, p. 89) argues punishment becomes an 'expression of the will of the community' rather than the power of a distant and alien government. When citizens embrace vigilante traditions and values, the 'affective bond from communal social control ... is transferred to state authority for executions and other serious punishment' (p. 99). As Messner et al. (2006) observe, 'he suggests that a vigilante tradition facilitates the embrace of harsh forms of punishment as a communal ritual'. The state becomes in the eyes of its citizens the willing executioner of the collective sentiments of the community, and of the felt necessity to restore its social cohesion. Their findings are generally supportive of Zimring's model, as both government distrust as well as a history of lynching increase support for capital punishment, however only amongst the white population.

On the individual level, the role of collective rather than individualistic attitudes for the formation of expressive punitiveness has been explored in a recent study by Anna King (2005). In her in-depth interviews and using both qualitative and quantitative methods, she found that strong attachment to a community, of which the individual's identity is seen as an integral part, is related to strong and extreme punitive attitudes. In contrast, those who define their identity through their own achievements are less punitive and more forgiving towards offenders. Often, definitions of identity in terms of the collectivity mirror a sense of loss of social cohesion and concern about moral values as well as declining social ties among people. For these individuals, harsh punishment and the dramaturgy of criminal justice evoke and strengthen those background moral-affective forces in society that they deem to be lost, but which are essential for their own identity.

Rather than individualization and ensuing insecurity, collective sentiments and the affective forces of strong social cohesion seem to be at the roots of re-emotionalization in criminal justice. This appears to be true for individuals and communities alike, with the latter naturally differing in how punishment is seen as enhancing or threatening the moral-affective forces within the community. The return of emotive punishment and the strong emotions that support it illuminate the complex and contingent possibilities for creating solidarity in contemporary societies.

# STATUS POLITICS, MORAL INDIGNATION AND THE DRAMATURGY OF PUNISHMENT

Social practices of status and power define the emotional tone and prevalent sensibilities in society, and they elicit powerful emotional responses. Criminal justice itself reflects these and uses punishment as a mechanism to do 'status politics'. Consequently, status and power differentials should indeed impact on punishment and its emotional content (Whitman, 2005). Durkheim ignored the impact of differences of status and power on punishment and its social evolution in favour of his concern with social cohesion. Danish social theorist Svend Ranulf (1938), who had had a comeback in recent years (Barbalet, 2002), explored the moral-affective forces in class society through a focus on the lower middle classes. In *Moral Indignation and the Middle Class Psychology*, he sought to understand the origins of the distanced and fragmented sphere of criminal justice or what he called the 'disinterested tendency to inflict punishment' (as opposed to personal vengeance). He connected a macro-level perspective of class analysis with a micro-level theory of collective emotional dynamics of punitiveness. According to Ranulf, the impulse to punish results from resentment, envy and moral indignation that arise from one's position within the class structure. Like other and subsequent proponents of structural theories of emotion (Kemper, Thamm), he links the experience of insufficient rewards, and the lack of fulfillment of legitimate expectations to shame, envy and resentment towards others. Notably, the envy that members of the middle class feel against the rich is channeled into resentment and moral indignation against those *below* them in the social hierarchy. In the social position of the 'middling sort' (Benjamin Franklin) moral indignation and the punishment of complete strangers function as powerful mechanisms to alleviate felt shame, and improve one's sense of self-esteem and pride in the precarious socioeconomic situation between the rich and poor.

Whilst Ranulf based his argument on the role of achievement and merit, contemporary societies are more defined by success than by achievement alone: status can be gained by luck, specific talents or just good looks, and it is debatable which kind and strength of emotions the status politics of *pure success* elicit (Neckel, 1999; Young, 2003). As much as resentment is still directed against those in lower status positions, strong punitive impulses are directed as well against the higher classes, in case they morally fail. Contemporary audiences seem to enjoy the spectacle of celebrities, high-ranking politicians and managers being accused of crimes, and severely punished (see Braithwaite & Drahos, 2002).

Ranulf's theory seems to be corroborated by the fact that higher levels of punitiveness are often found amongst those with less education and lower socio-economic status, although this is not necessarily so. The relations between economic insecurity and punitiveness were found to be inconclusive in recent studies (Useem et al., 2003; Maruna & King, forthcoming). Maruna and King who conducted the most intensive test of Ranulf's theory in the UK, found that members of the middle class, those who work in high-status and high-autonomy professions, have a high education and feel more financially secure, are generally less likely to espouse punitive views. However, higher income coincides with higher levels of moral indignation and punitiveness, and it seems that status anxiety is not restricted to the lower middle classes as Ranulf had thought. Most interestingly, they found that the strongest punitive attitudes were directed against young people. The theme of a lack of respect, anxieties about one's own status as an elderly person, and a felt loss of power over young people is pervasive in their in-depth interviews. Feelings of generational injustice and envy of the young appear as a strong undercurrent in these narratives. Maruna and King's subjects did not only feel the emotional consequences of a lack of power, but also a lack of cohesion between the generations. More than anything else, these interviews reflect a shift in the affective-moral forces connecting the young and the older generation that can explain the highly emotional punitive impulse against young people.

Structural theorists of emotion argue that shifts in status relations and redistribution of status elicit strong emotions. On the collective level these will change the emotional tone and the emotion culture of whole societies. In his book *Harsh Punishment* (2003), James Whitman explains the existing and widening differences between criminal justice in the United States and Europe through different pathways toward egalitarianism in the 19th century, and how status politics impacted on the forms and dramaturgy of punishment. European countries *leveled up*, i.e. they generalized forms of punishing high-status offenders to all, and modeled their criminal justice systems on the treatment of these offenders. In contrast, the United States *leveled down*, with the lowest status of slaves (or the most recent immigrants) as the model for the treatment of offenders. This led to the abolition of degrading punishments in Europe, and their retainment in the United States. Presently, these differences are clearly visible in the way how dignity of and respect for the prisoners (or the lack thereof) shape penal arrangements and prison regimes on both continents. Notably, public spectacles of humiliating and 'infamous' punishment which marked the degradation of offenders, were abolished in Europe in the course of the 19th century, and

only much later in the United States. These are highly emotive and ostentatious forms of punishment, designed as drama to arouse emotions in the
audience. The contemporary return of emotions to criminal justice in the
United States came with demands for and actual execution of such types of
humiliating punishments, mostly in small communities (see Karstedt, 2002;
Nussbaum, 2004).

The collective rites of status passages and status politics are part of the
affective-moral forces, and the 'injuries of class' (Sennet) as extended to
offenders and amplified in punishment are a defining feature of the emotional culture of societies. How different societies achieve solidarity and
attenuate the felt injustice of status differences, and how individuals cope
with the ensuing emotions, appears to shape differences in their 'retributive
temper' (Whitman, 2005). Were recent shifts in status politics and increasing
inequality in the United States as well as in Europe responsible for changes
in the 'retributive temper' on both continents, and the return of emotive and
ostentatious punishment to the scene?

## DURKHEIMIAN THEMES AND 'EMOTIONALLY INTELLIGENT JUSTICE'

Exploring the links between emotions, crime and justice through Durkheimian themes directs criminological inquiry towards a new set of
Durkheimian concepts. Ritual, collective representation, discourse, and
performance are coming to the fore (Smith & Alexander, 2005). Simultaneously, the themes lead to other strands of sociological theorizing on
emotions, like symbolic interactionism, exchange and structural theories, as
well as dramaturgical and cultural theories. We are presently confronted
with a richness of theoretical approaches in the sociology of emotions,
which is hardly backed by empirical studies, and criminology does not differ
in this respect. Besides Durkheim, both Elias and Foucault offer routes for
further research in the expanding field of the criminology of emotions.

The Durkheimian themes as explored here represent only a small number
of the themes that offer themselves in this field for further inquiry. They
illuminate however the problems and possibilities of creating 'emotionally
intelligent justice', and the difficulties that confront the 'education sentimentale' of criminal justice and the public. How does emotionally intelligent
justice position itself amongst the affective-moral forces of society? How can
emotionally intelligent justice accommodate demands from the public and

communities, and how and where should these be resisted? How are the emotional needs of victims and offenders to be balanced? Ultimately, how can affect be made 'safe' for emotionally intelligent justice?

# NOTES

1. See for a discussion of countervailing forces in particular Hirschmann's (1977) seminal work *The Passions and the Interests*. For the Scottish Enlightenment Buchan (2003) and Sznaider (1998), for Hume on justice and emotions, Sparks (forthcoming).

2. Garland (2001) in some ways is an exception to this. This differs widely from the simultaneous return of emotion to sociology (e.g. Barbalet, 1998) and political science (Goodwin, Jasper, & Polletta, 2001).

3. Mead's work on 'The psychology of punitive justice' (Mead, 1964/1918) is equally important and unfortunately mostly forgotten.

4. This mirrors Tilly's (1981) condemnation that Durkheim was 'useless' for historical sociology.

5. See e.g. Vester (1987) on Durkheim's ambivalence on the question if emotions are primordial to social practices or their consequences. This ambivalence is reflected in the three different strands of the constitutive, functional or indicative role of emotions for criminal justice (see above).

6. This implies that changes in social practices and concomitant shifts in the emotional culture are at the roots of the historical development of crime and punishment. Since this is the most contested part of Durkheim's theory, I will not refer to the 'dynamics' of his theory, but focus instead on its conceptual part as Braithwaite (1989) did.

7. See e.g. the recent US case of a husband who had murdered his wife; the fact that he did not show any emotions in court, was explicitly mentioned by the judge as aggravating circumstances.

8. Sherman (2003, p. 11) argues that these initiating 'negative' and exclusionary emotions should be avoided in restorative justice. My argument here is that avoidance would ignore the process of transformation and that these emotions should equally be engaged with in restorative justice settings in order to achieve the transformation.

9. Personal communication.

10. MacCoun (2005) reports the story of a defendant who wanted her day in court and to tell 'her story' before accepting a settlement; she was given a mock court session, after which she consented. MacCoun cites this as indicative of the dangers of manipulation inherent in procedural justice. I think it shows the potential of procedural justice of actually transforming emotions.

11. See for a critical discussion Gadd et al. (2005); Gadd and Jefferson (2006); Dixon and Gadd (2006); Messner, McHugh, and Felson (2004).

12. Anger as an emotional reaction towards injustice seems to be universal and culturally invariant (Scherer, 1997).

13. See for a discussion Pratt (2002), who uses Elias' *Civilizing Process* as a conceptual framework.

14. Similar results were obtained in a study on support for the death penalty in West Germany from 1950 to 1980, after it had been abolished in the constitution in 1949. Until the mid-1960s, support for the death penalty was lower amongst the working class and those with less education, who had mostly suffered from executions under the Nazi regime and during World War II. Since then until today, levels of support in these groups started to surpass those of higher social status and education (Reuband, 1980).

# REFERENCES

Ahmed, E., Harris, N., Braithwaite, J., & Braithwaite, V. (2001). *Shame management through reintegration.* Cambridge: Cambridge University Press.
Bandes, S. (Ed.). (1999). Introduction. In: *The passions of law* (pp. 1–18). New York: New York University Press.
Barbalet, J. M. (1998). *Emotion, social theory and social structure. A macrosociological approach.* Cambridge: Cambridge University Press.
Barbalet, J. M. (2002). Moral indignation, class inequality and justice. An exploration and revision of Ranulf. *Theoretical Criminology, 6,* 279–298.
Bourgois, P. (1995). *In search of respect. Selling crack in el Barrio.* Cambridge: Cambridge University Press.
Braithwaite, J. (1989). *Crime, shame and reintegration.* Cambridge: Cambridge University Press.
Braithwaite, J., & Drahos, P. (2002). Zero tolerance, naming and shaming: Is there a case for it with crimes of the powerful? *The Australian and New Zealand Journal of Criminology, 35,* 269–307.
Buchan, J. (2003). *Crowded with genius.* New York: HarperCollins.
Carlsson, B., & Hoff, D. (2000). Dealing with insolvency and indebted individuals in respect to law and morality. *Social and Legal Studies, 9,* 293–317.
Collins, R. (2001). Social movements and the focus of emotional attention. In: J. Goodwin, J. M. Jasper & F. Polletta (Eds), *Passionate politics. Emotions and social movements* (pp. 27–44). Chicago: University of Chicago Press.
Collins, R. (2004). *Interaction ritual chains.* Princeton: Princeton University Press.
De Haan, W., & Vos, J. (2003). A crying shame. The over-rationalized conception of man in the rational choice perspective. *Theoretical Criminology, 7,* 29–54.
Ditton, J., Farrall, S., Gilchrist, E., & Bannister, J. (2004). From imitation to intimidation. *British Journal of Criminology, 44,* 595–610.
Dixon, B., & Gadd, D. (2006). Getting the message? 'New' labour and the criminalization of 'hate'. *Criminology & Criminal Justice, 6.* forthcoming.
Durkheim, E. (1893/1964). *The division of labour in society.* New York: Free Press.
Durkheim, E. (1912/1995). *The elementary form of the religious life.* New York: Free Press.
Eisner, M. (2003). Long-term historical trends in violent crime. *Crime and Justice. An Annual Review of Research, 30,* 83–142.
Elster, J. (2004). *Closing the books. Transitional justice in historical perspective.* Cambridge: Cambridge University Press.
Feeley, M., & Simon, J. (1994). Actuarial justice: The emerging new criminal law. In: D. Nelken (Ed.), *The futures of criminology* (pp. 173–201). New York: Sage.
Fletcher, J. (1997). *Violence and civilization.* Cambridge: Polity Press.

Freiberg, A. (2001). Affective versus effective justice. Instrumentalism and emotionalism in criminal justice. *Punishment and Society, 3*, 265–278.

Gadd, D. (2006). The role of recognition in the desistance process: A case-study of a far-right activist. *Theoretical Criminology, 10*, 179–202.

Gadd, D., Dixon, B., & Jefferson, T. (2005). *Why do they do it? Racial harassment in North Staffordshire.* Keele: ESRC/ Keele University.

Gadd, D., & Jefferson, T. (2006). *Understanding the perpetrators of racial harassment.* Unpublished manuscript. Keele: Keele University.

Garland, D. (2001). *The culture of control.* Oxford: Oxford University Press.

Garland, D. (2005). Penal excess and surplus meaning: Public torture lynchings in twentieth century America. *Law and Society, 39*, 793–834.

Gault, B., & Sabini, J. (2000). The roles of empathy, anger and gender in predicting attitudes toward punitive, reparative, and preventative public policies. *Cognition and Emotion, 14*, 495–520.

Girling, E., Loader, I., & Sparks, R. (2000). *Crime and social change in Middle England.* London: Routledge.

Goodwin, J., Jasper, J. M., & Polletta, F. (Eds). (2001). *Passionate politics. Emotions and social movements.* Chicago: University of Chicago Press.

Hirschman, A. O. (1977). *The passions and the interests.* Princeton: Princeton University Press.

Hochschild, A. R. (2003). *The managed heart. Commercialization of human feeling.* 20th anniversary edition with a new afterword. Berkeley: University of California Press.

Hope, T., & Karstedt, S. (2003). Towards a new social crime prevention. In: H. Kury & J. Obergfell-Fuchs (Eds), *Crime prevention. New approaches* (pp. 461–489). Mainz: Weisser Ring.

Kahan, D. M. (1998). The progressive appropriation of disgust. In: S. Bandes (Ed.), *The passions of law* (pp. 63–79). New York: New York University Press.

Karstedt, S. (2001). Die moralische Staerke schwacher Bindungen: Individualismus and Gewalt im Kulturvergleich. *Monatsschrift fuer Kriminologie und Strafrechtsreform, 84*, 226–243.

Karstedt, S. (2002). Emotions, crime and justice. *Theoretical Criminology, 6*, 299–318.

Karstedt, S. (2005). Individualisme et Violence: Modernisation extreme ou re-traditionalisation de la societe? Une comparaison interculturelle. *Deviance et Societe, 29*, 273–284.

Katz, J. (1988). *The seductions of crime. Moral and sensual attractions of doing evil.* New York: Blackwell.

Kemper, T. (1978). *A social interactional theory of emotions.* New York: Wiley.

Kemper, T. (Ed.). (1990). Social relations and emotions: A structural approach. In: *Research agendas in the sociology of emotions* (pp. 207–237). Albany: State University of New York Press.

Kemper, T., & Collins, R. (1990). Dimensions of microinteraction. *American Journal of Sociology, 96*, 32–68.

King, A. (2005). *Self-understanding and attitudes towards offenders: Punitiveness as an element of identity management.* Unpublished doctoral dissertation. University of Cambridge, Cambridge.

Laster, K., & O'Malley, P. (1996). Sensitive new-age laws: The reassertion of emotionality in law. *International Journal of the Sociology of Law, 24*, 21–40.

Lawler, E. J., & Yoon, J. (1996). Commitment in exchange relations: A test of a theory of relational cohesion. *American Sociological Review, 61*, 89–108.

Lawler, E. J., & Yoon, J. (1998). Network structure and emotion in exchange relations. *American Sociological Review, 63*, 871–894.

Loader, I., & Mulcahy, A. (2003). *Policing and the condition of England*. Oxford: Oxford University Press.

MacCoun, R. (2005). Voice, control and belonging. *Annual Review of Law and Social Science, 1*, 171–202.

Markovsky, B., & Lawler, E. J. (1994). A new theory of group solidarity. *Advances in Group Processes, 11*, 113–137.

Maruna, S., & King, A. (forthcoming). Moral indignation in the East of England: An empirical look at Ranulf's thesis. In: S. Karstedt, I. Loader, & H. Strang (Eds.), *Emotions, crime and justice*. Oxford: Hart.

Mead, H. (1964). The psychology of punitive justice. In: A. J. Reck (Ed.), *Selected writings* (pp. 212–239). Chicago: University of Chicago Press.

Messerschmidt, J. W. (1997). *Crime as structured action. Gender, race, class and crime in the making*. Thousand Oaks: Sage.

Messner, S., Baumer, E. P., & Rosenfeld, R. (2002). Social capital, social trust and support for the death penalty: A multilevel analysis. Paper presented at the British Society of Criminology Conference. Keele.

Messner, S., Baumer, E. P., & Rosenfeld, R. (2006). Distrust of government, the vigilante tradition and support for capital punishment. *Law & Society Review*. forthcoming.

Messner, S., McHugh, S., & Felson, R. (2004). Distinctive characteristics of assualts motivated by bias. *Criminology, 42*, 585–618.

Neckel, S. (1999). Blanker Neid, blinde Wut. Sozialstruktur und kollektive Gefuehle. *Leviathan, 27*, 146–165.

Nunner-Winkler, G. (1998). Empathie, Scham und Schuld: Zur moralischen Bedeutung von Emotionen. In: M. Grundmann (Ed.), *Konstruktivistische Sozialisationsforschung* (pp. 118–143). Frankfurt: Suhrkamp.

Nussbaum, M. (2004). *Hiding from humanity. Disgust, shame and the law*. Princeton: Princeton University Press.

O'Malley, P. (2004). *Risk, uncertainy and government*. London: Glasshouse Press.

Plato (1987). *Protagoras*. Stuttgart: Philipp Reclam jun.

Pratt, J. (2000). Emotive and ostentatious punishment: Its decline and resurgence in modern society. *Punishment and Society, 2*, 417–441.

Pratt, J. (2002). *Punishment and civilization*. London: Sage.

Ranulf, S. (1938). *Moral indignation and middle class psychology*. New York: Schocken Books.

Ray, L., Smith, D., & Wastell, L. (2004). Shame, rage and racist violence. *British Journal of Criminology, 44*, 350–368.

Reiner, R. (1995). From sacred to profane: The thirty years' war of the British police. *Policing and Society, 5*, 121–128.

Reuband, K. H. (1980). Sanktionsverlangen im Wandel. Die Einstellung zur Todesstrafe in der Bundesrepublik Deutschland seit 1950. *Koelner Zeitschrift fuer Soziologie und Sozialpsychologie, 32*, 535–558.

Rossner, M. (forthcoming). Reintegrative ritual: Restorative justice and the sociology of emotions. In: S. Karstedt, I. Loader, & H. Strang (Eds), *Emotions, Crime and Justice*. Oxford: Hart.

Sarat, A. (2001). *When the state kills. Capital punishment and the American condition*. Princeton: Princeton University Press.

Scheff, T. (1990a). *Microsociology: Discourse, emotion and social structure*. Chicago: University of Chicago Press.

Scheff, T. (1990b). Review essay: A new Durkheim. *American Journal of Sociology, 96*, 741–746.

Scheff, T. (1994). *Bloody revenge: Emotions, nationalism and war*. Boulder: Westview.

Scheff, T. (1997). *Emotions, the social bond and human reality*. New York: Cambridge University Press.

Scheff, T. (forthcoming). A theory of runaway nationalism: 'Love' of country/hatred of others. In: S. Karstedt, I. Loader, & H. Strang (Eds), *Emotions, crime and justice*. Oxford: Hart.

Scherer, K. (1997). The role of culture in emotion – antecedent appraisal. *Journal of Personality and Social Psychology, 73*, 902–922.

Sherman, L. (2003). Reason for emotion: Reinventing justice with theories, innovations and research. The american society of criminology 2002 presidential address. *Criminology, 41*, 1–38.

Sherman, L., & Strang, H. (2004). Restorative justice: What we know and how we know it. Paper presented at Keele University.

Smith, P. (1996). Executing executions. Aesthetics, identity and the problematic narratives of capital punishment ritual. *Theory and Society, 25*, 235–261.

Smith, P. (2003). Narrating the Guillotine: Punishment technology as myth and symbol. *Theory, Culture and Society, 20*, 27–51.

Smith, P., & Alexander, J. C. (Eds). (2005). The new Durkheim. In: *The Cambridge companion to Durkheim* (pp. 1–40). Cambridge: Cambridge University Press.

Solomon, R. C. (1994). Sympathy and vengeance. In: S. van Goozen, N. van den Poll & J. Sergeant (Eds), *Emotions: Essays in emotion theory* (pp. 291–311). Hillsdale: Lawrence Erlbaum.

Strang, H. (2002). *Repair or revenge: Victims and restorative justice*. Oxford: Oxford University Press.

Sznaider, N. (1998). The sociology of compassion: A study in the sociology of morals. *Cultural Values, 2*, 117–139.

Sparks, R. (forthcoming). Sympathy and estrangement: Some arguments for a human criminology. In: S. Karstedt, I. Loader, & H. Strang (Eds), *Emotions, crime and justice*. Oxford: Hart.

Taylor, C. (1992). *Multiculturalism and the 'politics of recognition'. An essay*. Princeton: Princeton University Press.

Taylor, G. (1987). *Pride, shame and guilt*. Oxford: Clarendon.

Thamm, R. (2004). Towards a universal power and status theory of emotion. *Advances in Group Processes, 21*, 189–222.

Tilly, C. (1981). Useless Durkheim. In: C. Tilly (Ed.), *As sociology meets history* (pp. 95–108). New York: Academic Press.

Turner, J. H., & Stets, J. E. (2005). *The sociology of emotions*. Cambridge: Cambridge University Press.

Tyler, T. R. (1998). Trust and democratic governance. In: V. Braithwaite & M. Levi (Eds), *Trust and governance* (pp. 269–294). New York: Russell Sage Foundation.

Tyler, T. R., & Boeckmann, R. J. (1997). Three strikes and you are out, but why? The psychology of public support for punishing rule breakers. *Law & Society Review, 31*, 237–265.

Tyler, T. R., & Huo, Y. J. (2002). *Trust in the law. Encouraging public cooperation with the police and courts*. New York: Russell Sage Foundation.

Useem, B., Liedka, R. V., & Piehl, A. M. (2003). Popular support for prison build-up. *Punishment and Society, 5*, 5–32.

Van den Bos, K., & Lind, E. A. (2002). Uncertainty management by means of fariness judgments. In: M. P. Zanna (Ed.), *Advances in experimental social psychology* (Vol. 34, pp.
1–59). Amsterdam, Boston: Academic Press.

Vester, H. G. (1987). Zwischen Sakrileg und Sakralem. Durkheims Beitrag zur Sociologie der
Emotionen. In: R. Schumann & F. Stimmer (Eds), *Soziologie der Gefuehle* (pp. 1–26).
Muenchen: Sozialforschungsinstitut.

Whitman, J. (2003). *Harsh justice. Criminal punishment and the widening divide between America
and Europe.* Oxford: Oxford University Press.

Whitman, J. (2005). The comparative study of criminal punishment. *Annual Review of Law and
Social Science, 1,* 17–34.

Young, J. (2003). Merton with energy, Katz with structure: The sociology of vindictiveness and
the criminology of transgression. *Theoretical Criminology, 7,* 389–414.

Zimring, F. E. (2003). *The contradictions of American capital punishment.* Oxford: Oxford
University Press.

Zimring, F. E., Hawkins, G., & Kamin, S. (2001). *Punishment and democracy: Three strikes and
you are out in California.* Oxford: Oxford University Press.

Zimring, F. E., & Johnson, D. T. (2006). Public opinion and the governance of punishment in
democratic political systems. In: S. Karstedt, & G. LaFree (Eds), *Democracy, crime and
justice. The Annals of the American Academy of Political and Social Science, 605.* forthcoming.

# IN SEARCH OF CRIMINOLOGY'S EPISTEMOLOGICAL THRESHOLD

René van Swaaningen

## ABSTRACT

*This article examines criminology's epistemological threshold by relating its scientific development to its (autonomous) influence on (the professional and public debate on) crime and criminal justice politics, its dependency of hegemonic policy discussions and of commissioners of research and its institutionalisation as an academic discipline. After a brief historical introduction, we will focus on the developments of the last 30 years. We will conclude with a number of proposals to restructure criminology in such a way that it is the most relevant to today's social reality.*

## INTRODUCTION

Criminology's epistemological threshold is said to be low. As a so-called 'object–discipline' criminology lends the analytic and methodological tools from other social sciences and quite eclectically applies it to its object of research: crime and its control. Our field of knowledge would furthermore be more susceptible to pressures and interests generated elsewhere than is the case in other social sciences (Garland, 2002, p. 17). According to David Garland (2002, p. 17), criminology's contingent character is based in a historical development that is characterised by "constant reformulation in response to shifting political pressures, changes in institutional and

Sociological Theory and Criminological Research: Views from Europe and the United States
Sociology of Crime, Law and Deviance, Volume 7, 249–270
Copyright © 2006 by Elsevier Ltd.
All rights of reproduction in any form reserved
ISSN: 1521-6136/doi:10.1016/S1521-6136(06)07012-6

administrative arrangements, intellectual developments occurring in adjacent disciplines, and the changing ideological commitments of its practitioners." Let us see to what extent this analysis holds in the Dutch case.

If we are to examine criminology's epistemological threshold, as I propose to do in this article, it seems particularly pressing to analyse the factors that determine how research questions are formulated. In this respect, the following themes will be addressed:

• the role of criminologists in the political and professional debate on crime and criminal justice;
• the infrastructure of and tradition in (empirical) criminological research;
• the use of criminological studies in policy making;
• the expectations students, law enforcers and politicians hold of criminology;
• the job perspectives of criminologists; and
• the extent to which criminologists are able to address today's key problems.

## STARTING WITH A HISTORICAL AND COMPARATIVE PERSPECTIVE

Criminology's cradle stood, in the 19th century, in Belgium (around the statistical school of Quetelet of the 1830s), Italy (around the positivist or criminal-anthropological school of Lombroso, Ferri and Garofalo of the 1870s) and France (around the environmental school of Lacassagne, Manouvrier and Tarde of the 1880s). Of these three countries, criminology is today only a well-established academic field in Belgium. In France and Italy there is still plenty of 'criminological' research, but it is mostly called differently, and researchers tend to present themselves as scholars in political sciences, sociology, social psychology or history rather than as 'criminologists'.

On the other hand, the European country that at present probably has the largest number of criminologists, Britain, is a relative newcomer. Continental Europeans like Max Grünhut, Hermann Mannheim and Sir Leon Radzinowicz introduced it only in the 1930s (Garland, 2002). In that era, the criminology of many continental European countries had been 'intoxicated' by an ideology that spoke of crime-prone inferior races and the superiority of the Nordic race. The present situation in Germany, a country with an impressive tradition in social sciences where criminology is only marginally represented at the universities, is still blamed on the heritage of that period in which criminologists had lost any moral authority. The question why in

2006 criminology is still relatively *un*popular in Germany could make a very interesting article (see Oberwittler & Höfer, 2005).

Or take Spain, where at present one university after the other starts master-programmes in criminology. Spain has, partly due to 40 years of Franquist dictatorship, hardly any tradition in (empirical) social sciences. But, nearly 30 years after Franco's death, very traditional lawyers *still* think they are the only ones who can think properly and keep dominating the study in humanities. How did criminology suddenly become so popular in this country? There seems to be little institutional support, and there is only a very modest empirical research tradition (Barberet, 2005). The question how viable the position of criminology at Spanish universities will actually be would also make a very interesting article.

This brief paragraph serves to show that history may not determine everything, but that historical analyses are indispensable if we are to understand criminology's current popularity and epistemological status. A related question is whether the existence of a well-institutionalised criminology also implies that criminological research is of more influence on crime and criminal justice policy? In order to answer this question, we have to dig into rather specific historical and political developments. Because we cannot do this Europe-wide, we focus on one specific country here: the Netherlands.

It has taken quite a long time before criminology became a full-fledged academic discipline in the Netherlands, and before the rich research tradition we have now was established. Both have only begun in the late 1960s and early 1970s, whereas criminology already entered the university by the end of the 19th century. It is neither a history of steady progress. In 2006 criminology may be a very popular field of study in the Netherlands, but less than 10 years ago criminology had nearly disappeared from most Dutch universities. As a field of research, criminology is currently flourishing. Not only at the universities, but also at two major research institutes, dozens of private consultancy bureaus, research departments of the larger cities and mid-size towns and of various police forces, hundreds, if not thousands of criminologists are currently employed. The fields where criminologists are currently employed are, moreover, far wider than say 20 years ago. How can all this be explained?

# A BIRD'S EYE VIEW OF ONE CENTURY OF DUTCH CRIMINOLOGY

David Garland's (2002, p. 8) portrayal of criminology as a convergence between 'the governmental project' of criminal lawyers aiming at penal reform and the 'Lombrosian project' of medical scholars aiming at social hygiene is also visible in the Netherlands. In the 1880s, a number of lawyers, who were inspired by criminological debates about deterministic and indeterminist explanations of criminal behaviour, had a considerable impact – mainly through the Modern School in Penal Sciences – on the penal practice. Modern legal scholars in the Netherlands have developed a far more functionalist vision of criminal law than the preceding Classical School of Beccaria. Yet, they did not start from a particular, coherent criminological theory. They quite eclectically applied various criminological insights to the penal practice, and by doing so they were able to change criminal justice quite substantially from a system oriented at the offence to a system oriented at the offender (van Swaaningen, 1997, pp. 29–49).

In the Dutch case, the 'governmental project' actually preceded the 'Lombrosian project'. The latter only came off the ground in 1899, with the appointment of physician Arnold Aletrino as the first Reader in what was then called 'criminal-anthropology' at Amsterdam's Municipal University. Aletrino is an interesting figure in Dutch criminology, mainly because he linked theories of atavism and degeneration to a radical, anti-penal, abolitionist if you like, political agenda. His reasoning was not illogical: if a person cannot be blamed for what he has done, it is pointless and inhuman to punish him (Aletrino, 1906). In criminology Aletrino remained, however, a solitary individual who has not been of great influence on later developments in the discipline. Moreover, despite an important tradition in clinical psychological criminological studies, Lombrosian positivism has not at all been that influential in the Netherlands.

A truly sociological criminology emerged slightly later, when Willem Bonger published in 1905 his famous book *Criminality and Economic Conditions* (Bonger, 1916). In 1922, Bonger was appointed at the first 'real' professorial chair in criminology at Amsterdam's Municipal University. Bonger has been of great importance to Dutch criminology – if only because his, rather critical introduction to criminology of 1934 was for a long time the *only* Dutch language textbook available. Till World War II, virtually everybody was taught criminology from Bonger's historic–materialist perspective. Bonger did, however, not found any 'school' in criminology, and neither did he invest a lot of energy in the institutionalisation of criminology as an academic discipline. According to his biographer Bart van Heerikhuizen (1987), Bonger remained the 'professor in the Dutch Labour party and the socialist in the university'. His influence on the political and professional debate on crime and criminal justice was also mainly through the Dutch Labour Party. Consistent with his historic–materialist theory, his main policy recommendation to reduce crime was to improve people's economic conditions. This changed in the mid-1930s, when he felt forced to explicitly take issue with the derailment of democracy, the emerging authoritarian Law and Order politics of the Nazi's and the sudden preoccupation of so many criminologists with racial determinants of crime. But then again, Bonger did not specifically argue against the new criminal justice politics, but against the emerging authoritarian and racist politics at large (van Swaaningen, 1997, pp. 59–62). On the day of the Dutch capitulation Bonger took his own life, and soon after World War II, his sociological materialism in criminology was forgotten and replaced by a humanist-inspired approach of penal reform (van Swaaningen, 1997, pp. 62–73).

The first criminological institute in the Netherlands was founded in 1934 at the University of Utrecht by a professor of criminal law, Willem Pompe. This historical connection to criminal law is an important reason why criminology at Dutch universities is based in the Faculty of Law rather than in that of social sciences. The main Utrecht criminologist, Gerrit Theodoor Kempe, has revised the post-war editions of Bonger's introduction. But from the early 1950s on there came quite a number of other introductions to criminology that were, as it was argued, more in line with the new spirit of the time. In the case of Kempe, it meant a larger influence of existentialist thought and subsequent attempts to try and understand the motives of the delinquent. Another Utrecht scholar, Rijk Rijksen, was a major advocate of a more sociological criminology in the Netherlands. For him, this mainly meant asking the delinquent what he thought about criminal justice, probation and corrections. For those days, that was a revolutionary project. The main importance of the Utrecht School lies, however, in the influence it had on the penal practice of the 1950s: they were *the* advocates of rehabilitation in the Netherlands. With the barbarism of the late 1930s and 1940s still fresh in the minds of the general public and penal practitioners alike, this working groups of lawyers, criminologists, sociologists and psychiatrists succeeded to make its humanitarian, penal reductionist agenda the dominant perspective in Dutch criminal justice. It facilitated, to use Willem de Haan's (1990, p. 69) words, a 'politics of bad conscience' among penal practitioners. But again, little attempts were made to institutionalise criminology as an academic discipline, and, with today's eyes, the research designs still look rather primitive.

The process of institutionalisation and scientific elaboration slowly started in 1959, with the establishment of the *Netherlands' Journal for Criminology* by lawyers, psychiatrists and a few sociologists, such as Kempe and Rijksen, Willem Nagel and (the later abolitionist) Herman Bianchi. In 1963 followed the foundation, by roughly the same group of professors, of the first occupational association, the *Foundation Interuniversity Criminology Contact Organ* (SICCO). Though there have been (nearly) annual gatherings of criminologists in the Netherlands since 1938 (Bouman, van Bemmelen, & Kranenburg, 1938), the establishment of the Netherlands' journal and of SICCO were the first attempts to institutionalise criminology as an autonomous academic discipline. These initiatives were only carried by a relatively small group of senior professors in criminal law or forensic psychiatry, and do not witness any ambitions with respect to influencing crime and criminal justice politics.

Till the 1960s, criminology was at the universities a subject that was merely taught by lawyers and psychiatrists, and they were seldom engaged in empirical research. This changed in the 1960s, when young, methodologically more qualified researchers were employed at the universities. The development resulted in the foundation of the *Netherlands' Society of Criminology* (NVK) in 1974 (van Swaaningen & Bovenkerk, 1992). The NVK was the first national professional association that was carried by a younger generation of criminologists, and not by the older professors alone. The NVK does not have any political colour, and mainly acted as a professional association that was to advance criminology as an academic discipline.

From the outset, criminology's influence on the penal practice in the Netherlands has been quite large. We cannot really say that this was guided by any (policy) theory, but we can say that criminologists took a rather autonomous position in the political debates, and crime and criminal justice. We can, however, also argue that the dominant theoretical perspectives echoed the spirit of the time. The institutionalisation of criminology as an academic discipline only took place in the late 1960s and early 1970s, when younger criminologists found a place at the universities as assistant professors. Criminology's early development as an academic discipline may as such have been more determined by external factors than by scientific elaboration, but with respect to the content, it was not determined by any political forces either.

## THE 1970s AND 1980s: INSTITUTIONALISATION AND DOWNFALL

Though criminology's tradition at Dutch universities is quite comparable to that of neighbouring Belgium, its institutionalisation was far weaker in the Netherlands. An important reason for this is the different position of criminology as an occupational training. Unlike the Belgian case, the possession of a university degree in criminology has never been stipulated as an entrance requirement for any occupational group in the Netherlands. Eligibility to the higher ranks of the police force requires a diploma of the Netherlands' Police Academy (NPA), and prison directors and their staff always had a diversity of previous training – from clergyman and jurist in the old days to sociologist or management scholar at present – and they receive more specific training within their own institution. Probation officers and higher prison staff need a general training in social work, clinical psychology and similar training. There is not a single function in the Dutch criminal justice system for which an academic degree in criminology is required. In this sense, Belgian criminology has always been far more interwoven with the penal practice than Dutch criminology.

The absence of a specific occupational field of activity has, on the other hand, been one of the most important reasons for the relative marginality of criminology at Dutch universities. The growth of academic criminology staff, which took place in the late 1960s and 1970s, was mainly based on the allocation of research money and much less on stable teaching needs. Departments of criminology only offered a number of optional courses within the curriculum of lawyers or sociologists. Only in 1968, Herman Bianchi developed an autonomous criminological curriculum at the Free University Amsterdam (VU). Around the same time we witness the emergence of some more modest specialisations in criminology at the universities of Nijmegen and Leiden. These latter two have, however, never really taken off, mainly because of a lack of occupational interest. As such, the establishment of new criminology curricula seems to have more to do with internal factors, such as the advance of criminology as an autonomous academic discipline, than with political or practical demands.

In the late 1960s, the labelling approach was introduced in the Netherlands by Herman Bianchi in Amsterdam and by Peter Hoefnagels in Rotterdam. This approach, followed by critical perspectives of stigmatisation, criminalisation and abolitionism, put a dominant mark on the Dutch academic criminology of the 1970s. They were particularly influential on the research agendas of the criminology departments of the Free University Amsterdam and the Erasmus University Rotterdam. In the public debate, (these) criminologists mainly acted as fierce opponents of a criminal justice system that only makes new victims and is not of any help to anybody.

The most significant academic criminological research institute of the 1970s was, however, established by Riekent Jongman at the University of Groningen. This department worked from a Mertonian anomie and strain perspective, and its main focus in those days was the selectivity of the criminal justice system – to be followed by more aetiological studies from a mixed perspective of strain, conflict theory and social control in the 1980s. The Groningen criminologists mingled much less in the political and professional debate on crime and criminal justice than their colleagues from Amsterdam and Rotterdam, but they did dominate the academic criminological debate. Yet, in Groningen, the position of criminology as a field of teaching remained marginal. But, research money was in ample supply during those years and thus criminology did pretty well everywhere.

Not surprisingly, the position of criminology, which was mainly based on research money, collapsed when, in the 1980s, the allocation of university financing came to depend more and more on teaching needs. It became the victim of its marginal status in this respect and of a positivist swing back within the Law schools in which they were embedded. In the 1970s, it was a rather commonly shared idea that one could only be a good lawyer if one had sufficient knowledge of social sciences as well. In this context criminology had a more or less obvious place on the lawyer's curriculum. In the 1980s, the idea of the good lawyer changed into that of a good craftsman, a good technician. Criminology was now considered as unnecessary frills, and criminology staff was reduced everywhere.

But, there are also other reasons for this cold reorganisation. In the 1980s, academic criminology was also affected by a serious image problem (van Swaaningen, 2000). Led by the idea that 'nothing works' and that those who work 'in the system' will be co-opted by a punitive rationale, there was very little work that criminologists could actually do. Their strong normative beliefs often blocked them from doing anything at all. From the 1980s onwards, it had become a widespread opinion that criminologists at Dutch universities were more interested in delivering disengaged ideology critique than in conducting solid empirical research on serious problems. The – initially rather small – research institute of the Ministry of Justice had already taken advantage of this situation in 1973 by expanding in a major way and by adopting a new name: the Scientific Research and Documentation Centre (WODC).

In 1974, Herman Bianchi wrote a seminal article on 'governmental' and 'non-governmental' criminology as a paradigmatic problem. He saw an important role for both, but argued that the first started from an immanent position, within the logic of a certain system of social control, whereas the task of latter was mainly to offer an external, meta-sociological critique of this hegemonic system of social control (Bianchi, 1974). It was actually a rather balanced article, but it was widely interpreted as a plea for polarisation ... either you are with us, or you are with the law enforcers, so to say.

Starting from this – mistaken – plea for polarisation, academic criminologists did not want to engage in policy research. Partly because of this, the WODC has, particularly in the 1980s, maintained a strong research position in the Netherlands: they had the money, the power and the staff. Though it should be stressed that the WODC had quite an autonomous position as a scientific research institute, it is clear that the research questions were led by policy questions rather than by academic curiosity or theoretical interests. This was looked upon with frown by academic, non-governmental criminologists – who were also plainly jealous of the WODC's financial possibilities.

In the early 1980s, the scientific credibility of academic criminologists was challenged because they were often sloppy in methodology, and their credibility as a professional education was challenged because too many students found no job – at least no job that was related to their study. Finally, we should mention that many academic criminologists themselves shared the opinion that their subject area did not have enough academic stature to warrant its existence as an independent specialisation at the university. These criminologists have not sufficiently defended the right of existence of criminology at the universities. The idea was: let students first study one of the root-disciplines (law, sociology, psychology, medicine, etc.) and then specialise in criminology in their last year or so.

Looking back we must conclude that in this 'crisis period', a considerable amount of criminological research was undertaken at the universities; less reflexive than before, but often with a better empirical base (van Swaaningen & Blad, 1992, 1999). In all probability, this has protected Dutch academic criminology against a definitive downfall. But, as far as criminology's popularity as a subject of study is concerned, the situation was pretty bad. Looking for example at the number of Dutch lingual criminological textbooks that appeared is quite illustrative in this respect. Quite a substantial number of textbooks appeared between 1969 and 1980, but then it took till the mid-1990s before any introduction to criminology in Dutch appeared! In other words, between 1980 and 1995 there was apparently no need for a textbook in criminology that is oriented at the Dutch situation. The current lack of good criminological lecturers and researchers finds its basis in the free fall of academic criminology in the 1980s.

The 1980s mark a turning point in Dutch criminology. Till the 1980s, criminologists tried to influence the penal practice from an autonomous, if you like partisan or even insurgent position – or refrained from explicit political positions. In the 1980s, we see that policy considerations come to determine the development of criminology. After the contrast between 'administrative' and 'academic' criminology had been stressed in the 1970s, this alleged difference got increasingly blurred in the mid-1980s. Criminology got more or less modelled after public administration, a sister multi-disciplinary object-science that was, so much unlike criminology, extremely popular in the 1980s. Not only the criminology of the Ministry of Justice's research department WODC, but also academic criminology was increasingly led by policy questions. Senior civil servant at the Minister of Justice, Director of the WODC from 1982 to 1988 and later professor of criminology in Leyden, Jan van Dijk (1985) even argued that the status of criminological theories depends on their usefulness for criminal justice policy and practice. Jongman's Mertonian inspired conflict theory and Bianchi's labelling approach were, in this view, of course completely useless, and opportunity theories were the most useful. In the 1980s, rational choice, routine activities and last but not the least Travis Hirschi's attachment theory had become the most influential criminological perspectives.

Criminology's recent history shows a rather paradoxical picture. On the one hand, criminology's scientific development is more and more determined by external circumstances – such as the grown importance of research-led policy or an emerging neo-positivism in the Law schools. But on the other, we can also conclude that a dominantly critical criminology that was continuously afraid of making 'dirty hands' has also dug its own grave, because it alienated a new generation of optimistic young students and let the terrain open for technocratic 'crime administrators'. Another paradox is that, though the 1980s was intellectually not the most exciting era in Dutch criminology, its role in the development (and evaluation) of innovative crime and criminal justice policies has probably been larger than ever (van Swaaningen & Blad, 1992).

## THE 1990s: A GROWING NEED FOR CRIMINOLOGICAL RESEARCHERS AND EXPERTS

The position of criminology improved again in the mid-1990s. Criminality had increased dramatically till the mid-1980s and is, especially from the time on when it began to stabilise a bit, considered one of the most important societal problems. The criminologist is seen as the expert who should 'solve' this problem. Criminologists are appointed to a variety of commissions of (parliamentary) enquiry and they increasingly appear in the media. We can also observe a populist development in politics, where more attention is paid to public statements than to actual research. In this context, the insights criminologists offer in the media and in the commissions of enquiry seem to play a more important role in political debate than their research. One's status as a criminologist is increasingly influenced by media performances.

The 'mediatisation' of crime and disorder has, on the other hand, also contributed largely to the growth of criminology in the 1990s. This gave the academic criminologist, in particular, a diametrically different image than in the preceding decade. Instead of the notorious insurgent critic he is now treated as a constructive partner in law enforcement. Policy makers are now inclined to expect too much from criminologists rather than too little (van de Bunt, 1999). Also the expectation of students has changed: they do not study criminology to change the disruptive criminal justice system – or indeed create a more just world – as many did in the 1970s and early 1980s, but rather to 'solve' the crime problem.

Since the early 1970s, policy-making is strongly expert-led in the Netherlands. Among policy makers of the early 1990s there was a strong need for expert knowledge about 'new' types of criminality: cyber-crime, domestic violence, apparently random (youth) violence, ethnically based youth gangs, trans-national organised crime, human smuggling, environmental crime, stock fraud, corporate crime, collusion, genocide, human rights violations ... and some years later terrorism. Till then, criminologists had actually little to say about these issues. The prevention and tackling of these phenomena also raised new scientific questions. From the 1990s onwards, criminologists have definitely contributed to increase the empirical knowledge on quite a number of these terrains. It is difficult to say to what extent an external demand for this knowledge has facilitated the scientific progress in criminology, but criminologists have at least seriously engaged with these issues and thereby also played an important role in the improvement of criminology's image.

Also the emergence of the victim and related debates about compensation, redress, mediation and emotional support has changed ideas on crime control in an important way. In short, much action now occurs outside the boundaries of the traditional institutions of criminal justice. Private criminal investigation is growing as well as the role of local government and governmental control agencies in the curbing of insecurity. The research territory of criminology is expanding correspondingly and necessitates an enlargement of the knowledge base beyond traditional penal applications. These developments create not only new knowledge questions, but also new jobs: jobs for criminologists. That too has been an important reason for criminology's growth in the 1990s.

According to a questionnaire set out among potential employers of future criminologists, there is much demand for people who have knowledge of and insight into the political 'responsibilisation strategy', and the actual functioning of all organisations involved in modern forms of crime control (van Swaaningen & van de Bunt, 2003). Lawyers do not have this knowledge; and neither do sociologists nor public administration experts. When David Garland (2001) argues that the (political) role of the expert is pushed to the sideline in the new populist culture of control, he seems to overstate the point he is trying to make – at least in the Dutch context. 'The' expert is probably *more* influential than before. What has really changed is the expert's jargon and the role he plays. A researcher no longer looks for causes and analyses, but develops risk profiles. A youth worker or a psychiatrist does not help people, but manages risk groups. Social work or community work no longer serves the fight against deprivation or the emancipation of vulnerable groups, but contributes to the security in the society. Next to these changes of the roles of existing professionals, a whole range of new disciplines, from forensic accountants in the financial world to security managers in the public and semi-public domain, have emerged. All these new experts have become extremely influential; they actually feed the 'information brokers' of our risk society (Ericson & Haggerty, 1997).

In the 1990s, there is also a renewed demand for 'real' criminological researchers: lawyers have not been taught empirical research skills and social scientists often do not have enough eye for the juridical-normative context of the research field. Slowly, the realisation has grown that the policy of financial cutbacks in the academic teaching area of criminology of the 1980s needs to be reversed by the allocation of extra investments – be it that there is little interest in funding more fundamental and longitudinal research. At the same time the WODC has lost much of its influence. Here we see an opposite effect: the near monopoly of the 1980s has made many WODC researchers intellectually lazy, and their reports became very predictable and little innovative. The 'new themes' indicated above were hardly addressed by WODC researchers, and they did neither participate anymore in the academic debate by publishing in peer-reviewed scientific journals. Against this background, a more fundamental (or at least less applied) counterpart of the WODC, a new large criminological research institute was established in 1995 at the University of Leyden: the Netherlands' Study Centre for Criminality and Law Enforcement (NSCR). Three institutions finance the NSCR: the Ministry of Justice, the Dutch foundation for scientific research (NWO) and the University of Leyden. In the vacuum of a declining WODC and dismantled research institutes at the universities, a wide range of private research organisations with a certain expertise in criminological matters has also emerged.

It is too simple to say that these developments were all just beneficial for academic criminology. The demand for a policy-oriented criminology, as advocated by Jan van Dijk in 1985, has also led to the decline of criminology's autonomy as an academic discipline. Ten years later, a leading Dutch criminologist would sigh: "I know of no other object-science that is so strongly directed by the authorities as criminology" (van den Heuvel, 1994, p. 40). Reece Walters (2003) has made an interesting analysis of how regulatory and governing authorities set research agendas, manipulate the processes and production of knowledge, and suppress critical voices in criminology in Britain, Australia, New Zealand and the US. This development is unfortunately not systematically charted out for the Dutch case, but the analyses from a book on the way the pharmaceutical industry influences the Dutch medical and biological discipline may well be applicable to criminology as well. In their book, Köbben and Tromp (1999) analyse a number of cases in which researchers have been silenced mainly by the power of money, i.e. by the promise of lots of expensive research facilities, or indeed by the threat that finances will be withdrawn. The amounts of money involved in criminological research are far less significant, but nonetheless we can in the corridors also hear lots of complaints among criminological researchers of how authorities that commission research tend to choose research institutes of whom they can expect they will say what the authorities like to hear, delay the publication of unwanted research findings till a moment they are made politically harmless, declare certain parts of a research 'confidential', try to influence the way in which research findings or conclusions are formulated, or plainly threat dissenting researchers that they will not get any future research contracts. A lot of research is currently only published in reports, which are not subjected to the scrutiny of other academics. This development blocks the scientific development of criminology and poses a serious threat to academic freedom.

Köbben and Tromp's (1999, pp. 170–177) main advice to counter this undesirable threat of academic freedom is not to give in too easily, and develop counter-strategies such as (threats to) bring 'undesirable' research findings in the media, try to mobilise befriended politicians or indeed go to court. They also advocate the establishment of a 'trusted representative of the scientific community', a kind of ombudsman for researchers, now professional associations also lend their ear too much to the people who commission research rather than to the researchers. As said, the question whether Köbben and Tromp's analysis also holds in criminology still has to be tested, but if we assume that it does – at least to some extent – we can also think of other ways out of this dilemma. One of these could be the creation of strong criminology departments at universities, in order to reduce the dependency of external research contracts.

In this latter context, a growing need for a stronger educational position developed within the criminological academic community. The experiences of the recent past have taught us that the university position of criminology is greatly determined by teaching needs. Thus it was necessary in order to gain a solid position for academic criminological research, to concentrate first on establishing a strong teaching base. It was only possible to capitalise in an effective way on the growing knowledge need, if its continued existence was no longer dependent on all sorts of short-term research contracts. Another advantage of being able to pay staff members out of a teaching budget is that this avoids structural dependence on (the priorities of) commissioners of research, it allows for more staff continuity (and hence in the extant knowledge) and for more consistency in the research agenda. In other words: a new, independent criminology curriculum was gradually seen to offer the best guarantee for the re-establishment in the Netherlands of an independent academic criminology.

Once again we can conclude that the development of criminology is partly determined by external forces, such as the grown concern about crime and safety and changes in the criminal justice system, and by more internal factors, such as the grown 'willingness' of criminologists to provide new knowledge that can be used by the new 'information brokers of the risk society'. And once again we can observe a number of paradoxes. On the one hand, the role research plays in the development of policy has probably decreased. Undesirable findings are prevented or neutralised by contracting researchers who are willing to echo 'His Master's Voice', by subtle and less subtle financial threats of researchers, by discrediting certain – mainly qualitative – research designs, by declaring certain research findings 'confidential' or by 'rephrasing' certain passages or conclusions that challenge dominant policy lines. Though I have not gathered sufficient empirical evidence to support this thesis yet, it is my hypothesis that (populist) political considerations determine what will happen and that research currently plays a merely legitimising role.

Yet, on the other hand, we see a whole range of new experts – risk analysts, security experts – that have a tremendous influence on the practice of criminal justice ... albeit on the conditions dictated by the new 'culture of control' one may argue. In order to challenge the dictate of this culture of control, we need a critical mass of academics and practitioners who can feed a latent discontent about the current politics of law and order with sound arguments and working practices. A good, reflexive educational programme in criminology, with the doors wide open to other social sciences, seems a *conditio sine qua non* in this respect. As academics, we are often preoccupied with the effect our research has, but we seem much less concerned about the impact of our teaching. Yet, the students we educate today are tomorrow's policy makers.

## HOW THE CHANGES ARE REFLECTED IN EDUCATIONAL PROGRAMMES

The intellectually dun 1980s may well have been a reaction to the unrealistic romanticism of the 1970s. If we agree that now in the new millennium the time has come for a more intellectually challenging criminology again, and for some more 'deviant knowledge' on crime and crime control, it seems particularly pressing to avoid the mistakes that were made in the 1970s. Let us therefore take a look at the criminology programme Herman Bianchi developed in 1968 – and that continued with some obvious modifications till the early 1980s – and see what it can contribute to the development of criminology in the new millennium.

A first striking characteristic of the educational philosophy of the 1970s is the strong accent on learning to think independently and form ones own opinion. Students were from the outset confronted with the implicit views of the world and of mankind that underlie criminological theory. At present, the crime problem is too often taken in rather essentialist terms and students tend to reproduce rather easily what they are told on the news and what they hear in parliament. When I once asked an as such clever enough student of mine why she just reiterated this chatter instead of thinking for herself, she answered the current educational system is too much oriented at reproducing facts and that she was hardly ever challenged to think outside of the hegemonic paradigm of knowledge. This answer taught me that a reflexive attitude should form the basis of any academic educational programme.

A second striking characteristic of the criminology programmes of the 1970s was the 'holistic' vision that was offered on the inter-connectedness of historical, social, political, cultural developments, and the development of crime and crime control. At present, there is, also from the side of the students, mainly demand for a 'quick fix', for immediately applicable 'concrete' solutions for very specific, yet partial problems. Some contextualisation and insight in the slow process in which social developments take place can be very helpful to prevent disappointment if such 'quick fixes', again, turn out not to exist.

There were also elements of the 1970s programmes that strike us now in a more negative sense. At times it was just a bit too free floating, too one-sided and too sloppy. Too often students were taught mere *opinions*, without any credible scientific foundation. The simplistic idea of a malfunctioning criminal justice system of which everyone – 'deviants', victims and society as a whole – was the victim was actually the patchwork on which these programmes were built. A balanced transmission of the whole spectrum of scientific knowledge, with the up-to-date state of the art in criminology was notably lacking.

From the mid-1980s onwards, when it went downhill with Dutch criminology as an independent academic discipline, we also have to admit with hindsight that criminologists got back with their feet on the ground. A large part of the criminologist's 'core business', that had got lost in the era that was dominated by labelling, abolitionism and studies on the selectivity of the criminal justice system, was taken up again: plain, positivist aetiological and evaluation studies. We should also admit that the research climate in criminology became quite a bit more serious and – let us be frank – people started to work quite a bit harder too. The critical spirit of the 1960s and 1970s is sometimes glorified just a bit too much. In our nostalgia we should also admit that it is a true relief that we have got rid of the indolence and laziness that characterised that era just as well.

Of course the 1980s and 1990s had important shadow-sides as well. Gradually, another kind of one-sidedness crept into 'the criminological enterprise'. We have seen above how the agenda of the police and the Ministry of Justice became the alpha and omega of virtually all research. If the word 'vision' was used at all in these days, it was mostly in combination with the words 'lack of'. Instead of trend *setting*, and autonomously indicating what are important developments from an academic point of view, criminologists now merely *follow* political trends in order to attract some external research money – of which they have become nearly fully dependent.

Another weird thing is that so many years after the debate over positivism in social sciences and just a decade after a predominantly anti-positivist movement in criminology, new bio- and developmental psychological insights on aggression are as of old taken to be the 'new truth', without any reflection and with very little eye for processes of (de-) criminalisation, problems of causality, relations with social reactions and implications or long-term developments. In the early 1990s, Dutch criminology had become rather positivistic and applied, and more fundamental questions – particularly in the areas of penology or victimology – were left to lawyers. To me, that is just as undesirable and idiosyncratic as the irresponsible armchair radicalism of the 1970s.

Visions of crime and the 'appropriate' reactions to crime are currently strongly dominated by control talk. If we think this is a politically and scientifically undesirable development, we need to (re-)create a space for 'deviant knowledge' on crime control (Walters, 2003). This starts with the way a new generation of criminologists is educated. So, studying criminology must be intellectually challenging again. We should not transmit the idea that criminology is a technical discipline to assist law enforcers, but rather an independent, academic study of deviance and social control. In a way, it seems worthwhile to take up some of the basic epistemological premises of the 'non-governmental' criminology of the 1970s again, without falling into the trap of polarisation it has led to in those days. A lesson that also needs to be learned from the 1970s is that a criminology study must also transmit solid knowledge based on empirical research about criminality and the control of it, and it must offer extensive training in methods and techniques of social science research. In order to produce 'deviant knowledge' you need to know exactly what you criticise and why.

## DIFFICULTIES AND CHALLENGES

With the free fall of Dutch criminology in the 1980s still vividly in mind, we must conclude that it is undesirable that somebody can obtain a degree in criminology without being able to work with all the theories, research methods and techniques available in the field. Criminologists should be able to find a job, and we should not be too preoccupied beforehand with the question whether or not they 'strengthen the system' at certain positions. We are no missionaries, but lecturers. We can try and give our students some critical awareness, but it is up to them what they do with it.

Solid methodology classes seem a prerequisite for the future of criminology as a viable academic discipline and professional field of work. Yet, as Reece Walters (2003, p. 81) observes: "Methodological textbooks in criminology often omit any discussion of the difficulties and tensions of conducting criminological research. Such books share similar patterns by including chapters on sampling, questionnaires, bivariate analysis, correlations, control groups, interview techniques, statistical modelling and so on. (...) This literature conveys an impression that criminological research is a technical, scientific exercise."

If we want to create a more reflexive research environment, we first need to point out in what respects criminological methods are differentiated from regular social science methodology. We can point at (1) the kind of sources (from police files to hospital data and from self-reports by offenders to data from and about victims); (2) the relatively greater unreliability of our data (all sources have their own specific biases); (3) the nature of the research population (*dangerous fieldwork* with criminal groups, the forced situation of prison respondents, the fact that participant observation is only possible on a limited basis); and (4) the emotional (e.g. in case of rape) or political (e.g. the feeding of gut reactions) sensitive material. By showing the connection between explanations on the one hand, and conceptions and social reactions on the other, we secondly forestall that aetiological notions are conceived in a too clinical way or are given a too absolute predictive significance.

Summed up in this way, it may seem all too obvious, but in concrete research projects we often miss this awareness. In order to replace the current dominance of 'voodoo criminology', with its quasi-scientific correlations of three figures behind the comma, by a methodology that is reflecting the reality of crime in its full complexity, Jock Young (2004, p. 26) argues: "What is needed is a theoretical position which can enter in to the real world of existential joy, fear, false certainty and doubt (...). What we need is an ethnographic method that can deal with reflexivity, contradiction, tentativeness, change of opinion, posturing and concealment. (...) Our problems will not be solved by a fake scientificity but by a critical ethnography honed to the potentialities of human creativity and meaning."

Also theoretically we need to broaden our horizon beyond the traditional realm of criminology. We need, in other words, to measure ourselves with other social scientists, rather than keep circling around all too concrete policy questions. I do not want to suggest that we should not be concerned with policy questions at all, but I do like to stress that for truly creative and realistic answers to policy questions we need to throw out our nets out far wider than we do now. With the huge expansion of the criminological research field, particularly after 2000, we can already observe how for example sociological and economic studies on globalisation, ethnographic research methods from cultural anthropology or indeed bio-psychological or neurological findings on activation and arousal have put a strong mark on Dutch criminology. We can only make real sense of contemporary themes around trans-national organised crime (international drug trade, child pornography networks and other *cyber crimes*, people smuggling, prostitution networks, terrorism, the abduction industry, and such) if we link them to sociological theories about the globalisation of the neo-liberal economic model, the digitalisation of society and the growing gap between rich and poor, between *jihad* and *McWorld*. Likewise, fashionable policy-issues like security-management and risk-assessment can be explained by theories on the risk-society and a course on crime policy to theories on general developments in society and in politics.

The answer to the question what is a 'useful' criminology is today very different than 20 years ago. Jan van Dijk's (1985) idea of 'policy-oriented' criminology may have caused a useful stir in the 1980s, but today it totally misses the point. Crime and criminal justice policies are currently based on a very partial empiricist studies and subsequently limited visions of reality. Thus the logic needs to be turned around and we should offer replacement discourses to make a different vision – and policy – visible. An interesting experiment in this respect is Hugh Barlow's (1995) attempt to put various theories to work, but this book remains limited to the more traditional criminological theories and the more traditional criminological questions. It would be a big challenge to see whether the idea behind it can be expanded to the new criminological questions and the new social theories outlined in the last paragraph.

With respect to the question how to move on with criminology, there are also a number of matters for which there is no clear answer; issues where it will remain navigating between Scylla and Charybdis. There will, for example, always remain a paradoxical relationship between the wish to develop a solid, empirically based criminology and the attempt to deal with topical, not yet fully crystallised themes. When the former is dominant, we will inevitably run behind, but when the latter dominates, we run the risk of delivering free opinions with no more value than a journalistic piece. To avoid this dilemma we need to combine innovative instruction with innovative research.

If we look at two scenario studies (Bruinsma, van de Bunt, & Marshall, 2001; Hoogenboom, 2001), there is a long list of disciplines and crimes which in the next 10 years criminologists will have to pay attention to: biogenetics and biometry, economics, cultural studies, political criminality, genocide, terrorism, internet criminality, corruption or collusion, economic abuse of power, industrial espionage, large-scale fraud or domestic violence. This long list raises again the important question how we can develop the tools to actually research these problems. Traditional criminological methodology is mainly oriented towards everyday street criminality by deprived youth. If we are really serious about dealing with these new themes, and are not satisfied with the position of a dilettante, a drastic renovation of criminological methodology will be necessary.

Another problem is posed by the emergence of new surveillance and control mechanisms – special investigating methods, protection of public and private order, private and semi-private control services, risk profiling and camera surveillance. If lawyers are concerned about these matters at all, they raise questions about legal permissibility or about how a particular practice can be made to conform to the law. Criminologists have a tendency to restrict themselves to the instrumental question '*what works?*' in the fight against crime. It seems a good suggestion to stimulate more long-term effects studies in this area, but this is not sufficient. A science with inter-disciplinary intentions needs to address, first of all, normative questions about the desirability of a particular measure. And secondly, a science, with a conceptual apparatus and analysis framework derived to a considerable extent from sociology, must also be able to say something about the *societal* significance of certain developments. It is incumbent on us as serious ac-ademics to study as a topic in its own right, *separate* from the problem of crime control, the societal context within which certain forms of reaction are born and the implications of these for society. This poses as a great chal-lenge to actualise and revitalise the social reaction approach in criminology, which has been in the slumps since the 1980s. In the present curriculum this dimension is still insufficiently integrated.

And then there is the interpretation, embedding and contextualisation of all the debates we have mentioned. Both the scenario studies discuss ex-tensively the liberalisation, internationalisation and digitalisation of society, the globalisation of the economy, the 'pulverising state' and the 'network society'. They talk about growing 'horizontal supervision' and a decline in 'vertical authority', and about changing norms and values and sexual re-lationships, whether or not under the influence of a multicultural society. Everybody seems to agree that these are important developments for crim-inology, but what is our actual response? Do we really incorporate them in our research? Do we *seriously* address them in our courses or do we only give lip service to them?

At present, criminology is a discipline where pre-eminently 'precision re-garding details' is more in fashion than a broad approach or the big picture. But criminologists will not be able to successfully take on the roles assigned to them in the scenario studies, as bridge builders or knowledge brokers who make connections and engage in a dialogue with a variety of experts, unless they do have a picture of the whole. Knowledge of the broad context and of new societal and scientific developments enables us to signalise earlier crim-inological relevant trends; it sensitises us to new, future criminological themes; it improves our ability to develop a vision and to interpret new phenomena and problems. The old saying "a good theory is the most prac-tical tool" can still serve as a pretty good guideline for promoting a scientific and, at the same time, practice-oriented criminology.

# CONCLUSION

The factors that have determined criminology's historical development in the Netherlands should have become clear in this article. Some of them are quite independent of what we academics have done – e.g. the political and media attention for crime and safety – some only have an indirect relation with our own efforts – e.g. developments in the labour-market and the image and reputation of criminology as an academic discipline – and some are fully dependent of ourselves – e.g. an interesting and sound curriculum that also prepares for a job and useful 'tools' to analyse today's reality.

Looking at these developments, we must admit that the influence of external factors on criminology is rather large, and has probably only increased since the 1980s. In order to answer the question whether this is more so than in other social sciences, we should analyse these too. Yet, it seems likely that the external pressure on criminology is particularly high, now crime and insecurity have become such 'hot' political issues. Very few social sciences touch so much on the heart of the state than criminology.

Yet, we cannot say that criminologists are just puppets on a string in the hands of those authorities who develop policies and commission research. There have been many moments in history in which criminologists were able to put an important mark on crime and criminal justice politics with an autonomous agenda. Often, this happened through professionals that worked in the field – from civil servants to judges and from chiefs of police to social workers. This restructuring role of the practitioners has to be rediscovered.

An important thing that still needs to be improved with respect to the creation of a new, 'useful' criminology is the development of an adequate methodology to do research into the 'new' themes mentioned above, for which our traditional research techniques are insufficiently suited. In order to reach that aim we need to do our own research in these fields. In the last paragraph I have tried to give some examples of how a more reflexive research environment and how the production of necessary deviant knowledge about our current culture of control can be facilitated.

# REFERENCES

Aletrino, A. (1906). *Is celstraf nog langer geoorloofd en gewenscht?* Amsterdam: Van Maas & Van Suchtelen.

Barberet, R. (2005). Country survey Spain. *European Journal of Criminology, 2*(3), 341–368.

Barlow, H. D. (Ed.) (1995). *Crime and public policy: Putting theory to work.* Boulder, CO: Westview Press.

Bianchi, H. (1974). Goevernementele en non-goevernementele kriminologie: een meta-probleem. *Tijdschrift voor Criminologie*, 16, 201–216.

Bonger, W. A. (1916). *Criminology and economic conditions*. Boston: Little, Brown & Co (French original 1905).

Bouman, K. H., van Bemmelen, J. W., & Kranenburg, F. (1938). *Verslag van den Criminologendag*. Amsterdam: NVGV/Psychiatrisch-Juridisch Gezelschap.

Bruinsma, G. J. N., van de Bunt, H.G., & Marshall, I. H. (2001). *Met het oog op de toekomst; verkenning naar de kennisvragen over misdaad en misdaadbestrijding in 2010*. The Hague: Adviesraad voor het Wetenschaps- en Technologiebeleid. www.awt.nl

de Haan, W. (1990). *The politics of redress: Crime, punishment and penal abolition*. London: Unwin Hyman.

Ericson, R. V., & Haggerty, K. D. (1997). *Policing the risk society*. Oxford: Clarendon Press.

Garland, D. (2001). *The culture of control: Crime and social order in contemporary society*. Oxford: Oxford University Press.

Garland, D. (2002). Of crimes and criminals: The development of criminology in Britain. In: M. Maguire, R. Morgan & R. Reiner (Eds), *The Oxford handbook of criminology* (pp. 7–50). Oxford: Oxford University Press.

Hoogenboom, A. B. (2001). *t Neemt toe, men weet niet hoe; scenariostudie financieel-economische criminaliteit in 2010*. Lelystad: Vermande.

Köbben, A. J. F., & Tromp, H. (1999). *De onwelkome boodschap: of hoe de vrijheid van wetenschap bedreigd wordt*. Amsterdam: Mets.

Oberwittler, D., & Höfer, S. (2005). Crime and justice in Germany: An analysis of recent trends and research. *European Journal of Criminology*, 2(4), 465–508.

van de Bunt, H. G. (1999). Beleid uit wetenschap. *Justitiële Verkenningen*, 25(6), 13–21.

van den Heuvel, G. (1994). Het justitiële afbraakbeleid van de overheid. *Tijdschrift voor Criminologie*, 36(1), 37–41.

van Dijk, J. J. M. (1985). Beleidsimplicaties van criminologische theorieën en implicaties van het beleid voor de theoretische criminologie. *Tijdschrift voor Criminologie*, 27(5), 320–345.

van Heerikhuizen, B. (1987). *W.A. Bonger: socioloog en socialist*. Groningen: Wolters-Noordhoff.

van Swaaningen, R. (1997). *Critical criminology – visions from Europe*. London: Sage.

van Swaaningen, R. (2000). Zoek de tien verschillen! Criminologie in België en Nederland. In: J. Vanderborght, J. Vanacker & E. Maes (red.), *Criminologie, de wetenschap, de mens* (pp. 61–80). Brussel: Politeia.

van Swaaningen, R., & Blad, J. R. (1992). *A decade of criminological research and penal policy in the Netherlands, the 1980s – the era of business – management ideology*. Rotterdam: Erasmus Universiteit CGS. Working Document no. 4.

van Swaaningen, R., & Blad, J. R. (1999). La recherche criminologique aux Pays-Bas dans les annees 1990. In: L. van Outrive & Ph. Robert (Eds), *Crime et Justice en Europe depuis 1990; état des recherches, ecaluation et recommendations* (pp. 193–246). Paris: L 'Harmattan.

van Swaaningen, R., & Bovenkerk, F. (Eds). (1992). *Criminologie-beoefening in Nederland anno 1992; een overzicht naar onderzoek en onderwijs samengesteld door de Nederlandse Vereniging voor Criminologie (NVK)*. Unpublished document. Netherlands' Society of Criminology (NVK).

van Swaaningen, R., & van de Bunt, H. G. (2003). Een nieuwe opleiding criminologie in Nederland. *Panopticon; tijdschrift voor strafrecht, criminologie en forensisch welzijnswerk*, 25(1), 79–89.

Walters, R. (2003). *Deviant knowledge: Criminology, politics and policy*. Cullompton: Willan.

Young, J. (2004). Voodoo criminology and the numbers game. In: J. Ferrell, K. Hayward, W. Morrison & M. Presdee (Eds), *Cultural criminology unleashed* (pp. 13–28). London: Glasshouse Press.

# COMMENTARY ON PART II: THE FIELDS OF SOCIOLOGY AND CRIMINOLOGY

Fritz Sack

## ABSTRACT

*Commenting on the chapters in Part II, Fritz Sack argues for the theoretical underpinnings of sociological work on crime and its control on the basis of the work of Pierre Bourdieu. He additionally comments on the chapters in terms of their exemplary qualities as contributions to the study of the control of crime, rather than the aetiology of criminal behaviour.*

As with Part I, this is a mixed collection of authors coming from both sides of the Atlantic, with three authors who have changed sides during their professional career – Joachim J. Savelsberg and Susanne Karstedt, who both completed their academic socialization in Germany before they entered the world of science in the United States and the United Kingdom, respectively – and another colleague who went the other way around, though not while pursuing his scientific trajectory but in terms of political experience, as Nigel F. Fielding describes his ideological and professional development. The other two authors are full-blown "indigenous" scientists, each coming from one side of the Atlantic: René van Swaaningen from the Netherlands, and Robert G. Crutchfield from the United States. As will be shown in my

Sociological Theory and Criminological Research: Views from Europe and the United States
Sociology of Crime, Law and Deviance, Volume 7, 271–282
ISSN: 1521-6136/doi:10.1016/S1521-6136(06)07013-8

following comments of their respective articles, the biographically particular context is explicitly or unwittingly reflected in the specific interest or emphasis of their respective articles.

## GENERAL COMMENTS

Before entering into a more detailed and specific discussion of the chapters in Part II, some general remarks may be in order. Notwithstanding the overall rationale of this collection, which is presumably explained and dealt with at some length in the introduction by the volume's editor, and even without knowing actually what Mathieu Deflem told the reader about the "generative grammar" of the selected authors and topics, I would like to reflect somewhat about the remarkable title of the book. The title of the collection, as I understand it, implies a specific disciplinary understanding that needs emphasis from the outset.

Colleagues and readers whose disciplinary identity and conception not only tends towards criminology but is criminological in essence might feel somewhat embarrassed to be confronted with "criminological" research and "sociological" theory. This immediately raises questions, first, about criminological theory and its sociological counterpart; and second, its relation to other theoretical fields and sources outside of criminology itself. And, indeed, there is absolutely no serious and affirmative reference towards and mentioning of criminological theory, in the sense that this term is discussed in the literature of criminology under the title of "theory". I will return to this issue in the end of my comments. Likewise, there is no attempt to treat the relationship of sociological theoretical reasoning to theoretical issues of psychology, let alone of biology or neurobiological approaches that again are haunting our field since some time. All this boils down to a kind of sociological prerogative and preference as far as the theoretical dimension of analysis is concerned. In this sense, one could refer to Emile Durkheim's famous principle of explaining social phenomena by social phenomena only, which, of course, treats crime and its control theoretically as social facts and nothing else, without making any reference to and borrowing from other disciplines. There is no need to mention the service Durkheim delivered, not only to sociology but also to criminology itself when he constructed the concept of anomie and, above all, when he discovered the functional sides of crime and its normalcy for every society – against any commonsense conception and also against the most expert knowledge. The article of Susanne Karstedt is a vivid example of the scientific profit from the recollection of

Durkheim's wisdom for present purposes.[1] This knowledge and insight has to be regained and revitalized in a world in which crime is used to create moral panics, leads to literal "wars against crime," produces overcrowded prisons and a constantly growing army of prisoners, and in which the illusion of a crime-free society finally ends up in the vision of a societal utopia, which comes close to a kind of "magical denial of reality," to use an apt phrase from the late great French sociologist of our times, Pierre Bourdieu.[2]

## LESSONS FROM BOURDIEU

Although Bourdieu, unlike his predecessor Durkheim and unlike some other genuine sociologists, has never extensively and specifically dealt with problems of crime or deviant behaviour and its control, criminology could profit enormously from his sociological wisdom, analytical concepts and methodological devices. In his general sociological orientation, he sticks to the aforementioned Durkheimian principle to an extent, and in a way that could contribute considerably to the task of criminology and that would deserve a far greater resonance and relevance for our discipline as is actually the case. In direct reference to Durkheim's known dictum "society is God," Bourdieu holds that whatever people expect from god, they will get it from society. The most pertinent use criminology could get from Bourdieu's analytic tools refers to the way he includes the micro-level dimension in his theoretical edifice. He does not separate and exclude individual behaviour as a realm of its own that needs a separate analytical treatment but that has to be incorporated into the frame of sociology. Being fully aware of a criminological premise that goes to the contrary of such an assumption, it seems perfectly necessary for our discipline to go beyond this kind of epistemological precondition of analysis. It should be emphasized that sociology, contrary to what one can find in some criminological literature, aims at the interpretation and explanation of the behaviour of individuals, as is witnessed by the different approaches of action theory and as can be demonstrated also by the methods in use for doing criminological research. One needs only to throw a superficial look at prominent sociological authors in the field to become aware of the way sociologists try to come to grips with this theoretical problem. This can be shown in the work of the grounding fathers as well as their present representatives, whether it be Max Weber with his action theory and his vocabulary of intentions and concepts, or indeed Pierre Bourdieu with his central concept of "habitus."

As a matter of fact, I wonder a little bit about the reasons why Bourdieu's work and theoretical tools do not show up in any of the chapters in this second group. Some of the arguments and findings could have easily theoretically been framed by Bourdieu's thinking and approach. The central point of Crutchfield's article, which I understand is the historical dimension and reproduction of social structure and its manifestation in actual behaviour, would lend itself easily to getting theoretically explained and interpreted by the relational and historical concepts Bourdieu is stressing in all his work. In the same vein, the biographical and reflexive aspect, which gets a prominent place in Fielding's article, resonates with a very central component of Bourdieu's sociological reasoning. Probably no other science than criminology stands so much in need of a postulate that Bourdieu placed at the beginning of his distinguished inaugural lecture "Leçon sur la leçon" and which might be quoted at some length: "The sociology of sociology which can be used to call into question and to argue against its own knowledge and results, is an indispensable part of the sociological method" (Bourdieu, 1985, p. 50). And Bourdieu extends this principle on science in general and then he immediately continues: "One does science – above all sociology – by and against its existence" (*Ibid.*).

I would like to make one more remark in connection with the theoretical input and investment of the articles in this section of the book. The richness and, I should rather say, the relevance and significance of Bourdieu's work help me one more time to make my point. What strikes me considerably, especially in the chapters of authors whose empirical evidence is taken from the United States, is the almost complete lack and absence of tackling or working upon what is considered to be the most under-researched and under-explained development of the crime problem in modern advanced societies, notably in the United States. My remark, of course, aims at what has aptly been called the American "imprisonment binge" (Irwin & Austin, 2000) – an expression which for non-native readers needs the help of a dictionary where they would eventually find the hint to its slang context. What is still more important about this expression is its metaphorical quality which implies surrender and resignation instead of explanation vis-à-vis this obvious "social fact" in the field of crime and criminal policy. Except in the article by Savelsberg – but even there only to a marginal and minor extent and more indirectly and incidentally than focussed – does one find mention of this crucial development in our area of scientific interest.

Interesting as it surely is to learn about the "risks of unintended and even counter-productive consequences" of the rules and practice of "sentencing guidelines" in the tradition of structural functionalism, and undoubtedly just as creditable as it is to show that and how criminology would profit from Max Weber's conceptual tools and empirical findings,[3] other questions could have been raised – if only with the benefit of hindsight – with respect to this conspicuous measure in criminal policy. Probably, one should, for instance, drop the assumption of "unintended" consequences which, of course, would mean not so much to take at face value what politicians like to declare to their voters about certain measures and policies in the area in question, which in turn would raise a further question – which is not at all, incidentally, unfamiliar to functional analysis – of the functionality of crime in modern societies. This in turn would generate a whole series of still other assumptions and hypotheses, which would be worthwhile pursuing empirically, theoretically and politically.

Let me finally add a last point as to the advantage or benefit criminology could derive from Bourdieu's work. I will present my argument by way of a short discussion about a kind of preferential order between different positions in "social theory" – as opposed to "sociological theory", to refer to a distinction that Anthony Giddens (1984) has proposed in his *Constitution of Society*. "Social theory" cannot wholly be tested empirically, but relates "to conceptions about the essence and nature of man and social action" (Giddens, 1988, p. 31, my translation). On the level of a thusly conceived social theory there is a decisive antagonism between Bourdieu's and Giddens' conception of man and society, as Bourdieu once underscored in a straightforward and offensive way when he accused his British colleague of advocating and holding a view of society *"bien vulgaire"*[4] in favour and defence of neo-liberalism and its political representatives. Bourdieu's conception of society and man is thoroughly and firmly based on the French (Durkheimian) tradition of conceiving society against economic imperialism and omnipresence.

How does this issue relate to and affect criminological research and thinking, especially with respect to the chapters in this section? As a matter of fact, this social theory level of sociological analysis is hardly touched upon by any of the authors and their articles, however surprising this may be in view of an already well-established discourse on it. To be sure, Nigel Fielding takes Giddens' structuration theory – modified and elaborated by Margaret Archer's concept of morphogenesis – as a theoretical baseline of his empirical study of community policing, but this reference is far off of any comparative differential treatment of the social theory by Bourdieu and Giddens, let alone of any discussion about the implications of neo-liberalism for crime and criminal policy. This task, it seems to me, is left to others in the field who do not show up in the texts and their bibliographies – with one exception that will be mentioned in a moment. To be more specific, a search, say for the criminological work of Loïc Wacquant, probably the most intimate collaborator of Bourdieu, would be in vain, as would be – in three of the five cases – a search for the highly praised *The Culture of Control* by David Garland (2001), which was reviewed in the oldest sociological journal, the *American Journal of Sociology*, as "sociology at its best" (Lyon, 2003), to name only two known sociological criminologists out of a lot of others who have dwelt with crime and criminal policy on the level of social theory.

Let me finish this longer critical comment with a qualifying note. My remarks should not be taken so much as criticism of the mentioned chapters and arguments. Nor are they meant to put blame on the editor or the authors for treating the topics they have chosen or have been asked for in the way in which they did. There is essentially nothing wrong with the way the authors dealt with their subject matter in terms of the central aim of this book, which is, as I understand it, the demonstration of the profit and productivity criminology could gain from a more forceful and open-minded use of sociological theories and methods. Needless to say that all the authors of this volume are certainly fully aware of the multiplicity and variety of theoretical approaches and positions, even of "camps" or schools in the science of sociology. A certain "bias" or tendency of a book like this is therefore inevitable and no point of serious criticism.

## THE CENTRALITY OF SOCIAL CONTROL

I will now turn to a next point that has also to do with theoretical issues, moving into the direction of epistemological questions that touch the heart of criminology as a scientific discipline. I will not, however, restrict my remarks to van Swaaningen's piece, from whose title I have borrowed the epistemological accent. The spontaneous association that came up with me when I read the title of this chapter was a reminiscent note that was published several years ago in *Social Problems'* 50th anniversary issue by Troy Duster, an author who once belonged to the group of ethnomethodologists on the west coast of the US. In this short text, Duster (2001) reminds the criminological community of today of "the epistemological challenge of the early attack on 'rate construction'" by referring to the then celebrated, "now classic article" in *Social Problems* by Aaron V. Cicourel and John I. Kitsuse on the methodological status of official crime statistics. This attack took place more than four decades ago, in 1963, which was in the same year when

Howard Becker's "Outsiders" was published. This almost nostalgic recollection of authors and articles during the period of my own professional socialization – actually I spent a couple of months in the academic year of 1965/1966 on the Berkeley campus of the University of California – brings me to a closer look at the chapters of Part II to find out what is left of the agenda and the orientation in the field at that time.

In view of my own bias and theoretical prejudice on this matter, if only in the eyes of some of my German colleagues who reproach me for taking too radical a labelling position, I will practice some self-restraint and will use a "soft," although, I think, symptomatic indicator for an answer to the raised question. To take the data of crime statistics not as indicators of criminal behaviour, but, first of all, of the product of the processes of control and of acts of "rate-producing," what Cicourel and Kitsuse proposed in 1963 and what Duster reminded us in 2001, comes down indeed to a methodological, even epistemological shift in the perspective towards the subject matter of our discipline. The case of this inverse look on crime statistics may be too sensitive, not to say destructive for a discipline that has based its methods, theories and research activities overwhelmingly on the premise that these data possess and reflect an ontological reality. There is no need, however, to argue about this particular epistemological problem in order to drive my point home.

What I would like to emphasize with my reference to Duster, Cicourel and Kitsuse, to Becker, of course, and to numerous others not mentioned here but belonging to the same epistemological camp, is the very fact that since the 1960s and with the work of these authors the control side of crime and criminality has become an accepted, legitimate and respected part of the subject matter of criminology. This widening of the substantial object and scope of criminology is nicely reflected in this section of the book. Two of the chapters – Fielding's and Savelsberg's – deal with issues of the resources and strategies of the official social control process. Fielding's reflections of the professional socialization of the police and its hidden informal and biographical curriculum, as well as his findings about the organizational, personal and motivational prerequisites of the introduction and operation of the strategy of community policing reminds me somewhat of Howard Becker's work on "Boys in White" and medical socialization – a topic Becker studied before he entered the world of crime and deviance. Savelsberg's theoretical reinterpretation of three different empirical studies on the implementation and the results of sentencing guidelines, likewise, has nothing in common with questions and research about the aetiology and the causes of crime, the obsessional issue of traditional criminology.

Traditionally, criminology indeed focussed almost exclusively on crime, despite the fact that the probably most influential textbook of criminology – the one by Sutherland and, later, Sutherland and Cressey – included "reactions to law-breaking" besides "law-making" and "law-breaking" in the definition of the subject matter of criminology. But the breakthrough of criminology along political and legal lines was not achieved and established until the appearance of the social control camp during the 1960s. Empirical research and theoretical reflections on the processes of formal social control have from then on been transformed from a mere criminological programme in the books to a sheer matter of course of criminology in action. This has not, however, resulted in the complete exclusion of aetiological interests and studies, as is demonstrated by Crutchfield's sophisticated and elaborate revisiting of the crime-generating forces and factors of the vertical economic and power structure of society and its reproductive mechanisms of intergenerational family life and of the allocation patterns on the labour market. The empirical and theoretical study and research on the system of control and its institutions has become "normal science" for criminology and cannot be any longer considered as belonging to a different "paradigm" in the discipline, to use a Kuhnian rhetoric that was produced at about the same time when this widening of the criminological agenda gained momentum.

If, therefore, we endorse the observation of Jock Young in his circumstantial review article of Garland's *Culture of Control* that criminology has changed its interest and agenda of the "last century" from the search for the causes of crime rise to that of the "rise in punishment" (Young, 2002, p. 228), this collection of chapters is also an indicator of this change. This tendency will surely continue in the future, at least with respect to further empirical research and study. Whether this might lead, however, to a theoretical shift and "revolution" in criminology, can only be speculated upon rather than predicted. To be more precise, could this development end up with a further epistemological or theoretical upheaval in our discipline that could easily result in a destructive disruption of cataclysmic scope which criminology was confronted with during its history several times? What I am referring to is a kind of theoretical undercurrent in criminological reasoning that goes back beyond the 1960s and the "young Turks" of that time in criminology and which has intrigued me in all my sociological commitments with crime and the reactions to it.

It was nobody else than the internationally known German sociologist Niklas Luhmann who, in his famous work on the sociology of law, gave expression to the theoretical current in criminology I am alluding to.

When dealing with the different criminological positions and schools in his extensive discussion of the penal law and its social relevance, he expressed his conviction that "in principle the theoretical analysis of deviant behavior cannot be separated from the sociology of law" (Luhmann, 1972, p. 121, n. 162). Luhmann's remark was placed in a footnote and its elaboration postponed for a later occasion, which, however, did not arrive before his death. This theoretical suggestion is completely in line and continuity with a lot of criminological authors. In fact, again, it was one of the big figures in our field who can be quoted for this position. William Chambliss has reminded criminology already some time ago of a theoretical statement in the first edition of Sutherland's textbook that goes back more than 80 years (1924) and which deserves to be recollected not for historical but for systematic and analytical reasons: "A complete explanation of the origin and enforcement of laws would be, also, an explanation of the violation of laws" (Chambliss & Mankoff, 1976, p. 23). This statement of Sutherland is almost identical with the aforementioned suggestion of Luhmann and it hits exactly a point which, incidentally, I myself have discussed years ago (Sack, 1978, p. 269ff).

Let me conclude this reflection about the theoretical and epistemological issues of criminology by some comments on the van Swaaningen chapter and his "voice" from the European side of the Atlantic. I have to qualify the comment about criminological "normal science" I made a moment ago. What is probably the case in the United States or elsewhere outside Europe does not hold also for the latter. This seems to me a further lesson one has to learn from van Swaaningen's cursory view on the European situation of the discipline in general and the more detailed scrutiny of the development of criminology in his own country, the Netherlands. One who would like a sweeping and catchy phrase would probably characterize the state and development of the discipline in Europe as being in a constant "process of making and unmaking," thereby reproducing a well-known pattern of criminology's past.

The observation that of the three European countries that gave birth to criminology in the 19th century – Belgium, Italy and France – only Belgium can at present boast itself of a full-fledged institutionalization of the discipline under the title that was invented by the French anthropologist Paul Topinard in the 80s of that century. In contrast to these countries, Great Britain, a virtual late-comer in the discipline, has experienced during the last some decades an unparalleled explosive growth in criminology to the effect that its achievement and output in the field are irrefutably first-rate and challenge the traditional US position in criminology with some success.

With respect to my own country whose criminology has not at all succeeded in getting rid and emancipated from its legal superego – an equally contributing factor to its backwardness as the blame and shame it has put on its own shoulders during the Nazi period – the discipline suffers from a defective and truncated existence insofar as there exists no full-blown academic institutionalization of the field. In Germany, an academic chair in criminology can be held only in connection with parts of penal law, with sociology keeping aloof from the field.

The particular case of Dutch criminology, which has lived through dramatic ups and downs after World War II despite its early and lasting contribution to our science by William Bonger, is of instructive significance beyond its regional and national limits. What may sound as elementary essentials to most of the US readers and what should go without special saying and mentioning – sound methods and research, diligence in theory building, and the "dialectics of research and teaching," among others – is owned to the necessary self-defence of criminology against its general vulnerability and precariousness, and the specific defamation and attack Dutch criminology experienced during that period.

There is still another danger criminology is sometimes faced with. To put it somewhat dramatically and provocatively, I would call it the danger of Trojan horses in criminology. It refers to persons as well as to certain strategies that could affect the existence of criminology. For instance, van Swaaningen discusses several times the detrimental influence Jan van Dijk, the former director of the internationally known Dutch Scientific Research and Documentation Center (WODC) of the Ministry of Justice, has had on criminology's existence.

Two factors were responsible for this attack on the state of the discipline, a practical one and a theoretical one. The specific situation that criminology is confronted with and which is unique among the several sub-disciplines of the social sciences is its affinity and closeness to and accessibility for practical and political purposes and advice from the outside. Again and a next time I yield to the temptation to quote my favourite sociological authority, Bourdieu, who has this to say about expectations from the political and practical arena towards science: "Societal demand is always also a mixture of pressure, command and seduction – and therefore the greatest service one could do to sociology could perhaps be to expect nothing from it" (Bourdieu, 1985, p. 61, my translation from the German). It is in this spirit that a recent book by Reed Walters (2003) with the nice title *Deviant Knowledge* is written, and which van Swaaningen rightly recommends as a must-read for scientists working in the field of criminology.

The theoretical factor that particularly haunts and damages criminology like a Trojan horse, and which was also the theoretical stance and the "political" basis of the decline of Dutch criminology, was the adoption of the Rational Choice Theory model of criminal behaviour – for both explanatory and practical purposes. The imperialist invasion of economic reasoning into criminology began with a famous article of Nobel Prize winner Gary S. Becker almost 40 years ago and was accompanied by a recommendation to leave and renounce criminology as it was at that time. This advice was not in vain: rational choice theory plays a prominent role as the basis of the "new criminologies of everyday," of "routine activity", "life style", and "situational crime prevention" (Garland, 2001, p. 127ff). Garland's comment on this criminological drive and drift is as follows: "With the certainty of armchair philosophers and economic modelers they insist that crime is, after all, simply a matter of individual choice – or anyway can be treated as if it were" (Garland, 2001, p. 130). Still more plain and sarcastic is Garland's British colleague Paul Rock, who calls rational choice theory simply "the criminological anti-theory" (Rock, 2002, p. 76).

In order to prevent criminology from going down this anti-theoretical road, articles and books like the chapters in this volume are urgently needed. Especially, in view of the connection between sociology and criminology, this volume might serve as a warning against a state of affairs which Dick Hobbs, a British colleague of Paul Rock, describes as follows: "Criminology is no longer a branch of sociology, it's karaoke" (quoted in Rock, 2005, p. 484).

# NOTES

1. Unfortunately, I could not fully incorporate the chapter of Susanne Karstedt in my commentary because it arrived too late.

2. Pierre Bourdieu, who died in 2002, made this fine remark in his famous inaugural lecture when he took over the chair of sociology at the French most prestigious institution of Higher Education, the "Collège de France" in 1981. I translated the phrase into English from its German version in (Bourdieu, 1985, p. 57).

3. The interest in and the recourse to Max Weber's voluminous and unsurpassed work continues up to our days, without, however, much impact on criminological research and reflection. There has just been published the most detailed and biggest biography of Weber's personal and professional life and career by a German historian that has ever appeared (Radkau, 2005). Controversial as it is already upon the arrival of this book, it will surely further stimulate the reception and application of his analytical tools.

4. I take this quotation from an obituary of A. Hahn (2002), who himself refers to Bourdieu (2002, p. 471).

# REFERENCES

Bourdieu, P. (1985). *Sozialer Raum und Klassen. Leçon sur la leçon.* Frankfurt/Main: Suhrkamp Verlag.

Bourdieu, P. (2002). *Interventions, 1961–2001. Science sociale et action politique.* Paris: Agone.

Chambliss, W. C., & Mankoff, M. (Eds) (1976). *Whose law, what order. A conflict approach to criminology.* New York: Wiley.

Duster, T. (2001). The epistemological challenge of the early attack on 'rate construction'. *Social Problems, 48,* 134–136.

Garland, D. (2001). The culture of control. *Crime and Social Order in Contemporary Society.*

Giddens, A. (1984). *The constitution of society. Outline of a theory of structuration.* Cambridge, UK: Polity Press [German edition: Die Konstitution der Gesellschaft. Grundzüge einer Theorie der Strukturierung, 1988].

Hahn, A. (2002). In memoriam Pierre Bourdieu. *Kölner Zeitschrift für Soziologie und Sozialpsychologie, 54,* 403–405. 1.08.1930–23.01.2002.

Irwin, J., & Austin, J. (2000). *It's about time. America's imprisonment binge* (3rd ed.). Belmont, CA: Wadsworth.

Luhmann, N. (1972). *Rechtssoziologie, Band 1.* Reinbek bei Hamburg: Rowohlt Verlag.

Lyon, D. (2003). Review of D. Garland, the culture of control. Crime and social order in contemporary society. *American Journal of Sociology, 109,* 258–259.

Radkau, J. (2005). *Max Weber. Die Leidenschaft des Denkens.* München: Carl Hanser Verlag.

Rock, P. (2002). Sociological theories of crime. In: M. Maguire, R. Morgan & R. Reiner (Eds), *The Oxford handbook of criminology,* (3rd ed.) (pp. 51–82). Oxford, UK: Oxford University Press.

Rock, P. (2005). Chronocentrism and British criminology. *The British Journal of Sociology, 56,* 473–491.

Sack, F. (1978). Probleme der Kriminalsoziologie. In: R. König (Ed.), *Handbuch der empirischen Sozialforschung. Paperback edition,* (Vol. 12, pp. 192–492). Stuttgart: Enke-Verlag.

Walters, R. (2003). *Deviant Knowledge: Criminology, Politics and Policy.* Portland, OR: Willan Publishing.

Young, J. (2002). Searching for a new criminology of everyday life: A review of the culture of control, by David Garland. *The British Journal of Criminology, 42,* 228–261.

# SUBJECT INDEX

family 29–30, 32–38, 40, 42–43, 45, 50,
52–54, 91, 94, 100, 110, 112–113, 116,
119, 121, 126–127, 139, 143–145,
153–154, 204–205, 210, 212,
237, 278
female peer groups 122
femininity 112, 114–115, 118, 122, 125,
129–130
feminist theory 110–111, 152–153
financial security 33
formal rationality 187–191, 201
France 219–220, 233, 250, 279, 281
Franklin, Benjamin 24, 240
functionalism 174, 274

Garland, David 278, 281
gatekeeper 166
gender 45–51, 53, 109–130, 139, 142,
152–155, 166, 172, 195
gender definitions 111–113,
115–116, 118–119, 121, 125,
128, 130
gender gap 109–110, 117–121, 124,
126–130
general strain theory 65, 127, 142,
145–146, 149
generalized other 84–85, 87, 90–91, 94,
99, 101–104
genocide 259, 267
Germany 16–17, 45, 186–187, 202, 219,
234, 244, 250–251, 271, 280
Giddens, Anthony 174–175, 177, 275
Gilligan, Carol 123–124
globalization 219

hegemonic gender definitions 5, 112,
114–115, 117–121, 125, 127–129,
153–154
Hendon Police College 161–162
Hughes, Everett 164
human agency 5, 60, 63, 67–70, 73,
77–79, 85, 89–92, 95–97, 102, 140,
148–151, 175

human capital 12, 19, 209
hydraulic displacement 194, 199, 201

ideal types 5, 88, 185–188, 193, 195,
199, 201
identity 77–79, 88, 93, 99, 104, 118, 149,
151, 159, 161–162, 164, 178, 239, 272
ideology 26, 171, 220, 229, 250, 256
illegitimate means 31, 59, 72, 144, 146
immigrants 220, 234, 241
impulse 80–85, 88, 94, 240–241
incarceration 93, 95, 195–196, 211
inclusionary emotions 230
income 12, 34–35, 37, 43, 140, 207,
212, 241
income inequality 11
individual strain 66
industrial societies 25, 143
informal socialisation 159, 162
innovation 31, 33, 61, 65, 71, 91, 144,
163, 169, 173, 175, 178, 192, 227
instantiation 175–176
institutionalized means 31–33, 71, 147
intellectual deviance 160
interactional theory 12
internet criminality 267
interview data 14
Iowa School 78, 102
iron cage 188

jihad 266
Joas, Hans 78
juvenile delinquency 5, 16, 64, 109,
119, 217
juvenile justice 17, 190–191

King, Rodney 207, 235

labeling 17, 78–79, 92–95, 104, 139–140,
150–151, 153
labor market 10, 12–13, 19, 91, 209,
211–214, 216–219
Laub, John 139, 151

# SET UP A CONTINUATION ORDER TODAY!

Did you know  that you can set up a continuation order on all Elsevier-JAI series and have each new volume sent directly to you upon publication? For details on how to set up a **continuation order**, contact your nearest regional sales office listed below.

To view related series in Sociology, please visit:

## www.elsevier.com/sociology